TRAUMA-INFORMED PEDAGOGY IN HIGHER EDUCATION

This volume explores the current state of student mental health and trauma while offering theories and practice of trauma-informed teaching and learning.

The interdisciplinary authors gathered in this collection discuss the roles, practices, and structures in higher education that can support the wellness and academic success of students who suffer from the effects of traumatic experiences. Chapters cover topics on teaching traumatic materials ethically and effectively, reading and writing to support recovery and healing from trauma, inclusive pedagogies responsive to systemically inflicted trauma, and developing institutional structures to support trauma-informed pedagogies.

This timely and important book is designed for faculty in institutions of higher education seeking to meaningfully cultivate trauma-informed classes and learning experiences for their students.

Ernest Stromberg is Professor of Rhetoric and Communication at California State University, Monterey Bay, USA.

TRAUMA-INFORMED PEDAGOGY IN HIGHER EDUCATION

A Faculty Guide for Teaching and Learning

Edited by Ernest Stromberg

NEW YORK AND LONDON

Designed cover image: © Getty Images

First published 2023
by Routledge
605 Third Avenue, New York, NY 10158

and by Routledge
4 Park Square, Milton Park, Abingdon, Oxon, OX14 4RN

Routledge is an imprint of the Taylor & Francis Group, an informa business

© 2023 selection and editorial matter, Ernest Stromberg; individual chapters, the contributors

The right of Ernest Stromberg to be identified as the author of the editorial material, and of the authors for their individual chapters, has been asserted in accordance with sections 77 and 78 of the Copyright, Designs and Patents Act 1988.

All rights reserved. No part of this book may be reprinted or reproduced or utilised in any form or by any electronic, mechanical, or other means, now known or hereafter invented, including photocopying and recording, or in any information storage or retrieval system, without permission in writing from the publishers.

Trademark notice: Product or corporate names may be trademarks or registered trademarks, and are used only for identification and explanation without intent to infringe.

Library of Congress Cataloging-in-Publication Data
Names: Stromberg, Ernest, editor.
Title: Trauma informed pedagogy in higher education: a faculty guide for teaching and learning/edited by Ernest Stromberg.
Description: New York, NY: Routledge, 2023. | Includes bibliographical references. | Identifiers: LCCN 2022053918 (print) | LCCN 2022053919 (ebook) | ISBN 9781032185064 (hardback) | ISBN 9781032197708 (paperback) | ISBN 9781003260776 (ebook)
Subjects: LCSH: College students–United States–Psychology. | College students–Mental health–United States. | College students–Mental health services–United States. | Psychic trauma in adolescence–United States. | College teaching–Psychological aspects.
Classification: LCC LB3609 .T695 2023 (print) | LCC LB3609 (ebook) | DDC 378.1/9713–dc23/eng/20230217
LC record available at https://lccn.loc.gov/2022053918
LC ebook record available at https://lccn.loc.gov/2022053919

ISBN: 978-1-032-18506-4 (hbk)
ISBN: 978-1-032-19770-8 (pbk)
ISBN: 978-1-003-26077-6 (ebk)

DOI: 10.4324/9781003260776

Typeset in Bembo std
by Deanta Global Publishing Services, Chennai, India

To all the students surviving and even thriving in the wake of traumas known and unknown. With great appreciation to all the contributors whose compassion, intellect, and effort made this project a reality. And last but never least to my partner in work, play, and love, Dr. Maria J. Villaseñor, who provided support, insight, and encouragement throughout the process.

CONTENTS

1 Introduction   1
  Ernest Stromberg

SECTION I
Transforming the Institution and the Classroom   11

2 Considerations for Developing a First-Year Seminar on
  Psychological Trauma   13
  Christine Valdez

3 Trauma-Informed Pedagogy at the Grassroots: Building
  and Sustaining a Trauma-Informed Movement at a Large
  Public Institution   29
  Sarah Le Pichon and Steve Lundy

4 Racial Trauma: Dismantling Anti-Black Racism in
  Classrooms and Academia   43
  Vanessa Lopez-Littleton and Dennis Kombe

5 When Embodied Histories Meet Institutional Stories:
  Trauma as Pedagogical Possibility   55
  *Whitney J. Archer, Carina M. Buzo Tipton, Cassandra L. Hall,
  and Emma L. Larkins*

viii Contents

6 Affective Solidarity and Trauma-Informed Possibilities: A Comparative Analysis of the Classroom and the Clinic   69
Kriti Prasad and Pritha Prasad

7 Trauma-Informed Mindfulness Meditation in the College Classroom   89
Ernest Stromberg

8 Examining Authority Through Trauma: Reflections From Student to Teacher   100
Angela Moore

SECTION II
Reading and Writing to Recover and Heal   **113**

9 Trauma Together: Rethinking Collaborative Learning   115
Brynn Fitzsimmons

10 Insights in Trauma-Informed Pedagogy From the Field of Bibliotherapy, Literary Trauma Studies and Creative Writing   131
Katarina Båth

11 Trigger Warnings With Conscience: Presenting Texts About Sexual Assault With Respect   148
Rose Gubele

12 LGBTQ+ Trauma-informed Pedagogy in a Transnational Context   163
Jason Lee, Beverley Hancock-Smith, Zara Hooley, and Eleanor McSherry

List of Contributors   *181*
Index   *185*

1
INTRODUCTION

Ernest Stromberg

As I write these words in the waning days of the summer of 2022, the COVID-19 pandemic continues to rage on. While increased knowledge and the development of vaccines have slowed the spread and reduced the risk factors, a glance at the World Health Organization website indicates over 600,000 new cases within the last 24 hours and a cumulative global death toll nearing 6,500,000. Masks remain mandatory when indoors at my campus. And we have only begun to recognize the psychological toll exacted by the pandemic. Meanwhile, the Russian invasion of Ukraine passes the six-month marker with no end in sight. Around the globe, record heat waves contribute to wildfires and hazardous air quality. In the United States, the former president continues to foment rage and violence by perpetuating the lie that the presidential election of 2020 was stolen. And we can anticipate more potentially triggering images and testimony as the January 6 hearings prepare to resume. Indeed, it would be a gross understatement to state that these are traumatic times of a collective nature.

The development of this project on trauma-informed pedagogy was in its germinal stages when the pandemic struck the United States in 2020. When the shelter-in-place orders were enacted, including the lockdown of the institution where I teach and the subsequent move to online teaching and learning, work on this project took a backseat to other priorities—especially becoming a 24/7 parent and co-educator to two young children. The ensuing two years have brought a new presidential administration, vaccines, and additional experience with an online existence, and yet, as noted above, the urgency of this project on trauma-informed pedagogy is as great if not greater than it was two years ago. Yet to be clear, even prior to the pandemic and the chaos generated by the death throes of the 45th presidential administration, we lived in traumatic times. Indeed, some scholars have defined the 20th and now 21st

DOI: 10.4324/9781003260776-1

centuries as the age of trauma (Barber, 2013). Global conflicts and political instability have prompted unprecedented migrations, resulting in millions of people occupying refugee status. Climate change and the existential threat to humanity haunt the collective psyche. Oppression and violence based on race, ethnicity, gender, and sexuality continue to traumatize specific populations. Mass shootings have become almost commonplace. And the ever-widening gap between the absurdly affluent and the great majority of the world's population provides a breeding ground for fear, anger, and violence. Indeed, none of us are immune to the causes and conditions of a trauma-filled world.

As a teacher in higher education, the initial impulse behind this collection began years ago. After nearly two decades of teaching in a variety of institutions of higher education, I began to notice increasing evidence of psychological distress among my students. More of my students were self-reporting suffering from mental health disorders, especially anxiety and depression. Additionally, I noticed more students who seemed to "disappear" from my classes or who were simply failing to complete assigned projects. It may be that significant numbers of the students in my classes had always been exhibiting these patterns, and I had simply failed to take notice. It could also be that the normalization of discussions of mental health disorders supported students in the sharing of their situations with me in ways they would not have done in the past. That noted, data nationally indicates that an ever-increasing number of students are seeking out psychological support on campuses. Indeed, the requests for support have increased at such a rate that many campus counselling centers lack the staff and resources to provide the requested support. As Melissa Wood reports in her article, "The State of Mental Health on College Campuses":

> According to the National Association of Student Personnel Administrators (2009), approximately 1.6 million students solicited counseling assistance in the previous year. In addition, in the past two decades the number of college students presenting with clinical depression and suicidal tendencies has tripled. Likewise, twice as many students with anxiety issues now seek help from their college counseling departments than in 1989 (National Association of Student Personnel Administrators, 2009).
> *(Wood, 2012, p. 6)*

What I was observing and what the data confirms is that many of the students enrolled in higher education are afflicted with a range of mental health disorders. While I am not a mental health professional, and my official responsibilities are to facilitate student learning in a variety of subjects within the fields of humanities, communication, and ethnic studies, the question arose: What might I, as a classroom instructor and mentor to my students, do to facilitate their wellness beyond effectively teaching the assigned content of my courses? It did not take a great deal of research to realize that I was not alone in grappling with this question. A conversation with a colleague from the sciences resulted in our authoring and being awarded a campus grant to provide training in mindfulness-based stress reduction (MBSR) to faculty across the campus. Our pilot program was a success as we enrolled over 30 participants from a range of disciplinary areas in the training. Participants were provided the training for free with the stipulation that they integrate aspects of what they learned into the classes they were teaching. In my own contribution to this collection, I will discuss and analyze the results of my efforts.

Our local efforts to integrate practices into our pedagogies that might promote wellness and even contribute to healing among our students are mirrored in similar endeavors nationally and globally. More than 20 years ago, in the mid-1990s, James Penabacker, a professor of psychology, published on the therapeutic benefits of writing about emotional disorders and traumatic experiences. His work was subsequently taken up by scholars in the field of Composition and Rhetoric, most notably in Charles Anderson and Marian MacCurdy's 1999 edited collection, *Writing and Healing: Toward an Informed Practice*. This collection, focused on teachers of writing, advocates for and provides examples of ways to allow and even encourage students to write about traumatic experiences as a vehicle for healing from the impact of trauma. Anderson and MacCurdy and the authors they included in the book envisioned an integration of healing with learning. However, efforts such as these to invite students to explore trauma and traumatic experience are not without their critics, a point I shall return to momentarily.

Even as scholars and teachers in the field of Composition and Rhetoric were exploring ways to facilitate student wellness into their pedagogical practices, the work of scholars in a variety of humanities and social sciences began coalescing around an interdisciplinary field of inquiry that has come to be known as trauma studies. In the humanities generally and the field of literary studies particularly, a "flood of scholarship in the 1990s arose to examine the concept of trauma and its role in literature and society most prominently by Cathy Caruth, Shoshana Felman, and Geoffrey Hartman" (Marmbrol, 2018). As a field, trauma studies focuses on representations of trauma in literature, film, and other media in order to analyze and understand its "psychological, rhetorical, and cultural significance" (Mambrol, 2018). While traumatic experiences and their representations have always been a part of human experience and cultural expressions, the catastrophic wars of the 20th century and the American Psychiatric Association's classification of posttraumatic stress disorder (PTSD) in the *Diagnostic and Statistical Manual of Mental Disorders, Third Edition (DSM-III)* in 1980 both named the affliction and provided widespread evidence of its existence as a significant cultural experience. Thus, humanities and social science scholars found both a designation and the urgent impetus for the focus of trauma studies.

The work in both Composition Studies and in other fields of the Humanities and Social Sciences reflect an understanding of trauma as both an individual and cultural experience, an element of culture to be studied and analyzed beyond the field of psychology, and, most germane to this collection, a sense that teaching and learning in these fields has the potential to contribute to cultural and individual healing from trauma. In the ensuing years, publications in the field of trauma studies have proliferated.

However, these interdisciplinary approaches to the study and teaching of trauma have not been universally applauded. Scholars and practitioners in the field of psychology have sounded cautionary notes about the potential risks incurred when exposing students to intense media representations of trauma or inviting students to reflect upon and write about their own trauma. Perhaps the most pointed critique, "Potentially Perilous Pedagogies: Teaching Trauma Is Not the Same as Trauma-Informed Teaching," by Janice Carello and Lisa D. Butler, argues that the study of trauma "in nonclinical courses such as literature, women's studies, film, education, anthropology, cultural studies, composition, and creative writing" risks "retraumatization and secondary traumatization" among students with histories of trauma (2014, p. 153). Carello and Butler assert that, "although these educators appear to appreciate some of the force and significance of traumatic experience, their practice does not reflect an understanding of the implications of trauma, retraumatization, or secondary traumatization for student adjustment and academic performance" (p. 159). While it may be tempting to dismiss their critique as disciplinary boundary policing, they do acknowledge that "As educators we undoubtedly need to teach about trauma; at the same time, we must also *be mindful of how we teach i*t as well as how we teach trauma survivors" (p. 163). However, while their article raises important and even necessary concerns, beyond a brief checklist of items for instructors to keep in mind when teaching about trauma, it does not provide much guidance for what a trauma-informed pedagogy for higher education might look like in practice. Indeed, in their concluding remarks they note, "As theory and research concerning this topic develop, and the ethical necessity to protect student safety becomes more widely recognized, resources and guidance will ideally become available to aid instructors to become trauma-informed in the classroom" (p. 163). It is to this need that the present collection responds.

Before proceeding, let me offer a brief overview of what is meant by the term "trauma." The current edition of the American Psychiatric Association's *Diagnostic and Statistical Manual of Mental Disorders*, the *DSM-5*, defines trauma as "'actual or threatened death, serious injury, or sexual violence.' Stressful events not involving an immediate threat to life or physical injury such as psychosocial stressors (e.g., divorce or job loss) are not considered trauma in this definition" (Pai et al., 2017). The most recent edition of the *DSM* reflects significantly revised definitions of trauma and post-traumatic stress disorder. The revisions were in part made in response to concerns that the criterion for designating an experience as traumatic were "too inclusive [and] … it was modified to restrict its inclusiveness" (Pai et al., 2017). Yet the revisions and the term itself remain debated and controversial. Even as the *DSM-5* has limited the clinical definition of trauma, the American Psychiatric Association nevertheless notes that while a "diagnosis of PTSD requires exposure to an upsetting traumatic event ... the exposure could be indirect rather than first hand" (2020). Complicating the *DSM-5*'s definition of trauma and the criteria for a diagnosis of PTSD is research indicating that traumatic symptoms may be transmitted across generations to family members who have not directly experienced a "threatened death, serious injury, or sexual violence." Indeed, research on the children of Holocaust survivors produced compelling evidence that the symptoms of PTSD could be identified in the offspring of Holocaust survivors even though the children had never directly experienced the trauma of the Holocaust (Kellerman, 2001). Furthermore, research among Indigenous communities in Canada and the United States suggests that the legacies of colonization, displacement, genocidal efforts, and assimilation-oriented boarding school experiences have resulted in what is known as intergenerational and historic trauma (Brave Heart et al., 2011). Furthermore, the nation's legacy of slavery, racial oppression, and discrimination has led Joy DeGruy (2017) to coin the term "post traumatic slave syndrome" as a diagnosis for the cultural trauma inflicted upon African Americans. These findings are united in indicating that trauma is not limited to an immediate and direct experience of violence and danger but rather that trauma may also be a cumulative and social experience, and that the symptoms of trauma that manifest as PTSD may also be indirectly transmitted across generations. The authors in this collection respond both to the clinical definition provided by the *DSM-5* and to the broader traumas inflicted by the cultural violence targeting communities based on race, ethnicity, gender, and sexuality: cultural violence that is systemic, historic, and ongoing. Given this more inclusive understanding of trauma, while the data indicates that more than half of all college students have directly experienced trauma, faculty in institutions of higher education need to consider that an even greater percentage of students suffer from the impact of these broader forms of cultural trauma.

Because significant numbers of the students enrolled in our classes are suffering from the effects of direct or indirect trauma, and because, for many of us, teaching about trauma and traumatic events is integral to our academic fields, and because student success is directly tied to students' wellness, the question of how we teach about trauma, when relevant, in ways that "do no harm," and may even promote and facilitate student recovery and healing from trauma, is of vital concern. The authors gathered in this collection, from a range of disciplines and experiences, take these questions to heart and in the following chapters provide both theoretical, institutional, and classroom responses and models for practice. Each contributor takes seriously the concerns expressed by Carello and Butler who argue that, as teachers, our pedagogical practices must "reflect an understanding of the implications of trauma, retraumatization, or secondary traumatization for student adjustment and academic performance" (p. 159). The essays in this anthology take up the question, "What roles, practices, and structures can higher education provide to support the wellness and by extension academic success of students who suffer from the effects of traumatic experiences?" Included are chapters that cover topics on how to create institutional structures to support trauma-informed pedagogies, how to teach traumatic materials ethically and effectively, how to employ reading and writing to support recovery and healing from trauma, and the use of inclusive pedagogies responsive to systemically inflicted trauma.

In Chapter 2, "Considerations for Developing a First-Year Seminar on Psychological Trauma," professor of psychology Christina Valdez provides an overview of trauma, research on the trauma experienced by our students, and an introduction to trauma-informed pedagogy. Valdez argues that, as educators, we must consider the ability of our students to learn in the context of previous and/or ongoing trauma and develop ways to ensure that we help our students feel safe, empowered, and connected, and thus, able to learn. As a psychologist specializing in trauma, she notes that the foundation for effective trauma-informed pedagogy is a keen awareness of how trauma impacts students intra- and interpersonally, and an intentional effort to incorporate strategies aimed at increasing educational success for those who may be trauma-impacted. In this chapter she defines psychological trauma and identifies current prevalence rates in college students; describes the clinical manifestations of traumatic stress; presents an evidence-informed psychological framework of posttraumatic sequelae to understand the behavioral manifestations of unresolved traumatic stress in the classroom; and discusses the development of a trauma-focused First Year Seminar aimed at teaching students about trauma and trauma-specific social-emotional skills to self-regulate.

In Chapter 3, Steve Lundy and Sarah Le Pichon's "Trauma-Informed Pedagogy at the Grassroots: Building and Sustaining a Trauma-Informed Movement at a Large Public Institution" describes and analyzes the challenges to implementing trauma-informed practices as an act of radical curricular transformation. This chapter details the grassroots efforts and processes that resulted in "trauma-informed pedagogy" (TIP) becoming a recognized and practiced approach to teaching and learning across campus at a major state university. The authors discuss and analyze the structural impediments faced in implementing TIP at scale and outline the collaborations and strategies engaged that yielded a successful cross-campus implementation of TIP.

Chapter 4, "Racial Trauma: Dismantling Anti-Black Racism in Classrooms and Academia," by Vanessa Lopez-Littleton and Dennis Kombe, directly challenges teachers and institutions to recognize the history and current culture of anti-Black racism and its impacts on Black students in higher education. These authors explore the deep roots of systemic anti-Black racism and the painful burden it places on Black students. They frame the history of racism as a history of trauma inflicted upon African Americans. Their contribution concludes with recommendations for institutional transformation and several practical approaches to counter anti-Black racism within the classroom.

In "When Embodied Histories Meet Institutional Stories: Trauma as Pedagogical Possibility," Whitney Archer, Carina Buzo, Cassandra Hall, and Emma Larkins trace how embodied histories of trauma—including trauma inflicted by the academy, intergenerational trauma, and/or historical trauma—disrupt dominant academic narratives. The authors position trauma-informed pedagogy as a framework for resisting prescribed metrics of academic success thrust upon both instructors and the students we teach and mentor. This chapter considers "trauma as possibility" through a focus on the ways in which embodied traumatic histories can create ruptures within the limiting and potentially traumatizing structures of institutions of higher education. The chapter argues for a pedagogy of care that de-pathologizes manifestations of trauma as we navigate institutions haunted by systems of racism, sexism, classicism, nationalism, and homophobia.

Pritha Prasad and Kriti Prasad in "Affective Solidarity and Trauma-Informed Possibilities: A Comparative Analysis of the Classroom and the Clinic," examine how historical race, gender, and sexuality-based traumas manifest in institutional spaces, from the classroom to the healthcare setting. In their exploration and analysis, Prasad and Prasad interrogate their own relationships to the postcolonial, transgenerational, and familial historical traumas that have shaped their overlapping approaches to social justice–oriented "pedagogy" as university instructors and healthcare workers, respectively. The chapter offers a framework of trauma-informed praxis that points to the generative possibilities of shared and relational trauma across care-oriented relationships. Considering trauma-informed pedagogy broadly, the authors analyze parallel pedagogical situations in higher education and medicine. Both analyses rethink care-oriented pedagogical relationships (clinician–patient, mother–baby, and instructor–student) and their political, pedagogical, and the therapeutic possibilities for addressing collective, communal, and transgenerational historical traumas as they manifest in present contexts.

In "Trauma-Informed Mindfulness Meditation in the College Classroom," Ernest Stromberg examines and analyzes the effects of integrating mindfulness-based stress reduction (MBSR) practices into the curriculum. Stromberg explains how the integration of MBSR into the classroom came as a response to the recognition that more college students are reporting mental health problems. Stromberg takes up the question of how instructors might teach subject matter, some of which by necessity deals with traumatic events and experiences, while supporting the psychological wellness of students. Drawing on over three years of practice and data gathered through student surveys, this chapter analyzes and argues for the benefits and limitations of integrating meditation in a trauma-informed manner into the curriculum.

Angela Moore, in "Examining Authority Through Trauma: Reflections From Student to Teacher," explores the concept of classroom authority in higher education through the lens of trauma-informed scholarship. Moore argues that we need to consider classroom authority in relationship to trauma and to explicitly recognize the role frequently played by authority figures in inflicting trauma. The chapter analyzes the implications that authority-related traumas may have, not just for students, but also for teachers, *specifically related to the student–teacher relationship*. The chapter concludes with recommendations for ways we might approach the student–teacher relationship in light of how authority-related traumas may impact students, and how we might go about effectively training and supporting new teachers who have authority-related traumas.

Brynn Fitzsimmons, in "Trauma Together: Rethinking Collaborative Learning," focuses on the student-to-student relationship in the composition course, specifically group projects. Fitzsimmons argues that student success in group projects, activities, and composing must be an inclusion and development of strategies for engaging with and/or *through* one's own trauma and/or the trauma of classmates. This chapter draws on existing literature in writing as healing as well as trauma-informed pedagogy to offer trauma-informed modifications for standard approaches in composition literature to group work with first-year students.

Turning to the study of literature, Katarina Båth, in "Insights in Trauma-Informed Pedagogy From the Field of Bibliotherapy, Literary Trauma Studies and Creative Writing," employs literary trauma theory to review the field of *creative bibliotherapy* (i.e., reading of fiction and poetry to improve mental health). The chapter examines the current "bibliotherapy" initiatives in Sweden and Finland from the theoretical vantage point of literary trauma theory, and discusses norms regarding reading as therapeutic. The chapter challenges and improves bibliotherapeutic conceptions of reading, trauma, and literature. The chapter advances new ways of thinking about trauma, reading, and the possible healing uses of literature.

Rose Gubele's "Trigger Warnings with Conscience: Presenting Texts about Sexual Assault with Respect," focuses on the teaching of American Indigenous literatures. Because the process of colonization has been, and continues to be, systemically violent and traumatizing, teaching this subject requires exposing students to potentially triggering materials. Gubele provides models for how we educate students about the historic and ongoing violence, including sexual assault and rape inflicted upon Indigenous peoples, without traumatizing or re-traumatizing them. Gubele argues for teaching this difficult material with trauma-informed principles that include providing the support and making choices available to students who themselves may be survivors of assault and sexual violence.

The final chapter, "LGBTQ+ Trauma-Informed Pedagogy in a Transnational Context," by Jason Lee, Beverley Hancock-Smith, Zara Hooley, and Eleanor McSherry, examines ways to address the needs of LGBTQ+ people in a trauma-informed manner within the context of teaching creative writing. Drawing on their experiences as university instructors in Great Britain and the research on the array of traumas experienced by LGBTQ+ youth, these authors argue for the importance of creating welcoming environments in which students feel free to be and express their authentic identities. The chapter provides three case studies to illustrate their approaches to trauma-informed pedagogies in the context of teaching creative expression.

While neither comprehensive or exhaustive, this collection of essay provides a range of interdisciplinary and transnational approaches to transforming both institutions and classrooms in trauma-informed ways. Drawing on the most current research from the field of psychology, sections of this book advance an understanding of the nature of trauma relevant to the setting of higher education. Refusing to be confined by the definition of trauma articulated by the fifth edition of the *Diagnostic and Statistical Manual of Mental Disorders* (*DSM-5*), several authors analyze trauma as a sociological phenomenon transmitted over time and embedded within institutional structures, including institutions of higher learning. As we grapple with the impact of the COVID-19 pandemic, political turmoil, and a global climate crisis, among other traumatic phenomenon, the authors in the collection offer both a direction forward and an invitation to continue the development of trauma-informed approaches to teaching and learning in higher education.

References

American Psychiatric Association. (2020). What Is Posttraumatic Stress Disorder (PTSD)? Psychiatry.org—Home, September 22, 2022. https://psychiatry.org/.

Anderson, C., & MacCurdy, M., editors. (2000). *Writing as Healing: Toward an Informed Practice*. NCTE, 1999.

Barber, C. (2013, May 20). We Live in the Age of Trauma. Salon. https://www.salon.com/2013/05/01/we_live_in_the_age_of_trauma/.

Brave Heart, M. Y. H., Chase, J., Elkins, J., & Altschul, D. B. (2011). Historical Trauma Among Indigenous Peoples of the Americas: Concepts, Research, and Clinical Considerations. *Journal of Psychoactive Drugs*, 43(4), 282–290.

Carello, J., & Butler, L. D. (2014). Potentially Perilous Pedagogies: Teaching Trauma Is Not the Same as Trauma-Informed Teaching. *Journal of Trauma and Dissociation*, 15(2), 153–168. https://doi-org.csumb.idm.oclc.org/10.1080/15299732.2014.867571.

DeGruy, J. (2017). *Post Traumatic Slave Syndrome: America's Legacy of Enduring Injury and Healing*. Joy DeGruy Publications Inc.

Kellerman, N. P. F. (2001). Psychopathology in Children of Holocaust Survivors: A Review of the Research Literature. *Israel Journal of Psychiatry and Related Sciences*, 38(1), 36–46.

Mambol, N. (2018). Trauma Studies: Literary Theory and Criticism. https://literariness.org/2018/12/19/trauma-studies/.

Pai, A., Suris, A. M., & North, C. S. (2017). Posttraumatic Stress Disorder in the DSM-5: Controversy, Change, and Conceptual Considerations. *Behavioral Sciences (Basel, Switzerland)*, 7(1), 7. https://doi.org/10.3390/bs7010007.

Wood, M. (2012). The State of Mental Health on College Campuses. *Inquiry: The Journal of the Virginia Community Colleges*, 17(1), 4–15. https://commons.vccs.edu/inquiry/vol17/iss1/1/.

SECTION I
Transforming the Institution and the Classroom

2
CONSIDERATIONS FOR DEVELOPING A FIRST-YEAR SEMINAR ON PSYCHOLOGICAL TRAUMA

Christine Valdez

Societal awareness of trauma and its effects have waxed and waned (van der Kolk et al., 1994), even though peoples and cultures have named and worked with trauma differently throughout the centuries. Recently, there has been renewed interest in trauma, perhaps in part because of efforts of the National Center for Trauma-Informed Care (NCTIC), who develop the knowledge base on trauma-informed services, which they define as:

> A program, organization, or system that is trauma-informed realizes the widespread impact of trauma and understands potential paths for recovery; recognizes the signs and symptoms of trauma in clients, families, staff, and others involved with the system; and responds by fully integrating knowledge about trauma into policies, procedures, and practices, and seeks to actively resist re-traumatization.
> *(Substance Abuse and Mental Health Services Administration [SAMHSA], 2014, p. 9).*

Trauma-informed care has increased in popularity since 2011 (Becker-Blease, 2017). At the core of this approach is a basic understanding of trauma and how trauma affects the life of those who interface with systems of care (e.g., welfare services, the criminal justice system, physical and mental health care systems, the military, and schools and universities) so that services and programs can be supportive and avoid exacerbating the impacts of trauma (SAMHSA, 2014). Such elevated insights have led to changes in organizational policies and practices designed to facilitate resilience and recovery for those who are trauma-impacted and are burgeoning in the education system as greater awareness of trauma among students is clarified. This chapter presents a psychological

DOI: 10.4324/9781003260776-3

framework to define trauma and contextualize trauma responses among students in the higher-educational setting, and to provide recommendations for responding to trauma appropriately. Lastly, applications for a trauma-informed and trauma-specific first-year seminar are provided.

A Psychological Framework for Trauma and Traumatic Stress

In the field of clinical psychology, trauma has a very distinct definition that aligns with clinical criteria outlined in the *Diagnostic and Statistical Manual of Mental Disorders* (*DSM*). At the broadest level, trauma has historically been defined as an event(s) or set of circumstances that is experienced by an individual as physically or emotionally harmful or threatening and that has lasting adverse effects on the individual's functioning and physical, social, emotional, and/or spiritual well-being. In its most recent iteration, the *DSM-Fifth Edition* (*DSM-5*) (American Psychiatric Association [APA], 2013) characterizes trauma as actual or threatened death, serious injury, or sexual violence that is directly experienced, witnessed in person as the event is occurring, learned about from a close other, and/or repeated or extreme exposure (not through media unless work-related) to adverse details of trauma (APA, 2013). These experiences create psychological trauma, extreme stress that emotionally, cognitively, and/or physically overwhelms a person's ability to cope, and it is an individual's subjective experience that determines whether an event(s) is traumatic. In this way, trauma threatens one's sense of physical, psychological, or emotional safety and survival.

The circumstances of potentially traumatic events commonly include abuse of power, betrayal of trust, helplessness, pain, and/or loss. Such events include one-time incidents like natural or human made disasters, motor vehicle accidents, being violently threatened or assaulted, the sudden and unexpected death of a loved one, or close call with death. It also includes chronic or repetitive experiences such as medical trauma, combat exposure, or living in a warzone, child abuse and maltreatment, community violence, experiencing or witnessing domestic violence, human trafficking, and other forms of repeated victimization. These types of traumatic experiences can be complex (i.e., complex traumatic experiences) in which such severe events that occur over an extended period of time undermine a developing person's personality, brain development, and fundamental trust in relationships (Ford & Courtois, 2009).

Symptoms of posttraumatic stress disorder (PTSD) are very common and a typical reaction in the immediate aftermath of a traumatic event, where upwards of 90% of those exposed to certain types of trauma will experience symptoms within the first month (Rothbaum et al., 1992). Symptoms are defined by psychological re-experiencing of the trauma (e.g., nightmares, flashbacks, intrusive memories); avoidance of internal (e.g., memories, emotions, sensations) and external (e.g., people, places, situations) reminders of the trauma; changes to the way one views the world, self, and others that are negative and distorted, and accompanied by negative emotions (e.g., guilt, anger) and/or loss of interest; and increased arousal (e.g., irritability, hyperstartle, hypervigilance), which in combination can lead to considerable social, occupational, and interpersonal dysfunction (APA, 2013).

In the case of complex trauma, adverse mental health outcomes typically extend beyond the symptoms captured by PTSD because complex trauma can lead to chronic problems across multiple domains of self-regulation, including affective, behavioral, physiological, cognitive/perceptual, relational, and self-attributional (Cook et al., 2005). Challenges to these domains of self-regulation can manifest as a myriad of psychiatric disorders and functional deficits in the areas of attachment, anxiety, mood, eating, substance abuse, attention and concentration, impulse control, dissociation, somatization and chronic medical problems, sexual behavior and development, and learning and scholastic performance (Cook et al., 2005).

Realizing Trauma and Risk Factors in College Students

The peak age of trauma exposure is 16 to 20 years of age (Breslau et al., 2008), and there is considerable evidence that the vast majority, in the range of up to 89%, of college students have experienced a potentially traumatic event (Anders et al., 2012; Frazier et al., 2009; Read et al., 2011). One study of over 3,000 matriculating students aged 18 to 24 at two mid-sized public universities in the northeastern and southeastern United States found that 66% of students reported exposure to trauma that met clinical criteria; 35% experienced a life-threatening illness, 34% experienced the sudden death of a loved one, 26% were exposed to an accident/natural disaster/fire, 24% experienced physical violence, 7% experienced sexual assault, 1% were exposed to combat, while 20% reported another type of psychological trauma (Read et al., 2011). The average number of traumatic events was 1.5, with 23% of students reporting one event, 20% of students reporting two events, and 25% of students reporting three or more events (Read et al., 2011). These rates increase when examining community college students. In a combined sample of 842 undergraduate students at a large public university and 242 students at a community college, the mean number of potentially traumatic events meeting clinical criteria was 3; community college students reported a significantly higher total number of potentially traumatic events than university students, as well as more exposure to witnessing family violence, being threatened, intimate partner violence, witnessing violence, childhood physical abuse, sexual abuse/assault, physical assault, and being robbed or mugged with threat (Anders et al., 2012).

Gender has been consistently shown to be a risk factor for trauma, where women are at heightened risk for interpersonal types of violence like sexual and physical violence, especially in college samples (e.g., Read et al., 2011; Smyth et al., 2008; Vrana & Lauterbach, 1994). There are also other demographic variables that have been consistently shown to be associated with increased risk for trauma exposure that are particularly relevant to universities that serve a diverse student body. In one college student sample of matriculating students, lower socioeconomic status (SES) was associated with trauma exposure, and of those with a trauma history, ethnic minority status and lower SES were associated with experiencing more traumatic events (Read et al., 2011). In another study, women who often or always had difficulty paying for basic needs had increased odds of a sexual assault while in college; the trend was similar for men (Mellins et al., 2017). In a sample of 1,198 ethnically diverse community college students from the west coast of the United States, it was found that Black and Latinx students reported more trauma exposure compared to White and Asian students, and also reported more experiences of interpersonal violence than White students (Edman et al., 2016). Overall, this line of research demonstrates that students who are most impacted by trauma are traditionally underserved students, students who may be at increased risk for adverse mental health outcomes following trauma due to compounding stressors associated with being marginalized in a way that can trigger and/or exacerbate traumatic stress.

Recognizing Posttraumatic Sequelae in College Students

Current estimates suggest lifetime, past 12-month, and past 6-month PTSD prevalence for a specific trauma to be 8.3%, 4.7%, and 3.8%, respectively (Kilpatrick et al., 2013). However, rates of current PTSD in college students exceed those reported in the general population, as they have been estimated to be in the range of 6%–17% (Read et al., 2011). One study of 2,310 freshmen entering college found that approximately 70% were exposed to at least one potentially traumatic event, and 34.4% of those exposed met criteria for probable PTSD (Cusack et al., 2018). Even more, other research has uncovered that students who experienced events that do not qualify under the *DSM* clinical criteria for trauma reported significantly greater PTSD symptoms and met all other criteria for PTSD more than students who reported exposure to a *DSM*-defined trauma (Gold et al., 2004), suggesting the scope of traumatic stress among college students may be more extensive than previously realized.

Thus, given that students enter college with significant trauma histories and PTSD symptoms, as educators we must realize that the scope of trauma among students is widespread, and further we must recognize the signs and symptoms of trauma in our students so that we can respond to trauma in those we serve by integrating our knowledge of trauma into our classroom policies, procedures, and practices to support student well-being, personal development, and academic success. Table 2.1 presents the core symptoms of PTSD and domains of impairment in those exposed to complex trauma aligned with a myriad of

TABLE 2.1 Behavioral Manifestations of PTSD Symptoms

Re-experiencing	Distraction
Avoidance	Excessive absences and missing assignments
Alterations in cognitions and mood	Negative self-talk, lack of sustained curiosity and problems completing tasks, difficulty connecting with peers
Increased arousal	Difficulty concentrating and focusing, sleep disturbance

Behavioral Manifestations of Complex Trauma Domains of Impairment

Attachment	Distrust of others; boundary-crossing; difficulty in interpersonal relationships, attuning to others' emotional states, perspective-taking
Biology	Frequently sick, chronic pain, hypersensitive stress response
Affect regulation	Emotion dysregulation and heightened states of affect, difficulty expressing feelings, difficulty communicating needs
Dissociation	Impaired memory, feeling detached from self and others, difficulty staying present, problems orienting to time and space
Behavioral control	Poor modulation of impulses (e.g., interrupting in class), addictive and obsessive behaviors, aggression toward self and others, oppositional behavior, excessive compliance
Cognition	Difficulty with executive functioning (e.g., planning and anticipating, organizing schedule, structuring tasks), processing novel information, understanding responsibility.
Self-concept	Poor sense of self identity and separateness (e.g., difficulty articulating own ideas and opinions)

behaviors that impact learning and integrating into the campus community that might reflect psychological trauma in students.

Responding to Trauma in College Students: Pillars of Trauma-Informed Pedagogy

A trauma-informed approach to pedagogy is built on six core principles: (1) safety; (2) trustworthiness and transparency; (3) peer support; (4) collaboration and mutuality; (5) empowerment, voice, and change; and (6) cultural, historical, and gender issues (SAMHSA, 2014). In the educational setting, these principles can work in tandem to increase educational success for students who may be trauma-impacted.

Safety

Safety is specified as both physical and psychological, which is promoted by creating a physically safe environment and establishing safe interpersonal interactions. In one study of undergraduate students from the United States, it was found that those who identify as having PTSD had a lower sense of belonging on their campus compared to those who do not have PTSD; perceptions of campus safety, stigma about mental health treatment, and perceptions of campus climate related to mental health contributed to the diminished sense of belonging among college students who experienced PTSD (Shalka & Leal, 2022). These findings underscore the need for members of a campus community to understand the trajectories of trauma so they can better anticipate how feelings of safety may be compromised and ways to support student trauma survivors. This understanding may come with broad education of administrators, faculty, staff, and students about the impacts of trauma, and additionally serve to reduce a sense of stigma by illuminating the high rates of trauma and traumatic stress.

Helping to establish connections and relationships may also mitigate the effects of "othering." In one study of 18 teachers who co-designed and/or adapted trauma-informed positive education for trauma-impacted primary and secondary school students, through qualitative analysis it was revealed that teachers designed their classrooms and adapted their interactive style to facilitate attachment and build classroom relationships (Brunzell et al., 2019). In higher-education classrooms instructors can be mindful of body positioning in relation to students that can contribute to power differentials, create activities that enhance group cohesion, and identify ways to anchor students positively in one's own mind to create unconditional positive regard and more tolerance when responding to challenging student behaviors.

Trustworthiness and Transparency

Being open and honest about decisions in organizational operations builds and maintains a sense of trust among those who are being served. Unfortunately, there have been notable occurrences of institutional betrayal (i.e., an institution fails to fulfill its obligations to institutional members who entrust and depend upon it by actively committing a transgression or violation against a member and/or failing to enact appropriate policies or respond adequately to an expressed concern) in higher education in the context of campus sexual assault (Smith & Freyd, 2013), university study abroad programs (Wright et al., 2017), and a global pandemic (Adams-Clar & Freyd, 2021).

For example, most students at a public university in the Northwest United States reported at least one type of COVID-19–related institutional betrayal, and higher ratings of institutional betrayal were associated with more trauma symptoms, above and beyond the effects of gender, personal and familial COVID-19 infection, and past trauma history (Adams-Clar & Freyd, 2021). These results emphasize that traumatic stress is influenced by institutional systems and policies. To reduce institutional betrayal and negative mental health consequences, members of educational institutions—administrators, staff, and faculty need to be thoughtful about the impact of institutional decisions on students.

Peer Support and Mutual Self-Help

Lived experiences can promote recovery by instilling hope, establishing safety, building trust, and enhancing collaboration. A study of over 1,000 students across 12 California colleges examining students' engagement with Active Minds, a student peer organization dedicated to promoting mental health, demonstrated the impact of peer-to-peer dialogue on campus climate (Sontag-Padilla et al., 2018). Students with increased familiarity with Active Minds over the course of an academic year demonstrated increases in perceived knowledge and decreases in stigma, and increased involvement in Active Minds was associated with increases in perceived knowledge and helping behaviors (Sontag-Padilla et al., 2018). Furthermore, improvements in aspects of mental well-being have been documented in students receiving peer-support services (Bryom, 2018) and in student mental health peer-support workers (Johnson et al., 2021). Thus, to meet the increasing need for mental health services for students, it is important to advocate for peer-support programs to be developed and implemented at universities. As these programs become more available, it will be important to assess the effectiveness for those impacted by trauma, and the feasibility and acceptability of trauma-specific programs.

Collaboration and Mutuality

Sharing of power and decision-making is promoted through partnering with those who are being served and by leveling out power differences. Within higher education, practices that center "students as partners" position students and other members of the campus community to contribute equally to further common educational goals. Students become co-teachers, co-inquirers, co-creators, and co-learners across all facets of the educational enterprise, an approach that has been associated with a plethora of positive outcomes for students (for a review, see Mercer-Mapstone et al., 2017).

An example of a pedagogical partnership program engaged undergraduate student partners to research resources during the 2020 global coronavirus pandemic on trauma-informed, anti-racist, and equitable approaches to hybrid and remote teaching and learning (Akua Ameyaa et al., 2021). Students met with academic staff across a ten-college consortium to consult on implementing recommendations and developing a publicly accessible web page of resources. An autoethnographic account of three Black, Asian, and minority student partners' experiences showed that this partnership created a space for affirming the lived experiences of marginalized students, supported students in developing language to voice their lived experiences to their campus community members, created institutional roles that remunerate students for their work, and inspired students to carry the partnership benefits forward (Akua Ameyaa et al., 2021). Thus, engaging students as partners in teaching and learning, especially in areas where students have lived experiences, can uniquely speak to student needs and avenues for success.

Empowerment, Voice, and Change

This principle recognizes and builds upon the strengths and experiences of those engaged with the organization—administrators, staff, and those being served. In the study by Brunzell et al. (2019) of teachers co-designing and/or adapting trauma-informed positive education for trauma-impacted students, teachers discussed positive learning outcomes to practical strategies that supported students in making and sustaining positive behaviors for learning, including teaching and framing in the learning process character strengths, a growth mindset, and reaching goals through flow. Teaching and utilizing a strength-based approach can enhance psychological capacities to support student learning.

Cultural, Historical, and Gender Issues

Lastly, it is important for organizations to actively move past cultural stereotypes and biases; offer access to gender responsive services; leverage traditional cultural connections; incorporate procedures that are responsive to the culturally diverse individual needs; and recognize and address historical trauma. For example, it has been found that racial minority students report more frequent experiences of discrimination than White students on their campus, and they perceive their campus racial climate as more negative; unfortunately, perceptions of discrimination and racial climate contribute significantly to trauma-related symptoms among racially marginalized students (Pieterse et al., 2010). Therefore, it is important that institutions and its members acknowledge their past history of exclusion and articulate a vision for a more inclusive future, increase structural diversity, implement systematic and comprehensive educational programs for members of the campus community to identify and confront stereotypes and biases, and increase opportunities for cross-cultural interactions through campus programs and activities (Hurtado et al., 1998).

Reducing Retraumatization During the College Transition

A considerable number of first-year college students evidence an increase in traumatic stress symptoms in their second semester (Read et al., 2016), suggesting the first year of college is a particularly challenging transition for those with a trauma background. Unfortunately, higher levels of PTSD symptoms in the first semester of college predict second-year enrollment, partly through effort regulation and first-year grade point average, suggesting that posttraumatic stress has deleterious effects on academic performance and college persistence (Boyraz et al., 2016). Further, the use of negative coping strategies for trauma-exposed students may exacerbate traumatic stress over the first three years of college (Read et al., 2014), particularly for those who do not have the skills to effectively manage the competing demands of mental health challenges with the stress of college life. Thus, as educators, we must consider the ability of our students to learn in the context of previous and/or ongoing trauma, and develop ways to ensure that we help our students feel safe, empowered, and connected, and thus, able to learn.

A first-year seminar (FYS) is a special course for first-year students to enhance their academic and social integration into college, and an ideal point of intervention to support students who are trauma-impacted to adjust to college. Studies have found that students who engage in FYSs have increased persistence and retention in college, more meaningful interactions with faculty and peers, increased levels of satisfaction with the college experience, more positive perceptions of themselves as learners, and achieve higher grades in college (Goodman & Pascarella, 2006). A FYS focused on psychological trauma and integrating trauma-informed practices may provide opportunities for students to understand concepts and stages associated with trauma recovery, and promote optimism and adjustment toward others who have experienced trauma or toward themselves if they are trauma survivors. What follows is an example of developing a FYS course on psychological trauma, as well as practical applications for teaching about trauma and establishing safety in learning in a FYS.

Reducing Stigma Through Enhanced Awareness of Self and Others

A significant number of student trauma survivors may enter college with internalized stigma that can increase barriers to connecting with peers, integrating into the campus community, and seeing themself as a capable and worthy student. As such, I developed a FYS focused on educating students about trauma, the impacts of trauma, and how to heal from trauma to debunk preconceived notions that contribute to self-stigma and other types of stigma. This course includes an overview of different types of trauma in relation to stressful events and highlights types of trauma that are uniquely associated with being a college student (e.g., sexual assault). Naming these different types of trauma can increase self-understanding and potentially motivate students to seek help. I also provide statistics on rates of trauma exposure and different trauma trajectories to increase a sense of universality and common humanity. That is, this course emphasizes that trauma is a universal experience of people where few people are not impacted by trauma either directly or indirectly, and that suffering and unpleasant feelings are part of the human experience. Course content is introduced in the sociopolitical context of trauma to help students honor historical trauma and understand, and ideally intervene in, complex dynamics that perpetuate gender-based violence, racially motivated violence, and other hate-based acts of violence that contribute to oppression and marginalization.

Although course content will change across disciplines, utilizing trauma-informed principles can serve to reduce self-stigma and other types of stigma in any disciplinary area. Instructors can socialize students in creating and establishing an inclusive classroom environment by incorporating student-centered learning methods that provide ongoing opportunities for diverse students to communicate, interact, and learn from each other. In doing so, students may feel more similar than different from each other, and less isolated in their experiences. Activities that increase awareness of biases and understanding the effects of such biases on others, modeling cultural humility, and integrating diversity as part of the course content may allow for feelings of empathy and compassion for themselves and others.

Establishing Trust: Norming, Socializing, and Co-Creating the Course Expectations

FYSs provide students with opportunities to interact with their peers and seminar leaders/instructors/facilitators to build a community of academic and personal support. Given the trauma-focused nature of my FYS course, it was important to co-create with students the guidelines for learning and developmental experiences. On the first day of class, I ask students to individually reflect on, then talk in small groups, and then share in the class what they need from each other and from me as the instructor to feel supported in the course as they learn about a potentially sensitive topic. I also post an anonymous survey on the Learning Management System in the first week to honor voice and choice for students who may feel more comfortable stating this privately and anonymously. In the anonymous and voluntary survey, I also invite students to share anything they believe is important for me to know about them. Guidelines and expectations introduced often include holding confidentiality between each other, showing compassion and kindness, offering validation and grace, encouraging curiosity and self-care, and avoiding shaming and fixing. In the anonymous survey, students often describe aspects of their identity they want acknowledged.

Instructors across disciplines can invite students into dialogue at the outset of a course to co-create a safe and inclusive environment for optimal learning. Instructors can foster trust by being clear, transparent, and reliable. This includes, for example, detailing policies and procedures for their course to establish clear expectations of students, articulating objectives of the course and aligning learning goals/outcomes with each assignment, specifying how each assignment will be evaluated, providing explanations and rationale for course changes to maintain integrity, and integrating student feedback into course policies or including student voices in decision-making processes. Given the high rates of trauma exposure, assume that trauma is in your presence, and consider building flexibility into course policies (e.g., percentage deductions for late assignments, allowing for a certain number of absences). Instructors can also create opportunities for more faculty–student interaction inside and outside of the classroom and modify course activities to reduce competition and hierarchical structures.

Increasing Safety and Developing Psychological Capacity to Learn

Invisible psychological challenges related to unresolved trauma can undermine academic success, especially during the college transition as students adapt to new developmental tasks and academic demands. Social connectedness, self-care behaviors, an optimistic cognitive style, and life skills have been associated with positive adaptation during the college transition (Leary & DeRosier, 2012). In my trauma-focused FYS course, students are assigned activities throughout the semester to develop social-emotional skills to contain stress- and trauma-related reactions that are informed by research. It is a hybrid course, with half of the units allocated to in-person activities to establish and enhance social connectedness, and the other half allocated to online activities to balance trauma-specific education with limiting exposure to trauma content. Online activities are experiential and enhance capacity for self-regulation, including mindfulness training and exercises to calm the nervous system, journaling with structured prompts to calm the mind, as well as comprehensive self-care activities to attend to areas of physical, psychological, emotional, spiritual, and professional health and well-being.

Instructors in other disciplines may consider a targeted curriculum at developing skills in self-care for incoming students who are learning to balance competing demands of self and study. Learning and practicing mindfulness and compassion skills may promote a healthy stress response in students transitioning to college by strengthening socioemotional competencies and by supporting the development of adaptive appraisal and psychological coping resources (Dvořáková et al., 2019). In a pilot study of 109 freshmen in a randomized control trial for Learning to BREATHE (L2B), a universal mindfulness program adapted to match the developmental tasks of college transition, it was observed that students in the intervention had significant increases in life satisfaction, significant decreases in depression and anxiety, and marginally significant decreases in sleep issues and alcohol consequences (Dvořáková et al., 2017). Thus, integrating mindfulness in FYS curriculum of any topic can support psychological resources for optimal learning.

Empowering Students Through Topics of Strengths, Resilience, and Growth

I have found it is also important to normalize trauma reactions and emphasize the arc of recovery in trauma trajectories to de-pathologize trauma responses and instill hope around recovery, respectively. The vast majority of trauma survivors are resilient—they evidence increased healthy, adaptive, or integrated positive functioning over time in the aftermath of adversity (Southwick et al., 2014), and I teach in my FYS course about factors (and students engage in activities) implicated in fostering these resilience outcomes. I also discuss experiences of positive change as a result of adversity, or what has been referred to as posttraumatic growth, benefit-finding, thriving, and stress-related growth, which can co-occur alongside distress (Linley & Joseph, 2004). For example, most trauma survivors report an increased appreciation for life, more meaningful interpersonal relationships, an enhanced sense of personal strength, changed priorities, or a richer existential life (Tedeschi & Calhoun, 1996).

In FYSs that are not trauma-focused, instructors may consider incorporating positive psychology (i.e., focus on well-being, human strengths, and optimal functioning) into classroom content and activities. For example, positive education, which draws from the positive psychology literature, positions well-being learning to be of equal importance to academic learning—it has been associated with a range of well-being outcomes, including hope, optimism, resilience, mindfulness, and character strengths (Brunzell et al., 2015). Increasing these types of strength-based competencies can promote healing and growth through planning opportunities to boost positive emotions, exploring character strengths through curricular connections, teaching and modeling a resilient mindset, and providing ways to action gratitude through student initiatives (Brunzell et al., 2015).

Enhancing Self Help and Collaboration with Resource Linkage and Advocacy Efforts

An important component of a FYS is to introduce students to the functions and resources of the university as they transition into the campus community. Increasing awareness about psychosocial resources available on and off campus can aid in linking students to support systems to address social-emotional needs, and direct them to avenues for healing. In my trauma-focused FYS course, students are introduced to a number of resources beneficial for those who are trauma-affected (directly or indirectly). General mental health resources include the campus counseling center, the National Alliance on Mental Illness (NAMI) (https://nami.org/Home), and NAMI on Campus (https://namica.org/nami-on-campus/). I invite a representative from at least one of these centers to come to class to speak about their services, and, if available, there is often a representative(s) who comes to speak about their lived experience with mental health–related challenges. Peer-support programs on my campus include Mental Health First Aid (https://www.mentalhealthfirstaid.org/), and students are encouraged to engage in this training through extra credit in the course. I also provide a list or resources in the syllabus and Learning Management System of targeted resources for students who are directly impacted by trauma, including the campus sexual assault advocate, campus and community veterans centers, rape crisis centers, and Trauma Recovery Centers (https://www.traumarecoverycentermodel.org/).

Integrating peer-support programs into assignments may be appropriate when learning goals are focused on developing professional skills, and they can also be learning opportunities for engaging in advocacy efforts. In addition to the ones I listed for my course, a general and popular mental health peer-support program is Active Minds (https://www.activeminds.org/) and a trauma-relevant peer-support program is Growing Veterans (https://growingveterans.org/peer-support-training), These resources can be made more visible to students in course syllabi, field trips to resource centers integrated into assignments, and/or having staff from such resource centers come to class to discuss their services or lecture on a topic relevant to the course content, thereby making connections with students and reducing barriers to seeking help. It is important to remember that many students are consumers of such programs, and they can broaden our awareness of student needs and available resources if we engage them as partners in resource linkage. For example, students can contribute to a shared course resource list.

Conclusion

Realizing the widespread prevalence of trauma among students, recognizing the signs and symptoms of unresolved trauma in the higher-educational setting, responding appropriately to the impacts of trauma at every institutional level, and implementing relevant university programming to reduce retraumatization during the most vulnerable times of the college years is imperative to addressing the whole embodied student. Teaching students about psychological trauma using a trauma-informed approach in a FYS can be positioned as a powerful place of intervention for posttraumatic awareness and healing, as it can empower students, build connection, enhance social-emotional development, and enable academic success. Integrating trauma-informed principles into FYSs that are not trauma-focused can also benefit students, especially those trauma-affected, to create safety in their learning and enhance their academic success.

References

Adams-Clark, A. A., & Freyd, J. J. (2021). COVID-19-related institutional betrayal associated with trauma symptoms among undergraduate students. *PLOS ONE*, *16*(10), e0258294. https://doi.org/10.1371/journal.pone.0258294

Akua Ameyaa, R., Cook-Sather, A., Ramo, K., & Tohfa, H. (2021). Undergraduate students partnering with staff to develop trauma-informed, anti-racist pedagogical approaches: Intersecting experiences of three student partners. *Journal of Educational Innovation, Partnership and Change, 7*(1). https://doi.org/10.21100/jeipc.v7i1.1020

American Psychiatric Association. (2013). *Diagnostic and Statistical Manual of Mental Disorders* (5th ed.). Arlington, VA: American Psychiatric Publishing.

Anders, S. L., Frazier, P. A., & Shallcross, S. L. (2012). Prevalence and effects of life event exposure among undergraduate and community college students. *Journal of Counseling Psychology, 59*(3), 449–457. https://doi.org/10.1037/a0027753

Becker-Blease, K. A. (2017). As the world becomes trauma-informed, work to do. *Journal of Trauma and Dissociation, 18*(2), 131–138. https://doi.org/10.1080/15299732.2017.1253401

Boyraz, G., Granda, R., Baker, C. N., Tidwell, L. L., & Waits, J. B. (2016). Posttraumatic stress, effort regulation, and academic outcomes among college students: A longitudinal study. *Journal of Counseling Psychology, 63*(4), 475–486. https://doi.org/10.1037/cou0000102

Breslau, N., Peterson, E. L., & Schultz, L. R. (2008). A second look at prior trauma and the posttraumatic stress disorder effects of subsequent trauma: A prospective epidemiological study. *Archives of General Psychiatry, 65*(4), 431–437. https://doi.org/10.1001/archpsyc.65.4.431

Brunzell, T., Stokes, H., & Waters, L. (2019). Shifting teacher practice in trauma-affected classrooms: Practice pedagogy strategies within a trauma-informed positive education model. *School Mental Health, 11*(3), 600–614. https://doi.org/10.1007/s12310-018-09308-8

Brunzell, T., Waters, L., & Stokes, H. (2015). Teaching with strengths in trauma-affected students: A new approach to healing and growth in the classroom. *Amerian Journal of Orthopsychiatry, 85*(1), 3–9. https://doi.org/10.1037/ort0000048

Bryom, N. (2018). An evaluaiton of a peer support intervention for student mental health. *Journal of Mental Health, 27*(3), 240–246. https://doi.org/10.1080/09638237.2018.1437605

Cook, A., Spinazzola, J., Ford, J., Lanktree, C., Blaustein, M., Cloitre, M., DeRosa, R., Hubbard, R., Kagan, R., Liautaud, J., Mallah, K., Olafson, E., & van der Kolk, B. (2005). Complex trauma in children and adolescents. *Psychiatric Annals, 35*(5), 390–398.

Cusack, S. E., Hicks, T. A., Bourdon, J., Sheerin, C. M., Overstreet, C. M., Kendler, K. S., Dick, D. M., & Amstadter, A. B. (2019, February–March). Prevalence and predictors of PTSD among a college sample. *Journal of American College of Health, 67*(2), 123–131. https://doi.org/10.1080/07448481.2018.1462824

Dvorakova, K., Greenberg, M. T., & Roeser, R. W. (2019). On the role of mindfulness and compassion skills in students' coping, well-being, and development across the transition to college: A conceptual analysis. *Stress and Health, 35*(2), 146–156. https://doi.org/10.1002/smi.2850

Dvorakova, K., Kishida, M., Li, J., Elavsky, S., Broderick, P. C., Agrusti, M. R., & Greenberg, M. T. (2017). Promoting healthy transition to college through mindfulness training with first-year college students: Pilot randomized controlled trial. *Journal of American College of Health, 65*(4), 259–267. https://doi.org/10.1080/07448481.2017.1278605

Edman, J. L., Watson, S. B., & Patron, D. J. (2016). Trauma and psychological distress among ethnically diverse community college students. *Community College Journal of Research and Practice, 40*(4), 335–342. https://doi.org/10.1080/10668926.2015.1065211

Ford, J. D., & Courtois, C. A. (2009). Defining and understanding complex trauma and complex traumatic stress disorders. In C. A. Courtois & J. D. Ford (Ed.), *Treating complex traumatic stress disorders: An evidence-based guide* (pp. 13–30). New York: The Guilford Press.

Frazier, P., Anders, S., Perera, S., Tomich, P., Tennen, H., Park, C., & Tashiro, T. (2009). Traumatic events among undergraduate students: Prevalence and associated symptoms. *Journal of Counseling Psychology, 56*(3), 450–460. https://doi.org/10.1037/a0016412

Gold, S. D., Marx, B. P., Soler-Baillo, J. M., & Sloan, D. M. (2005). Is life stress more traumatic than traumatic stress? *Journal of Anxiety Disorders, 19*(6), 687–698. https://doi.org/10.1016/j.janxdis.2004.06.002

Goodman, K., & Pascarella, E. T. (2006). First-year seminars increase persistence and retention: A summary of the evidence from how college affects students. *Summer 2006 peerReview, Published by the Association of American Colleges and Universities, 8*(3), 26–28.

Hurtado, S., Clayton-Pedersen, A. R., Allen, W. R., & Milem, J. F. (1998). Enhancing campus climates for racial/ethnic diversity: Educational policy and practice. *The Review of Higher Education, 21*(3), 279–302. https://doi.org/10.1353/rhe.1998.0003

Johnson, B. B., & Riley, J. B. (2021). Psychosocial impacts on college students providing mental health peer support. *Journal of American College of Health, 69*(2), 232–236. https://doi.org/10.1080/07448481.2019.1660351

Leary, K. A., & DeRosier, M. E. (2012). Factors promoting positive adaptation and resilience during the transition to college. *Psychology, 3*(12), 1215–1222. https://doi.org/10.4236/psych.2012.312A180

Linley, P. A., & Joseph, S. (2004). Positive change following trauma and adversity: A review. *Journal of Traumatic Stress, 17*(1), 11–21. https://doi.org/10.1023/B:JOTS.0000014671.27856.7e

Kilpatrick, D. G., Resnick, H. S., Milanak, M. E., Miller, M. W., Keyes, K. M., & Friedman, M. J. (2013). National estimtes of exposure to traumatic events and PTSD prevalence using DSM-IV and DSM-5 criteria. Journal of Traumatic Stress, 26(5), 537–547. https://doi.org/10.1002/jts.21848

Mellins, C. A., Walsh, K., Sarvet, A. L., Wall, M., Gilbert, L., Santelli, J. S., Thompson, M., Wilson, P. A., Khan, S., Benson, S., Bah, K., Kaufman, K. A., Reardon, L., & Hirsch, J. S. (2017). Sexual assault incidents among college undergraduates: Prevalence and factors associated with risk. *PLOS ONE, 12*(11), e0186471. https://doi.org/10.1371/journal.pone.0186471

Mercer-Mapstone, L., Dvorakova, S. L., Matthews, K. E., Abbott, S., Cheng, B., Felten, P., Knorr, K., Marquis, E., Shammas, R., & Swaim, K. (2017). A systematic literature review of students as partners in higher education. *International Journal of Students as Partners, 1*(1). https://doi.org/10.15173/ijsap.v1i1.3119

Pieterse, A. L., Carter, R. T., Evans, S. A., & Walter, R. A. (2010). An exploratory examination of the associations among racial and ethnic discrimination, racial climate, and trauma-related symptoms in a college student population. *Journal of Counseling Psychology, 57*(3), 255–263. https://doi.org/10.1037/a0020040

Read, J. P., Bachrach, R. L., Wright, A. G., & Colder, C. R. (2016). PTSD symptom course during the first year of college. *Psychological Trauma: Theory, Research, Practice, and Policy, 8*(3), 393–403. https://doi.org/10.1037/tra0000087

Read, J. P., Griffin, M. J., Wardell, J. D., & Ouimette, P. (2014). Coping, PTSD symptoms, and alcohol involvement in trauma-exposed college students in the first three years of college. *Psychology of Addictive Behaviors, 28*(4), 1052–1064. https://doi.org/10.1037/a0038348

Read, J. P., Ouimette, P., White, J., Colder, C., & Farrow, S. (2011). Rates of DSM-IV-TR trauma exposure and posttraumatic stress disorder among newly matriculated college students. *Psychological Trauma: Theory, Research, Practice, and Policy, 3*(2), 148–156. https://doi:10.1037/a0021260

Rothbaum, B. O., Foa, E. B., Riggs, D. S., Murdock, T., & Walsh, W. (1992). A prospective examination of post-traumatic stress disorder in rape victims. *Journal of Traumatic Stress, 5*(3), 455–475.

Shalka, R. T., & Leal, C. C. (2022). Sense of belonging for college students with PTSD: The role of safety, stigma, and campus climate. *Journal of American College of Health, 70*(3), 698–705. https://doi.org/10.1080/07448481.2020.1762608

Smith, C. P., & Freyd, J. J. (2013, February). Dangerous safe havens: Institutional betrayal exacerbates sexual trauma. *Journal of Traumatic Stress, 26*(1), 119–124. https://doi.org/10.1002/jts.21778

Smyth, J. M., Hockemeyer, J. R., Heron, K. E., Wonderlich, S., & Pennebaker, J. W. (2008). Prevalence, type, disclosure, and severity of adverse life events in college students. *Journal of American College of Health, 57*(1), 69–76. https://doi.org/10.3200/JACH.57.1.69-76

Sontag-Padilla, L., Dunbar, M. S., Ye, F., Kase, C., Fein, R., Abelson, S., Seelam, R., & Stein, B. D. (2018). Strengthening college students' mental health knowledge, awareness, and helping behaviors: The impact of active minds, a peer mental health organization. *Journal of the American Academy of Child and Adolescent Psychiatry, 57*(7), 500–507. https://doi.org/10.1016/j.jaac.2018.03.019

Southwick, S. M., Bonanno, G. A., Masten, A. S., Panter-Brick, C., & Yehuda, R. (2014). Resilience definitions, theory, and challenges: Interdisciplinary perspectives. *European Journal of Psychotraumatology, 5*. https://doi.org/10.3402/ejpt.v5.25338

Substance Abuse and Mental Health Services Administration. (2014). *SAMHSA's concept of trauma and guidance for a trauma-informed approach*. HHS Publication No. (SMA) 14-4884. Rockville, MD: Substance Abuse and Mental Health Services Administration.

Tedeschi, R. G., & Calhoun, L. G. (1996). The posttraumatic growth inventory: Measuring the positive legacy of trauma. *Journal of Traumatic Stress, 9*(3), 455–471. https://doi.org/10.1007/BF02103658

van der Kolk, B. A., Herron, N., & Hostetler, A. (1994). The history of trauma in psychiatry. *Psychiatric Clinics of North America, 17*(3), 583–600. https://doi.org/10.1016/S0193-953X(18)30102-3

Vrana, S., & Lauterbach, D. (1994). Prevalence of traumatic events and post-traumatic psychological symptoms in a nonclinical sample of college students. *Journal of Traumatic Stress, 7*(2). https://doi.org/10.1007/BF02102949

Wright, N. M., Smith, C. P., & Freyd, J. J. (2017). Experience of a lifetime: Study abroad, trauma, and institutional betrayal. *Journal of Aggression, Maltreatment and Trauma, 26*(1), 50–68. https://doi.org/10.1080/10926771.2016.1170088

3
TRAUMA-INFORMED PEDAGOGY AT THE GRASSROOTS

Building and Sustaining a Trauma-Informed Movement at a Large Public Institution

Sarah Le Pichon and Steve Lundy

For educators seeking to incorporate trauma-informed care in university settings, there are at least three reasons their well-intentioned efforts might be complicated and even thwarted by day-to-day experience. First, there is the reality of trauma itself, which occupies an intermediary space between the individual and the social, and the psychological and the embodied. As such, trauma implicates all members of a learning community, including those who are not ostensibly survivors of traumatic experiences. Yet trauma-informed policies tend to gravitate toward trauma as exceptional or a matter of crisis. This tendency is related to the second reason, the widespread "medicalization" of trauma in contemporary Western discourse, which identifies effective interventions against trauma as treatment within medical settings, rather than addressing trauma as systemic and resisted as a matter of the renegotiation of its lived political and social dimensions (Rajabi, 2021; Thompson, 2021). Third, as educators attempt to navigate orienting themselves along these first two vectors, they must consider their own roles: as individuals both "caring for"[1] and "caring with" students (cf. Waghid, 2019, p. vi); and as institutional agents embedded in the historical constitution and contradictions of higher education.

Because of these challenges, any educator trying to navigate a trauma-informed pedagogy on their own will likely experience some mixture of burnout, apathy, cynicism, and may even themselves experience trauma (e.g., Nikischer, 2019; Turner, 2021). In this chapter, we consider strategies for educators, staff, and administrators in higher education to mobilize a network of like-minded, supportive experts to develop and implement trauma-informed best practices in and out of the classroom. Our research is based on our experience cultivating such a network over many years at a large flagship R-1 public institution. During this time, our work culminated in, among other

DOI: 10.4324/9781003260776-4

assets, the publication of a trauma-informed pedagogy guide, a grant-funded learning community project, various digital resources, and regular workshops for educators and staff. Following a short review of efforts to institutionalize trauma-informed pedagogy (principally in K–12 settings), we identify the most important campus stakeholders in higher education who can help develop robust trauma-informed practices. We also clarify organizational and sociological considerations that may impact their success and sustainability. We close by discussing how our network was impacted by political public controversies among some of our early partners and conclude with some wider lessons for a durable trauma-informed community in higher-educational settings.

At the core of our experience is an ongoing dilemma over whether trauma-informed networks work most effectively as fully fledged institutional presences, or whether such networks should maintain a more informal, ad hoc status. There are clear benefits to official institutional status, including funding, permanent staff, and consistent research missions, deliverables, and organizational commitments. Indeed, much research into trauma-informed pedagogies stresses the value of building institutional presences that can support a diverse membership and a democratic vision for teachers, support staff, and administration invested in trauma-informed work (e.g., Webb & Wyandt-Hiebert, 2016; Chafouleas et al., 2016). These priorities, however, are sometimes at odds with the meritocratic, hierarchical, and siloed character of higher-education settings. As trauma-informed practices advance in their institutional grounding, their impact can be compromised by conflicting institutional priorities. While our response to this dilemma is ultimately equivocal, since different institutions serve different populations and have different needs, we nonetheless recommend that trauma-informed initiatives remain active at the grassroots throughout their lifespans in order to be responsive to the mobile and elusive nature of trauma in educational settings.

Trauma-Informed Pedagogy and Practices in Schools: History and Organizational Contexts

While it is not the purpose of this chapter to define trauma or provide a prevailing set of characteristics or practices of trauma-informed pedagogy, there are some preliminary assumptions that will bear on the account offered here. First, in addition to the concise definition of trauma offered by Rajabi—"something that shifts the way individuals conceive of their worlds" (2021, p. 7)—we understand trauma to be experienced within a frame of complex symbolic, psychological, and social dimensions. As a result, trauma-informed pedagogy does not seek to provide a "cure" for students' personal or social histories of trauma. But a trauma-informed pedagogy also entails that there are measures educators can adopt that do not exacerbate and may even mitigate trauma in the course of learning. This can start from "holding space" for the reality of trauma in a given context, and acknowledging how that context might be impacted by differential power and privilege among members of a learning community (cf. Quimby, 2021), but will unfold into diverse social practices and rituals depending on institutional positionality and opportunity.

Schools, therefore, play a decisive role in this social experience of trauma and can either aggravate or effectively engage and provide care for students' stressful and traumatic experiences (e.g., Zembylas, 2008). In recognition of the prevalence and impact of trauma in learning institutions, there has been a recent push in K–12 schools to provide trauma-informed practices and services (SAMHSA, 2014) and work toward the reduction of retraumatization and traumatic stress through school-based trauma-informed intervention (Rolfsnes & Idsoe, 2011). This move itself follows from the observation that those suffering from traumatic experiences (with or without instructor support or guidance) invariably attempt to manage their symptoms in the classroom, where "even traditional curricula and assignments can become overwhelming or triggering" (Emerson & Lovitt, 2003). Teachers also have "a front row seat to the behavioral, academic, and socioemotional issues that traumatized students encounter" (Crosby, 2015, p. 7), whether or not they have received training or information on how to best address trauma in the classroom as a part of their education (Splett et al., 2013). Consequently, many K–12 officials and teachers have successfully advocated for trauma-informed practices in their schools and across their districts. In Massachusetts, for example, *An Act Relative to Safe and Supportive Schools,* signed into law in 2014, serves as an example of a trauma-sensitive K–12 school initiative. However, the degree to which cultural sensitivity and trauma-informed practices can be implemented into the curriculum is most often at the discretion of teachers and staff who interact with students. Consequently, it is important that staff and teachers are knowledgeable about trauma and effective ways to address it (Crosby, 2015).

In order to effectively train instructors, provide support, and address pushback, implementation of trauma-informed practices in schools, therefore, looks to organization-wide policies and development. Chafouleas et al. (2016), for example, identify the following organizational requirements for effective trauma-informed programming:

1. Align with district goals.
2. Focus on measurable outcomes.
3. Make decisions based on data and local context characteristics.
4. Prioritize evidence-based practices.
5. Formally assess implementation integrity.

Webb and Wyandt-Hiebert similarly note that a single campus group cannot eradicate sexual and interpersonal violence by itself, so a campus should work together and acknowledge that violence on campus is a public health issue that affects everyone in the community. Webb and Wyandt-Hiebert advise that the campus should form a "robust, trauma-informed coalition" (p. 51). To create this coalition, they recommend:

1. Engaging in deliberate efforts at a positive campus climate through prevention and response strategies.
2. Providing regular training and support to all employees and students.
3. Using data-driven feedback from students, faculty, and staff to identify and reduce sexual and relationship violence (Webb and Wyandt-Hiebert, 2016, p. 51).

Various different frameworks have also been developed to standardize trauma-informed principles that can guide teachers and school administrators (Crosby, 2015). These models are primarily aimed at primary education and include the C.A.P.P.D model ("calm," "attuned," "present," "predictable," "don't let children's emotions escalate your own") (Perry, 2009); Making SPACE for Learning (Australian Childhood Foundation, 2010); the Flexible Framework (Cole et al., 2017); and the Compassionate Teaching model (Wolpow et al., 2009), which defines a compassionate school community as a space that is welcoming, affirming, and safe. Compassionate teaching also emphasizes shared control between the students and the teacher (Perry, 2009) and asks that teachers consistently challenge their own assumptions about students, and their pedagogical methods (Wolpow et al., 2009). Initial pilot studies demonstrated "that students' posttraumatic stress symptoms significantly decreased during a school year when school educational and support staff participated in ongoing trauma-informed training" (Crosby, 2015, quoting Day et al., in press).

A community-based or organization-wide approach to trauma-informed education also underscores the necessity for democratic partnerships among all school personnel for the care of students (Bloom, 1995) in which all classroom staff are included as equals (Anderson et al., 2015). According to Anderson et al., one of the biggest steps toward implementing a trauma-informed school is providing training to school staff during their professional development, and/ or during their regularly scheduled faculty and staff meetings. As part of this training, a workshop might begin with a nominal needs assessment in which the staff writes down their top five professional development needs, after which the researchers develop a series of four workshops based on these needs. Workshops may also include the neurohormonal impact of trauma and toxic stress on students' behavior and learning, and strategies for classroom intervention.

Thus, one of the key components of trauma-informed schools is professional development training, so that all teachers, staff, and school personnel understand the impact of trauma and develop the skills to "create an environment that is responsive to the needs of trauma-exposed students" (Chafouleas et al., 2016). Such training has been shown to change attitudes and build knowledge in favor of trauma-informed practices (Brown et al., 2011). Trauma-focused professional development training "typically aims to create a shared understanding of the problem of trauma exposure, build consensus for trauma-informed approaches, and engender attitudes, beliefs, and behaviors conducive to the adoption of system-wide trauma-informed approaches" (Overstreet & Chafouleas, 2016, p. 2). Simply receiving targeted professional development seems to positively influence school staff (Anderson et al., 2015). These trainings may also include a focus on the neurobiological impact of trauma, de-escalation strategies to avoid retraumatization, and staff self-care that touches on secondary trauma (Chafouleas et al., 2016).

Organizational Considerations for Trauma-Informed Approaches to Higher Education

As this brief survey shows, trauma-informed teaching and student support has received considerable attention in K–12 contexts in recent years, with greater movement toward organizational considerations for effective support. To be sure, recommendations oriented toward higher education professionals have also gained currency during this period, although these tend to be directed more toward specific classroom strategies (e.g., Carello & Butler, 2015), as well as debates around the politics of trauma-informed measures, such as the controversy over "safe spaces" and "trigger warnings" (e.g., Carter, 2015). A comparative lack of emphasis on organizational measures in higher education makes sense, at least in our experience in a large R-1 institution. Such institutions are relatively inconsistent in standardized measures for teacher training as a matter of professional certification and advancement, and often include many practical and political obstacles to implementing instructional policies across a large, diffuse campus. Recent experience of trauma-informed policies that emerged in the wake of the COVID-19 pandemic may suggest new directions for such implementation (e.g., Turner, 2021; Carello & Thompson, 2021 passim), although the durability of such measures remains to be seen.

However, after several years developing cross-organizational programming in such a setting, we believe that it is possible to work toward effective trauma-informed practices in higher education while providing organizational support for instructors and students in a trauma-informed classroom. This approach emphasizes a grassroots network of instructors, support staff, and administrators, at all ranks. It calls for critical reflection and praxis among members that address the impact of contemporary educational practices on members of the community experiencing trauma, and the possibilities of reform. The goal of our work remains the importance of interventions in student-facing contexts as the gold standard of trauma-informed pedagogies, but because we believe those interventions are informed by a potentially unlimited range of experiences and expertises, we have sought to establish practices designed for the classroom on an open-ended process of network-building outside of it.

Our movement began as we and other educators grappled with curricula containing disturbing content and were not able to identify existing practices for compassionate, effective instruction in our existing workplaces. As a first-time graduate student instructor, for example, Sarah found herself floundering for the right words to acknowledge a sexual assault scene in a movie required as part of a class curriculum. Steve, meanwhile, was tasked with creating a fully online course on Greek and Roman mythologies and was uncertain what methods existed for online course developers to handle discussions about violence and trauma outside a traditional classroom setting (cf. Rabinowitz & McHardy, 2014). When we independently approached a violence prevention program on our campus, Voices Against Violence, a social worker at the program connected us, and we began discussing the development of a TIP community. What started as a desperately sought-for learning opportunity about teaching problematic and difficult materials in the higher-education classroom soon turned into a years-long project to create a trauma-informed teaching community, in the hopes of helping current and future instructors better prepare for these discussions. A year or so after starting our work on TIP, we received a grant from our university's learning and teaching center, the Faculty Innovation Center. This grant allowed us to bring together professors, teachers, and students from across the campus, to form a community of like-minded pedagogues with whom we organized regular meetings to read about, discuss, and teach each other the principles of TIP. Long after the grant-funded project ended, this community endured, and we hope this chapter properly recognizes the participants' contribution to a grassroots movement that started with two confused teachers.

Our initial connection through Voices Against Violence was a significant first lesson in the orientation of our work in trauma-informed pedagogy. Located within the university's student counseling and mental health services, the anti-violence organization gave us access to social workers and counselors already equipped with experience and practices that work toward mitigating the impact of trauma on learning and students' experience. This was in part driven by staff members' expertise in mental health treatment and advocacy, but also stemmed from the organization's recognition of the structural roots of violence, pointing toward community-based resolutions and movement-building. By the same token, we expect that educators may similarly find productive collaborations within organizations working toward diversity, inclusion, equity, and belonging in their institutions, especially among activists and policymakers dismantling the violence inherent in traditional and/or normative higher-educational teaching practices and curricula (e.g., Chimbganda, 2015).

The balance between trauma-informed advocacy and structural analysis of trauma that we learned from our initial connection at Voices Against Violence set the stage for the growth of our network. Naturally, teachers working in the classroom were among the first to join us to research trauma-informed pedagogies. Among these instructors, the fields represented in our earliest cohorts seemed to naturally gravitate toward understanding trauma and its effects on learning, and it stands to reason that strong trauma-informed networks will benefit from experts in psychology (especially educational psychology), sociology, counseling, social work, among others directly engaged with human development and care. Over time, however, we learned that trauma-informed pedagogies benefit from the experience and expertise of scholars from any and all fields. Indeed, only by building on these diverse perspectives were we able to comprehensively understand the impact of trauma in the classroom. What united instructors committed to trauma-informed pedagogy was not their specific academic training and research areas, but rather a willingness to consider and implement critical perspectives on received modes of teaching and learning, especially those that have embraced feminist, anti-racist, and/or disability study critiques on the wide-ranging effects of symbolic and institutional trauma on the culture of modern disciplines and knowledge systems.

While effective trauma-informed teaching appears to coincide with an appreciation of critical theory—including the rise of trauma studies and its ancillary fields—we quickly recognized that of greater importance was a willingness to explore and adopt a critical pedagogical praxis in the classroom (one might compare Zembylas' (2008) emphasis on "critical emotional praxis" as a determining factor in the healing of trauma and conflict in school settings). In keeping with Carello and Butler's (2014) aphoristic reminder that "teaching trauma is not the same as trauma-informed teaching," we found that faculty who worked in fields whose curricula highlighted potentially disturbing material were most likely to facilitate successful and inclusive learning experiences, but only when coupled with strategies that eliminated the risk of retraumatization and secondary traumatization and prioritized student safety and wellbeing. Carello and Butler remind us that many instructors falsely believe that intense emotional responses and retraumatizations are signs of effective teaching of critical content (p. 159) and that students' ability to work through and resolve the experience is a pedagogical success (cf. Felman, 1991). Further, students often believe that papers and discussions recounting traumatic or highly emotional events earn the highest grades (cf. Swartzlander et al., 1993). These damaging beliefs exemplify a severe lack of understanding concerning trauma and retraumatization: "We know of no evidence to indicate that experiencing fear, horror, and helplessness are precursors to effective learning or that the development of PTSD symptoms is evidence of effective teaching" (Carello & Butler, 2014, p. 160).

Such an emphasis on critical praxis, rather than specific subject-matter expertise, also opened our constituency to non-teaching members of the university. We found that faculty and graduate students pursuing trauma-informed practices were similarly relevant to supportive instructional designers and technologists, whether working within campus pedagogy centers (like the University of Texas at Austin's Faculty Innovation Center) or units devoted to technological support. Creative partnerships between faculty and technologists were necessitated by the digital transformation of the higher-education campus in recent years, including the COVID-19 pandemic and the need to rapidly scale up digital learning. Given this development, what may have been straightforward trauma-informed interventions in the traditional classroom—for example, a "grace period" for students working on assignments—require technical knowledge that cannot be assumed. As numerous researchers have demonstrated, however, all kinds of digital media, from social media platforms to learning management systems, are not neutral spaces; they reproduce and exacerbate social iniquities and demand critical scrutiny and judicious implementation (e.g., Noble, 2018; Gilliard & Culik, 2016). In response, educational activists have advocated a "critical instructional pedagogy" (Morris, 2017) and/or "designing for care" (Stommel, 2020) that may accompany trauma-informed practices in the rollout of digitally mediated instruction. Thus, experience with technology needed to be accompanied by appreciation for cultural and socio-economic factors influencing the emergence of digitally mediated education.

Given the origins of our network at Voices Against Violence, student support and administrative units remained a third indispensable constituency, especially among staff and administrators with a deep understanding of student mental health counseling, anti-violence advocacy (such as the growing number of bystander intervention initiatives in higher education), and diversity, equity, and inclusion (DEI) initiatives. The support and guidance of counselors were critical not only for their expertise in the treatment of traumatic experiences and distress, but to underscore the distinction between trauma-informed practices employed by educators and therapeutic interventions (that, in other words, counselors are not teachers and teachers are not counselors). In defining and articulating trauma-informed pedagogy in workshops and discussions, we benefited by underlining that a trauma-informed approach, while empathetic, is not therapeutic. Teachers and mentors learned to acknowledge trauma and its deep influence on each and every one of our students, and thus learn to respond with pedagogical practices that allow for flexibility and provide students with autonomy in their learning process. They are not, however, typically trained to offer therapeutic guidance. Counselors, as a result, are well placed to advise teachers and staff on setting effective boundaries and scripting responses to distress that both promote empathy and respect while directing students to more appropriate, effective resources.

The situation is further complicated by the fact that, in most cases in the United States, instructors and staff members on college campuses are mandatory reporters.[1] In our conversations with educators and staff, we encountered frequent anxiety and misunderstandings about the requirements and procedures of Title IX reporting, especially among instructors whose fields might be especially given to discussion of violence and trauma. As a result, consulting with university officers with expertise in Title IX provided an effective solution for any instructor looking to help students navigate difficult material while abiding by the legal parameters of Title IX. Dr Gloria González-López, a UT-Austin professor and researcher on the sociology of sexual violence, suggested seeking out such recommendations before delivering courses in which students might make disclosures that prompted Title IX reporting: "I think for anyone who is interested in having those conversations in advance [of a course] … it's a good idea for them to have those personal conversations with Title IX representatives, so they can give them the specific language" (Le Pichon & Lundy, 2021). Following these conversations, Title IX representatives advised Dr González-López on pre-semester interviews with students and provided guidance on syllabus language.

Over time, our community came to draw on these constituencies evenly, although the importance of their contributions emerged more in hindsight than in planning. Simply, the impetus for a community of trauma-informed practitioners emerged from initial conversations between an instructor and an outreach specialist in a counseling center. Working together on best practices for trauma-informed instruction, this partnership yielded a workshop based on informational interviews conducted with a number of interested educators and administrators. We piloted a workshop among small groups of counselors and faculty before moving into regular iteration at events sponsored by UT's Faculty Innovation Center. This provided opportunity and visibility for further collaborations, and, eventually, we were able to secure a grant to establish an informal learning community for regular meet-ups, an online space based in the university's learning management system, and investment for further resources, including a website and podcast series. These assets, as well as providing a focal point for conversation and planning, allowed for a lasting impact despite the natural flux of community membership given its informal nature.

Trauma and Educational Institutions: Theory and Experience

Given the wide-ranging expertise and institutional knowledge provided by the diverse network of trauma-informed educators, support staff, and administrators comprising our community, it stands to reason that higher-education institutions would benefit from creating permanent organizations or units committed to consolidating this kind of work. In the final part of this chapter, however, we will clarify both theoretical and practical reasons why this may not always be the case.

From a general theoretical perspective, Zembylas (2008, pp. 25–26, following Bush & Saltarelli, 2001) remarks on the ambiguous status of schooling vis-à-vis trauma, with its capacity to reinscribe privilege, repression, and intolerance, or promote opportunity, tolerance, and reconciliation. Thompson (2021), meanwhile, provides a brief but illuminating intellectual history of trauma in the modern era, revealing how our understanding of trauma is inseparable from its institutional and disciplinary contexts (in particular, medicine and psychology). In Thompson's view, the conceptual evolution of trauma within medical and psychological disciplines in particular produces a concept of trauma as behavior aberrant to social institutions in general. It follows that trauma discourse defines traumatized behavior as a condition to be "cured" (that is, made more palatable to the normal functioning of institutions), made invisible, or otherwise marginalized. On the contrary, argues Thompson, trauma is an entirely "normal" reaction to the experience of modern institutions, and cannot, therefore, be conceived apart from those sociopolitical (i.e., institutional) factors.

Thompson's critique is usefully illustrated by how our network-building around trauma-informed work also took shape alongside an initiative evolving parallel to our own formative work and a public controversy that ensued. This public outcry called into question the durability of institutional support for potentially controversial programming and required us to reconsider our own institutional strategy. In 2018, as we were beginning our work, Voices Against Violence (the organization that had originally supported our endeavor) also inaugurated an outreach program titled "MasculinUT." The MasculinUT program aimed to help students define masculinity for themselves, and advocated for creative, flexible, and post-patriarchal models of masculinity. Its organizers also hoped that the program might draw more men to violence-prevention work, a field historically dominated by women. As the program's director explained, "We know that if we're not bringing men to the table and bringing them into the conversation about these issues, […] we're missing out on an important partner in doing this work" (Chris Brownson quoted in Hamdan, 2018). After its initial rollout, however, MasculinUT was "put on hold" for "treating masculinity as a mental health issue" (Hamdan). Believing it to pathologize masculinity, conservative media outlets drew attention to the MasculinUT program, claiming it painted masculinity as inherently problematic. Voices Against Violence subsequently faced intense scrutiny and external reviews from the Dean of Students (representatives claimed that the conservative media backlash had not influenced these reviews). After a hiatus, MasculinUT was briefly resuscitated within the purview of the Dean of Students (and with new branding and mission), although its mission has since dissipated at the university and its website has been removed.

During this period, Voices Against Violence offered to support pilots of trauma-informed pedagogy workshops in light of our initial conversations. In the wake of the MasculinUT affair, however, the involvement of Voices Against Violence in the trauma-informed pedagogy workshops came to an end, since it was no longer feasible for the organization to commit resources to new projects. Logistically, therefore, this avenue was no longer open to us, but strategically it also began to make sense for our work to be detached from specific institutional backing. Because of its implication for modern institutions (per Thompson), we realized that trauma-informed pedagogy may make recommendations that sit uneasily with received institutional norms and practices. Indeed, the way that much of trauma-informed pedagogical discourse in higher education has been consumed by backlash against "safe spaces" and "trigger warnings" would seem to bear this out. As we commenced our work, we believed that the decision either to articulate the critical positionality of trauma-informed pedagogy, or, conversely to reframe trauma-informed practices in different, less controversial ways, lay with practitioners delivering it. But we also felt that our ability to offer recommendations and advice would be constrained by other organizational norms and commitments, nor did we want to risk jeopardizing them ourselves. As a result, we decided not to seek permanent institutional status for the work we were doing, and relied instead on informal but committed grassroots movement-building.

If Thompson's argument for the inextricable situatedness of trauma as an inevitable fact of normal institutional operations is correct, it might be less surprising that cross-organizational, grassroots movements formed of diverse perspectives and diverse stakeholders can be more effective contexts for trauma-informed pedagogies. This too finds support in recent critical work on trauma and community formation. In a recent monograph on the modern emergence of online communities in response to trauma, Rajabi (2021) locates trauma at the point of rupture from the experience of the everyday. Those suffering violence in the face of everyday "modes of social and cultural domination" experience trauma when they are subjected simultaneously to the violent consequences of that domination coupled with the realization of others' complicity in its perpetuation as the status quo. Trauma (described by Rajabi as "symbolic trauma") then occurs because such agents can no longer tolerate such systems of power, Rajabi argues, but also have no context in which it can find effective expression. Trauma only finds articulation as such when agents move into a "third space" (p. 27, following Bhabha, 1994), in which the social and cultural conditions of the originating violence become liminal, and new forms of meaning-making around trauma become possible. In other words, in order for trauma-informed networks to articulate and implement practices that actively address and work against the reproduction of traumatizing conditions, educators may first need to identify provisional, transitional "third spaces" within their organizations as a precursor to effective intervention.

So, as the UT TIP network sought out mobile networks made up of instructors, professors, staff, and students, we were able to continue and further our work on campus. Per Rajabi and Thompson's analysis, this was not merely in the absence of institutional endorsement, but precisely because of it. The TIP community thus benefited from its existence as one that is provisional and agile, rather than one that is beholden to a specific organization or institutional context. In lieu of specific institutional backing, the TIP community continued its work across campus, partnering with many other departments, organizations, and programs along the way. Grassroots organizing also affords the most likely opportunity for democratic constituency building. One of the recurring themes in our conversations, and a research topic that certainly merits further exploration, is that in the absence of trauma-informed practices, the emotional labor of processing trauma in the classroom is directed to the institutional margins—typically, grad student TAs, contingent faculty, and, of course, other students. In other words, the distribution of emotional labor in higher education is apt to be inverse to academic rank, shielding senior faculty and administrators from the day-to-day realities of secondary trauma and retraumatization. Trauma-informed networks need to exist in spaces in which, as much as is realistically possible, participants can contribute without being beholden to rank or other markers of academic hierarchies.

Of course, such a provisional, grassroots network will not suit all organizations equally. As discussed above, K–12 schools that implement regular professional and pedagogical development based on district or organizational policy may be better served by a durable institutional TIP presence, and other institutions. Likewise, other higher-education institutions with different organizational structures may be able to pursue centralized TIP planning. Indeed, should conditions evolve to the point where large public institutions like ours are able to incorporate diverse perspectives and skillsets for the purpose of organization-wide training and policymaking, it may be possible to envision more expansive trauma-informed support. Even then, we believe, educators will always need to continue to practice critical scrutiny of their recommendations and advocacy to avoid succumbing to sedimentation within the larger demands of the organization and remain committed to those who benefit the most from their work.

Note

1 There are very few exceptions. These include counselors or wellness professionals who learn of an incident in the course of a session or appointment ("Exemptions to Mandated Reporting," Office of Equity & Title IX at UMKC: https://info.umkc.edu/title9/makingareport/mandated-reporting/).

References

Anderson, Elizabeth, Blitz, Lisa, & Saastamoinen, Monique (2015). "Exploring a School-University Model for Professional Development With Classroom Staff: Teaching Trauma-Informed Approaches." *School Community Journal*, 25(2), 113–135.

Australian Childhood Foundation. (2010). "Making SPACE for learning: Trauma informed practice in schools." http://burnside.slimlib.com.au:81/docs/MakingSpaceForLearning_Trauma_2010.pdf

Bhabha, H. K. (1994). *The Location of Culture*. London: Routledge.
Bloom, S. L. (1995). "Creating sanctuary in the classroom." *Psychological Trauma: Theory, Research, Practice, and Policy*, 1(4), 403–433.
Bush, Kenneth D. & Saltarelli, Diana (2001). *The 2 faces of education in ethnic conflict: towards a peacebuilding education for children*. UNICEF: UNICEF Innocenti Research Center.
Brown, S. M., Baker, C. N., & Wilcox, P. (2011). "Risking Connection Trauma Training: A Pathway Toward Trauma-Informed Care in Child Congregate Care Settings." *Psychological Trauma: Theory, Research, Practice, and Policy*, 4(5), 507–515. https://doi.org/10.1037/a0025269.
Butler, Lisa, & Carello, Janice (2014). "Potentially Perilous Pedagogies: Teaching Trauma Is Not the Same as Trauma-Informed Teaching." *Journal of Trauma & Dissociation*, 15(2), 153–168.
Butler, Lisa, & Carello, Janice (2015). "Practicing What We Teach: Trauma-Informed Educational Practice." *Journal of Teaching in Social Work*, 35(3), 262–278.
Carello, Janice, & Thompson, Phyllis (2021). *Lessons from the Pandemic: Trauma-Informed Approaches to College, Crisis, Change*. Palgrave Macmillan.
Carter, Angela (2015). "Teaching with Trauma: Disability Pedagogy, Feminism, and the Trigger Warnings Debate." *Disability Studies Quarterly*, 35(2), 9–19.
Chafouleas, Sandra, Johnson, Austin, Overstreet, Stacy, & Santos, Natascha (2016). "Towards a Blueprint for Trauma-Informed Service Delivery in Schools." *School Mental Health*, 8(1), 144–162.
Chimbganda, T. (2015). "Traumatic Pedagogy: When Epistemic Privilege and White Privilege Collide." In K. Fasching-Varner, K. Albert, R. Mitchell, & C. Allen (Eds.), *Racial Battle Fatigue in Higher Education: Exposing the Myth of Post-racial America* (pp. 29–36). Rowman and Littlefield.
Cole, Susan, Eisner, Anne, Gregory, Michael, & Ristuccia, Joel (2017). *A Vision for Trauma-Sensitive Schools Optimizing Learning Outcomes* (pp.166–179). Routledge.
Crosby, Shantel D. (2015). "An Ecological Perspective on Emerging Trauma-Informed Teaching Practices." *Children and Schools*, 37(4), 223–230.
Emerson, J., & Lovitt, T. (2003). "The Educational Plight of Foster Children in Schools and What Can Be Done about It." *Remedial and Special Education*, 244(4), 199–203. https://doi.org/10.1177/07419325030240040301.
Felman, Shoshana (1991). "Education and Crisis, or the Vicissitudes of Teaching." *Remedial and Special Education*, 13–73.
Gilliard, C., & Culik, H. (2016). "Digital Redlining, Access, and Privacy." https://www.commonsense.org/education/articles/digital-redlining-access-and-privacy. Published 05/24/2016.
Hamdan, Nadia. "UT Rethinks MasculinUT Program After Criticism From Conservative Groups." https://www.kut.org/education/2018-05-09/ut-austin-rethinks-masculinut-program-after-criticism-from-conservative-groups. Published 05/9/2018.
Le Pichon, Sarah, & Lundy, Steve. "Episode 3: Gloria Gonzalez-Lopez, part I. TIP@UT." June 9, 2021. Spotify.
Morris, S. M. (2017). "A Call for Critical Instructional Design." https://www.seanmichaelmorris.com/a-call-for-critical-instructional-design/. Published 10/27/2017.
Nikischer, A. (2019). "Vicarious Trauma inside the Academe: Understanding the Impact of Teaching, Researching and Writing Violence." *Higher Education*, 77(5), 905–916.

Noble, Safiya U. (2018). *Algorithms of Oppression: How Search Engines Reinforce Racism*. NYU Press.

Office of Equity & Title IX, UMKC. "Mandated Reporting." https://info.umkc.edu/title9/makingareport/mandated-reporting/. Published 1/15/2022.

Overstreet, Stacy, & Chafouleas, Sandra (2016). "Trauma-Informed Schools: Introduction to the Special Issue." *School Mental Health*, 8(1), 1–6.

Perry, B. D. (2009). "Examining Child Maltreatment through a Neurodevelopmental Lens: Clinical Applications of the Neurosequential Model of Therapeutics." *Journal of Loss and Trauma*, 12(4), 240–255. https://doi.org/10.1080/15325020903004350.

Rabinowitz, Nancy Sorkin, & McHardy, Fiona (2014). *From Abortion to Pederasty: Addressing Difficult Topics in the Classics Classroom*. Ohio State University Press.

Quimby, H. Michelann (2021). *Trauma-Informed Pedagogy for Primary and Secondary Trauma in Female and Minority Natural Sciences Undergraduates during COVID*. Palgrave Macmillian.

Rajabi, S. (2021). *All My Friends Live in My Computer: Trauma, Tactical Media, and Meaning*. Rutgers University Press.

Rolfsnes, E. S., & Idsoe, T. (2011). "School-Based Intervention Programs for PTSD Symptoms: A Review and Meta-analysis." *Journal of Traumatic Stress*, 24(2), 155–165. https://doi.org/10.1002/jts.20622.

Splett, J. W., Fowler, J., Weist, M. D., McDaniel, H., & Dvorsky, M. (2013). "The Critical Role of School Psychology in the School Mental Health Movement." *Psychology in the Schools*, 50(3), 245–257. https://doi.org/10.1002/pits.21677.

Stommel, J. (2020). "Designing for Care: Inclusive Pedagogies for Online Learning." https://www.jessestommel.com/designing-for-care/. Published 06/19/2020.

Substance Abuse and Mental Health Services Administration. (2014). "Key Terms: Definitions." SAMHSA News, 222. Retrieved from http://www.samhsa.gov/samhsaNewsLetter/Volume_22_Number_2/trauma_tip/key_term s.html.

Swartzlander, S., Pace, D., & Stamler, V. L.(1993). "Requiring students to write about their personal lives." *Feminism and Psychology*. http://chronicle.com/article/Requiring-Students-to-Write/70582/

Thompson, L. (2021). "Toward a Feminist Psychological Theory of 'Institutional Trauma'." *Feminism and Psychology*, 31(1), 99–118.

Turner, Nicole K. (2021). "Turning Emergency-Response to Standard Procedure Through a Trauma-Informed Attention to Crisis." In Lisa Carello & Phyllis Thompson (Eds.), *Lessons from the Pandemic: Trauma-Informed Approaches to College, Crisis, Change* (pp. 15–22). Palgrave Macmillan.

Waghid, Y. (2019). *Towards a Philosophy of Caring in Higher Education: Pedagogy and Nuances of Care*. Palgrave Macmillan.

Webb, Kim, & Wyandt-Hiebert, Mary A. (2016). "*Towards a Philosophy of Caring in Higher Education: Pedagogy and Nuances of Care*." American College Health Association Toolkit..

Wolpow, R., Johnson, M. M., Hertel, R., & Kincaid, S. O. (2009). *The Heart of Learning and Teaching: Compassion, Resiliency, and Academic Success*. Washington State Office of Superintendent of Public Instruction, Compassionate Schools.

Zembylas, M. (2008). *The Politics of Trauma in Education*. Palgrave Macmillan.

4
RACIAL TRAUMA

Dismantling Anti-Black Racism in Classrooms and Academia

Vanessa Lopez-Littleton and Dennis Kombe

Academic institutions in the United States are ground zero for anti-Black racism. From experiences with racial bullying, racial slurs, harassment, discrimination, and systems that minoritize, marginalize, and dehumanize, Black (across the African diaspora) students are exposed to unsafe racial climates with potential triggering and traumatizing effects (Government Accounting Office (GAO), 2021; Griffin et al., 2017). The heart of the problem is the fact that Black students are educated in a system grounded in white supremacy culture, "a political-economic social system of domination" (DiAngelo, 2012, p. 145). Structural racism—a macro-level system of policies, practices, cultural norms, and ideologies—shapes and reinforces racial group inequity (The Aspen Institute, n.d.). While race is a social construct, it brings with it a powerful sociopolitical reality that reinforces an environment whereby Black people are forced to struggle for their own survival (Love, 2019).

Anti-Black racism systematically marginalizes and devalues Blackness (identity, culture, social norms) and Black concerns (University of California San Francisco, 2022). Through a complex set of narratives about Black identity, anti-Black racism shapes perceptions and fuels negative sentiment regarding the abilities and lived experiences of Black people. According to the Substance Abuse and Mental Health Services Association (SAMHSA), trauma can be defined as an "event, series of events, or set of circumstances that is experienced by an individual as physically or emotionally harmful or life threatening and that has lasting adverse effects on the individual's functioning and mental, physical, social, emotional, or spiritual well-being" (SAMHSA, 2022, para 2). Black students experience both historical and current trauma that may emanate from everyday microaggressions, macroaggressions, bias, discrimination, and overt racism. Trauma can manifest in a number of ways including difficulty

DOI: 10.4324/9781003260776-5

focusing, absenteeism, anxiety, anger, helplessness, isolation, or dissociation when stressed. These can have serious impacts on students' learning.

This chapter explores anti-Black racism in education and how it contributes to racial trauma and the discriminatory outcomes experienced by Black students. We begin by discussing the roots of anti-Black racism in education and the history of racial trauma in academic institutions. Then, we present critical race theory as a conceptual framework for dismantling long-standing systems of oppression. We conclude by offering practical strategies for addressing anti-Black racism in academia (K-12 and higher education) and in the classroom.

Roots of Anti-Black Racism in Education

Anti-Black racism is a specific form of structural racism that perpetuates and sustains white supremacy culture, a complex dogma that advances social, economic, and political ideologies that center Eurocentric values (Feagin, 2006). This oppressive system has long roots in US history dating back to the arrival of enslaved Africans aboard the *White Lion* in 1619 (Hannah-Jones, 2021a). For 244 years (1619–1863), African slaves were held captive on American soil through a system born out of and reinforced by racial prejudice (Stevenson, 2017). Throughout history, the presence of anti-Black racism has served a distinct purpose of protecting and preserving a racial hierarchy that is undergirded by colorblindness, a racial ideology where race is considered an irrelevant and inconsequential factor in social, economic, and political outcomes (Annamma, 2015; Bonilla Silva, 2018).

Black education and literacy remain thwarted in educational systems that are designed for Black students to fail (e.g., underfunded, understaffed, issues of school safety, underprepared teachers, poor parental engagement, high-level of teacher burnout) (Love, 2019). While some Black students are able to successfully navigate through these troublesome systems, others experience varying levels of trauma from their exposure and experience in academic settings beginning in K-12 (Love, 2019; Menakem, 2017). This is not the fault of the student but of an educational system that has not fully come to grips with how to honor or educate Black students by dismantling these oppressive systems.

Racism as Trauma

White supremacy culture brings with it a harsh reality for Black Americans as cultural baggage is transmitted across generations (DeGruy, 2017). Racial trauma "occurs when members of a collectivity feel they have been subjected to a horrendous event that leaves indelible marks upon their group's consciousness, marking their memories forever and changing their future identities in fundamental and irrevocable ways" (Alexander, 2004, p. 1). Prolonged and repeated exposure to negative racial incidents is a known psychological, emotional, and physical stressor (Bryant-Davis & Ocampo, 2006; Carter et al., 2016, 2019). Racial trauma, which includes the cumulative effect of subtle difficult-to-detect events, has been linked to negative psychological symptoms, including psychological distress, low self-esteem, and suicidal ideation (Williams et al., 2018). Racism and the resulting racial trauma can be passed down across generations (epigenetic inheritance). "Research shows that people who live through high levels of toxic stress alter the genes of their children and, therefore, the lives they will lead" (Love, 2019, p. 76). This does not mean that every Black American will manifest symptoms of racial trauma. However, every Black American is the recipient of a cultural inheritance rooted in residing in a racialized society where their socially constructed racial identity is devalued and often exploited (Feagin, 2001; Love, 2019).

While discrimination and racial bias are capable of producing a traumatic stress response similar to those experienced with post-traumatic stress disorder (PTSD), racial trauma does not meet the criteria for PTSD, the category where this form of psychological trauma should naturally fit. The *Diagnostic and Statistical Manual of Mental Disorders (5th Edition)* limits the definition of trauma to "actual or threatened death, serious injury, or sexual violence" (American Psychological Association (APA), 2013, p. 271). According to the APA, any psychological event that does not involve an actual threat to life or bodily harm is excluded from what can be considered as trauma, including racial trauma (Pai et al., 2017). This is a gross limitation of *DSM-5* as a "growing body of evidence indicates that experiences of racial discrimination are an important type of psychosocial stressor that can lead to adverse changes in health status and altered behavioral patterns that increase health risks" (Williams & Mohammad 2013, p. 1). Some suggest the fact that racial trauma is not recognized as a triggering event for PTSD may be due to the lack of awareness regarding racial trauma, discomfort in discussing race-based topics, the lack of validated measures to assess racial trauma, or the lack of skill on the part of clinicians to identify characteristics of racial trauma (Williams et al., 2018).

Critical Race Theory in Academia

Critical race theory (CRT) posits that racism is real, ordinary, socially constructed, and engrained throughout society as a mechanism to exploit and oppress non-white people (Editors of Encyclopedia Britannica, n.d.). As a conceptual framework, CRT acknowledges that racism is an endemic and permanent aspect of the lived experiences of minoritized people and challenges the oppressive structures and discourses that seek to normalize

Eurocentric values (McCoy & Rodricks, 2015). The prolonged and protracted effect of white-supremacy culture is a form of racial violence that contributes to academic climates where Black students are ostracized and not fully integrated (Freire, 1970). The struggle to overcome anti-Blackness in education is the struggle to decolonize and transform society by shifting away from the dominant culture toward one that honors and values all students (hooks, 1994; Freire, 1970). Increasing critical consciousness is one of the ways in which educators can begin to address anti-Black racism. Critical consciousness is one's ability to recognize and acknowledge the social and political realities associated with exposure to systemic problems such as racism followed by action to address the problem (Mosley et al., 2021). The power of critical consciousness is that it is a reflective practice that allows educators to thoughtfully consider how their approaches to teaching and learning in the classroom are shaped and influenced by the environment in which the student exists. By grappling with the politics of dominance associated with racism and other forms of exploitation, educators are better equipped to recognize how these systems contribute to the marginalization and oppression of non-dominant groups (hooks, 1994). Thus, critical consciousness—through the lens of CRT—on the part of educators provides a pathway for challenging normative educational approaches, outcomes, and standards that persistently reproduce inequities.

Dismantling Anti-Black Racism in Academia

Dismantling anti-Black racism in academia requires educational professionals who are committed to creating an internal culture that is capable of addressing, challenging, and healing from racial trauma. Using CRT as a framework, education personnel and instructors can dismantle historic and contemporary inequalities. The following sections offer strategies for creating a positive learning environment where Black students can thrive. First, we present strategies to begin the process of decolonizing higher education. Then, we present strategies for dismantling anti-Black racism in the classroom.

Strategies for Decolonizing Higher Education

At its heart, decolonizing higher education refers to

> diverse efforts to resist the distinct but intertwined processes of colonization and racialization, to enact transformation and redress in reference to the historical and ongoing effects of these processes, and to create and keep alive modes of knowing, being, and relating that these processes seek to eradicate.
>
> *(Stein & de Oliveira Andreotti, 2018, para. 1)*

Explicit Acknowledgment

Addressing anti-Blackness or anti-Black racism requires a willingness for institutions to name, acknowledge, and understand detrimental effects of entrenched structural racism in academic settings before actions can be taken to change (Lopez & Jean-Marie, 2021). This goes beyond taking a broad stance against intolerance or racism, or an admission of the existence of white privilege or white supremacy. Administrators need to create opportunities to engage in honest and specific conversations about Blackness within the institutions and in the local community (Lopez & Jean-Marie, 2021). Administrators, faculty, and staff must examine their positionality and engage in self-reflection to individually and collectively make meaning of the contours of racial oppression. It is incumbent upon them to understand how anti-Blackness is manifested in students' everyday experiences and to come to terms with what they need to learn and unlearn. Having done so, they can then take steps to actively and intentionally create spaces to challenge anti-Black racism—be it in discourse around Black students, curriculum, pedagogy, resource allocation, and so forth (Lopez & Jean-Marie, 2021). This requires trust and commitment.

Bold Leadership

Academic institutions must be guided by bold and authentic leaders who are capable of recognizing and loving Black people in their full humanity (Love, 2019). These leaders must do the work of transforming the institution by examining the racialized complexities that serve as barriers to access, opportunities, and belongingness and design comprehensive plans that center equity and justice. Transformation calls for radical action undergirded by a firm notion of an inherent flaw in the system. Data from external campus climate surveys, for example, may reveal gaps in equity and inclusion, and offer opportunities to address internal organizational and operating issues. Similarly, conducting equity audits can serve as a means for analyzing policies and practices that shape and influence inequities. This information can be used to develop an anti-racist agenda. All campus personnel have a responsibility for ensuring Black students are provided with an environment where they feel welcome and included as well as able to see themselves represented in every aspect of academic life. Additional strategies that institutional leaders can explore include: the development of mentoring networks for Black faculty and staff; the use of dialogic approaches to campus-level discussions about the manifestations of anti-Black racism and other forms of oppression; and efforts to center and normalize Black achievement. Combined, these efforts can work to create a campus climate where Black students can experience the power and value of their cultural identity in a space that nurtures their well-being and supports their academic success.

Improved Academic Outcomes and Well-Being for Black Students

Academic institutions do not exist in a vacuum; thus, recognizing the broader systemic issues that contribute to the racialized oppression Black students and Black communities experience, decolonizing higher education must also include the K-12 system, where much of the harm and insults occur. Two factors driving the entrenchment of inequities are personnel and budgetary decisions. Academic hiring in predominantly Black communities is challenging at best. These schools tend to be under-resourced, poor performing, and unable to attract and retain highly qualified instructors. As a result, they are more likely to produce students who are underprepared for their college experience (Hammond, 2015). In this regard, there is a critical need to change traditional approaches to the education funding model. This disruption could be pivotal as the link between public education and property taxes is an inherent flaw that virtually guarantees differential experiences and outcomes. When it comes to hiring decisions, Black students are often educated in settings with few faculty of color in the front of the classroom to serve as effective role models and mentors. Schools must be intentional in developing pipelines for the recruitment and retention of highly qualified Black teachers. In much the same way, there is an important need for greater community participation in educational decision-making. Communities should be valued for the varied and unique perspectives on issues affecting their communities. These broad shifts are critical to laying the foundation for student success.

Strategies for Dismantling Anti-Black Racism in the Classroom

Anti-Black racism does not stop at the classroom door but leeches into affecting what, how, and from whom Black students learn. Truly educating Black students, including the ones who have been exposed to racial trauma, requires instructors to grow their capacity to care for the souls of their students. Success in this realm hinges on the ability of instructors to develop critical consciousness and adopt culturally responsive teaching practices. Combined, these practices can contribute to an inclusive classroom environment that honors diverse learners.

Unpacking Bias

Advancing critical consciousness and taking steps toward becoming an effective culturally responsive teacher is necessary in creating a learning environment where racial identities are acknowledged, honored, and reflected throughout the learning experience. Committing to self-examination is a crucial first step to helping teachers understand how their cultural values shape expectation in the classroom including interactions with students (Hammond, 2015). Increasing one's critical consciousness allows instructors to better contextualize their own life chances, experiences, and opportunities and fuels a deeper awareness of anti-Black racism as a source of racial trauma. Expanding one's worldview and deepening self-awareness about intersectionality enhances the ability to imagine what Black liberation and freedom means, not only to the individual but for the whole of society. Becoming a culturally responsive teacher means seeking opportunities to broaden cross-cultural knowledge and interrogate the biases behind triggered reactions. By unpacking their biases, reflective instructors recognize and examine their own worldview, intentionally design classrooms that are conducive to learning, and adopt pedagogical practices that meet the unique needs of individual diverse learners.

Understanding Learners

Instructors have a responsibility to understand what type of learners they have in their classroom, to design curricular material that responds to how students learn, and to integrate concepts in a way that promotes effective information processing (Hammond, 2015, p. 15). Recognizing the various cultural archetypes—universal patterns across groups, organizations, or cultures—can help instructors respond to student needs (Hammond, 2015). While Eurocentric cultures are grounded in individualism, African, Asian, Latinx, and Native American cultures operate from a more collectivist frame. In collectivist cultures, there is a stronger pull toward working collaboratively in groups and teams as a survival strategy. This approach may translate to Black students being more likely to engage and learn in environments where interdependence is fostered through collaborative processes or where there are opportunities for deep authentic relationships that nurture their heritage, identity, and culture (Hammond, 2015). Culturally responsive teaching is a critical tool for recognizing that students arrive in higher education at varying levels of readiness. Instructors should use cultural archetypes—not to stereotype or overgeneralize students or their identities but to better understand how to recognize behavioral patterns and how students from different cultures might arrive in the classroom.

Embracing a Culture of Care

The classroom climate is not singly affected by the teacher. Attitudes, actions, and behaviors of each individual student contribute in some way to the overall learning experience. For students, critical consciousness can assist in developing their capacity to identify their own implicit biases and unconscious attitudes that contribute to stereotypes, overgeneralizations, and negative perceptions of other (non-white or white) groups. It is important that educators take the time to understand the everyday manifestations of inequities with the education system and take steps to dismantle these. This is especially so in classrooms where students are exposed to hidden curriculums, biased (one-sided or narrowly focused) information and material, and ideas and perspectives that align with mainstream ideologies that fail to include ideas or perspectives of non-dominant groups. This conceptualization is powerful as it provides an opportunity for those in the front of the classroom to better identify with and understand how oppression works (Mosley et al., 2021).

Enacting Trauma-Informed Pedagogies

Caring, collaborative instructors recognize that racial trauma is real and has lasting effects that impact individual performance and the overall learning environment. Enacting trauma-informed pedagogies means showing compassion to students and responding to each student in a culturally appropriate manner. Recognizing the presence of such trauma and how it affects individual students is crucial to creating a safe, inclusive, and supportive system that allows each student to thrive. Enacting pedagogies that prioritize safety, choice, collaboration, and empowerment are crucial to supporting student learning (Harper & Neubauer, 2021). This includes helping Black students succeed at learning by developing their self-efficacy and capacity to persevere in academia (Hammond, 2015). Creating a trauma-informed classroom is important in dismantling anti-Black racism, but it ultimately comes down to how well instructors are prepared to teach, what they teach, how they teach it, and the environment in which teaching and learning occurs. Building honest relationships with students and creating space to openly talk about race, racism, and societal inequities should be a priority.

Creating An Anti-Black Racism Action Plan

Education is not a passive process, but one with deep connections to social organization, economics, and politics. Creating a classroom culture that honors and values Blackness and Black identity means strategically thinking about how to structure a space that centers agape love while allowing for radical self-love (Lopez-Littleton et al., 2022). The following activities are provided to aid instructors in creating a trauma-informed anti-racist learning environment. The requisite skills yield from knowledge and intentional practices that advance toward more just and equitable outcomes. First, we offer a reading list to provide an awareness and understanding of the power anti-Black racism has in shaping and influencing educational experiences. Second, we provide checklists for increasing critical consciousness and advancing culturally responsive teaching practices.

Suggested Reading List

The following reading list is provided to ensure instructors are prepared with a baseline of knowledge for creating a trauma-informed classroom. It is best to complete these readings with an accountability partner, who is capable of providing critical insights and reflections throughout the process.

- *How to Be an Antiracist* by Ibram X. Kendi
- *We Want to Do More Than Survive* by Bettina L. Love
- *The Sum of Us: What Racism Costs Everyone and How We Can Prosper* by Heather McGhee
- *The Racial Healing Handbook: Practical Activities to Help You Challenge Privilege, Confront Systemic Racism & Engage in Collective Healing* by Annaliese A. Singh
- *The 1619 Project* by Nikole Hannah-Jones
- *Culturally Responsive Teaching and the Brain: Promoting Authentic Engagement and Rigor Among Culturally and Linguistically Diverse Students* by Zaretta Hammond
- *My Grandmother's Hands: Racialized Trauma and the Pathway to Mending Our Hearts and Bodies* by Resmaa Menakem
- *Race Dialogues: A Facilitator's Guide to Tackling the Elephant in the Classroom* by Donna Rich Kaplowitz, Shayla Reese Griffin, and Sheri Seyka

The following checklists should be completed at the beginning and end of each academic year. Instructors should challenge themselves to increase the number of boxes they check each year. The list is presented in a progressive order of increasing levels of critical consciousness.

Increasing Critical Consciousness

- I have identified (met regularly with) an accountability partner who can increase my critical thinking around anti-Black racism.
- I understand my own positionality (power and privilege aligned with my identity, if any).
- I can recognize my own blind spots (areas where you may hold biases or fully understand the extent of the obvious harm that is caused by anti-Black racism).
- I can recognize anti-Black racism and how it occurs in society, academic settings, and classrooms.
- I make a habit of exploring counternarratives that challenge dominant ways of thinking.
- I have thoughtfully considered the role structural racism plays in perpetuating poverty, unrest, and (social, economic and political) disadvantage by

expanding my exposure to critical scholarship and thinking outside of my own worldview.
- I can recognize instances when issues of trust and distrust manifests among Black students or my colleagues.
- I use data-informed processes (not data-driven, but data-informed; context and perspectives matter) and best practices models that produce equitable outcomes.

Advancing Culturally Responsive Teaching Practices

- I have created a learning environment that is a safe space (sense of safety from physical and psychological harm) and a brave space (everyone is willing to take risks and authentically engage) in preparation for emotionally charged issues and discussions.
- I have designed a learning space and routine that is shaped and influenced by the cultural makeup of a broad cross-section of learners (particularly Black students).
- I am capable of affirming and validating historically and contemporarily marginalized student groups.
- I have created an environment (that is capable of supporting an optimal level of social-emotional development) where students can express a broad spectrum of emotions.
- I am capable of fostering an open and safe learning environment that recognizes, integrates, and honors cultural contexts through dialogue and reflective activities.
- I can contribute to the resiliency of students by acknowledging and honoring histories, communities, and shared narratives.
- I am capable of authentically involving students and community voices in the development of curriculum and co-curricular activities and matters.

Conclusion

Anti-Black racism is a blight on the fabric of US society. Taking steps to address anti-Black racism in institutions of higher education requires deliberate and concerted efforts. Critical race theory provides a useful lens for identifying and addressing oppressive structures and discourses that seek to normalize white-supremacy culture. In this regard, academic institutions must recognize the inherent challenges they face in creating environments that reject the idea of colorblindness or racial neutrality, in favor of one that recognizes and values differences and creates structures that are capable of adapting and supporting radical change. In this chapter, we have offered strategies for assuring institutional responses to anti-Black racism and underscored the need to promote critically conscious and culturally responsive teaching practice. Regardless of the prevailing conditions, it is important that we continue to persist in framing, analyzing, and discussing issues of race and access that will ultimately dismantle anti-Black racism and lead to academic and personal success of Black students.

References

Alexander, J. (2004). Toward a theory of cultural trauma. In J. Alexander, R. Eyerman, B. Gieson, N. Smleser, & P. Sztompka (Eds.), *Cultural trauma and collective identity*. University of California Press.

American Psychiatric Association. (2013). *Diagnostic and statistical manual of mental disorders* (5th ed.). American Psychiatric Association Publishing, Washington, DC.

Aspen Institute. (n.d.). *Glossary for understanding the dismantling structural racism/promoting racial equity analysis*. https://www.aspeninstitute.org/wp-content/uploads/files/content/docs/rcc/RCC-Structural-Racism-Glossary.pdf.

Bonilla-Silva, E. (2018). *Racism without racists: Color-blind racism and the persistence of racial inequality in America*. Rowman and Littlefield Publishers.

Bryant-Davis, T., & Ocampo, C. (2006). A therapeutic approach to the treatment of racist-incident-based trauma. *Journal of Emotional Abuse*. https://doi.org/10.1300/J135v06n04_01

Carter, R., Johnson, V. E., Muchow, C., Lyons, J., Forquer, E., & Galgay, C. (2016). Development of classes of racism of racism measures for frequency and stress reactions: Relationships to race-based traumatic stress. *Traumatology*, 22(1), 63–74. https://psycnet.apa.org/doi/10.1037/trm0000057

Carter, R. T., Kirkinis, K., & Johnson, V. E. (2019). *Relationship between trauma symptoms and race-based traumatic stress*. American Psychological Association. http://doi.org/10.1037/trm0000217

DeGruy, J. (2017). *Post traumatic slave syndrome, revised edition: America's legacy of enduring injury and healing*. Uptone Press.

DiAngelo, R. (2018). *White fragility: Why it's so hard for white people to talk about racism*. Beacon Press.

Editors of Encyclopedia Britannica. (n.d.). *Critical race theory*. https://www.britannica.com/topic/critical-race-theory

Feagin, J. R. (2006). *Racist America: Roots, current realities, & future reparations*. (1st ed.). Routledge. https://doi.org/10.4324/9781315880938

Feagin, J. R. (2001). *Racist America: Roots, current realities, & future reparations*. Routledge.

Freire, P. (1970). *Pedagogy of the oppressed*. Herder and Herder.

Griffin, C. B., Cooper, S., Metzger, I. W., Golden, A. R., & White, C. N. (2017). School racial climate and the academic achievement of African American high school students: The mediating role of school engagement. *Psychology in the Schools*, 54(7), 673–688.

Government Accounting Office (GAO). (2018). *K-12 education: Discipline disparities for black students, boys, and students with disabilities*. https://www.gao.gov/products/gao-18-258

Hammond, Z. (2015). *Culturally responsive teaching and the brain: Promoting authentic engagement and rigor among culturally and linguistically diverse students*. Corwin.

Hannah-Jones, N. (2021a). *A new origin story: The 1619 project*. One World.

Harper, G. W., & Neubauer, L. C. (2021). Teaching during a pandemic: A model for trauma-informed education and administration. *Pedagogy in Health Promotion*, 7(1), 14–24.

hooks, b. (1994). *Teaching to transgress*. Routledge/Taylor & Francis.

Kendi, I. X. (2019). *How to be an antiracist*. One World.

Lopez, A. E., & Jean-Marie, G. (2021). Challenging anti-black racism in everyday teaching, learning, and leading: From theory to practice. *Journal of School Leadership*, 31(1–2), 50–65.

Lopez-Littleton, V., Sampson, C., & Corpening, B. (2022). ADORE: A framework for community building to dismantle anti-black racism in academia. *Public Integrity*, 1–12. DOI: 10.1080/10999922.2022.2112869

Love, B. (2019). *We want to do more than survive: Abolitionist teaching and the pursuit of educational freedom*. Beacon Press.

McCoy, D. L., & Rodricks, D. J. (2015). Critical race theory in higher education: 20 years of theoretical and research innovations. *ASHE Higher Education Report*, 41(3), 1–117.

Menakem, R. (2017). *My grandmother's hands: Racialized trauma and the pathway to mending our hearts and bodies*. Central Recovery Press.

Mosley, D. V., Hargons, C. N., Meiller, C., Angyal, Bl., Wheeler, P., Davis, C., & Stevens-Watkins, D. (2021). Critical consciousness of anti-black racism: A practical model to prevent and resist racial trauma. *American Psychological Association*, 68(1), 1–16.

Pai, A., Suris, A. M., & North, C. S. (2017). Posttraumatic stress disorder in the DSM-5: Controversy, change, and conceptual considerations. *Behavioral Sciences (Basel, Switzerland)*, 7(1), 7. https://doi.org/10.3390/bs7010007

Substance Abuse and Mental Health Services Association (SAMHSA). (2022, March 22). *Trauma and violence*. SAMHSA. Retrieved May 28, 2022, from https://www.samhsa.gov/trauma-violence

Steele, C. M., Spencer, S. J., & Aronson, J. (2002). Contending with group image: The psychology of stereotype and social identity threat. In M.P. Zanna (Ed) *Advances in Experimental Social Psychology* (Vol. 34, pp. 379–440). Academic Press.

Stein, S., & de Oliveira Andreotti, V. (2018). Decolonization and higher education. *Encyclopedia of Educational Philosophy and Theory*. http://doi.org/10.1007/978-981-287-532-7_479-1

Stevenson, B. (2017). A presumption of guilt: The legacy of America's history of racial injustice. In D. Roberts (Ed.), *Killing the black body: Race, reproduction, and the meaning of liberty* (pp. 3–30). Penguin Random House.

University of California San Francisco Multicultural Resource Center. (2022). *Racial equity & anti-black racism*. https://mrc.ucsf.edu/racial-equity-anti-black-racism

Williams, D. R., & Mohammed, S. A. (2013). Racism and health I: Pathways and scientific evidence. *American Behavioral Science*, 57(8), 1–19.

Williams, M. T., Metzger, I. W., Liens, C., & DeLapp, C. (2018). Assessing racial trauma within a DSM-5 framework: The UConn racial/ethnic stress and trauma survey. *Practice Innovations*, 3(4), 242–260. https://doi.org/10.1037/pri0000076

5
WHEN EMBODIED HISTORIES MEET INSTITUTIONAL STORIES

Trauma as Pedagogical Possibility

Whitney J. Archer, Carina M. Buzo Tipton, Cassandra L. Hall, and Emma L. Larkins

Trauma is always in the room, in our bodies, classrooms, and the brick walkways that line our campus. As Charlene Carruthers (2019) reminds us, "We can and do show up … holding all of that trauma in our minds and that pain in our bodies" (p. 65). Following Carruthers, we consider how trauma-informed and healing-centered institutional practices are enabled when we account for these embodied stories (of trauma) within the university. Our focus on the university reflects our context as university scholars, practitioners, and administrators and recognizes the university is the location of historical and ongoing systemic violence. We grapple with our complicated positionalities within these fraught institutions and feel for how trauma may be engaged as lived and embodied wisdom through alternative pedagogies and practices. In making use of this lived and embodied wisdom, we hold close the lessons of the intellectual ancestors whom we follow in this work. We are guided by the words of Black feminist scholar bell hooks who became an ancestor as we co-created this project. As hooks tells us, "Teaching in a manner that respects and cares for the souls of our students is essential if we are to provide necessary conditions where learning can most deeply and intimately begin" (hooks, 1994, p. 13). We honor hooks and other teachers within and beyond the university by creating teaching-learning spaces where this tender learning and unlearning may flourish so that we can feel and imagine worlds beyond interlocking systems of oppression. Following hooks, we remember that allowing ourselves and our students to be whole is not distinct from the work of teaching and learning about these systems. Instead, these whole-making trauma-informed approaches are vital to academic rigor within anti-oppression teaching-learning spaces.

The institution of higher education is a "white supremacist capitalist patriarchy" (hooks, 1994) which traumatizes through the imposition of academic

DOI: 10.4324/9781003260776-6

and professional norms that reflect and maintain these oppressive systems. The university's function in maintaining hegemony is often veiled within "neutral" academic and professional norms. As such, part of the work of a trauma-informed institutional practice is to name the unnamed (Ahmed, 2012, 2017). Our critiques of the university are hopeful and reflect a desire to "make" a university in which harm is not inevitable (Powell, 2014, n.p.). In doing so, we illuminate trauma-informed approaches that account for how the university itself is traumatizing, particularly for those most impacted by interlocking systems of oppression (Combahee River Collective, 1977).

We **account for the embodied wisdom of our lived experiences**, including those related to the ongoing COVID-19 pandemic. This chapter reflects the flows of pandemic time and what we call "COVID grammar." We first came together for this project in a world before COVID-19, and we have continued to dream this work into being throughout the pandemic. This chapter was always intended to reflect our desire for a more livable future in which trauma-informed care and healing-centered practices are woven into university structures. While the focus of our work has not shifted, the exigency of the trauma-informed approaches that we advocate for here has. This chapter dreams of what might be possible if the university centered trauma-informed approaches rather than relegating them to those units, programs, or bodies positioned as "caring."

This bending of time echoes the lived experience of trauma in which time is not experienced as a "straightforward, orderly procession from the past through the present, to the future." Rather, "the future and past are intimately entwined, the present produced in their merging" (Morrigan, 2017, p. 50). Through attention to time and linearity as a colonial construct, Morrigan positions these queer experiences of time—and trauma more broadly—as sites of possibility rather than abject tragedy. Following Morrigan, we consider how trauma-informed practices allow us to attend to immediate violence in the present, grapple with traumatic histories, including those related to white supremacy and other interlocking systems of oppression, and illuminate transformative future possibilities for care within the university.

Transformative trauma-informed work requires us to engage with intention and allow space for reflection. We invite you to follow us as we feel for the possibilities that emerge when we position trauma as possibility. We invite you to slow down, challenge the ableist and capitalist pressures to produce, and quiet the sense of urgency that reflects a culture of white supremacy. We do this explicitly through the "praxis pauses" that we offer throughout this chapter, often through an intentional slowing down and reflection. In this deliberate slowing down, we are moved by Alexis Pauline Gumbs' (2020) question, "what if we could release ourselves from an internalized time clock and remember that slow is efficient, slow is effective, slow is beautiful?" (p. 141).

Praxis Pause: Slow down with us, dear reader, pour yourself a cup of tea, sit and have a conversation with us as you engage with our reflections and offerings. What are you carrying in your bodymind that holds possibility in your practices of trauma-informed pedagogy?

COVID Trauma and COVID Grammar

As feminist scholars, we approach trauma as we approach all oppressive and violent structures: through a critique of its violence, including the imposition of false binaries such as good–bad and traumatized–healed. These critiques are generative and aim to reveal what else might be possible when we attend to institutional harm and endeavor to do otherwise. We lean on trauma-informed approaches that account for how trauma—inclusive of intergenerational and historical trauma—emerges not only in anomalous moments in which we are "triggered" but serves as a constant presence and embodied knowing that shapes how we move through the university and our broader worlds. In the context of a mass traumatizing and disabling pandemic, we cannot abide by these clean binary notions of trauma.

COVID shifts our grammar, or the everyday structures and language through which we understand our worlds. In attending to how our grammar has shifted in COVID time—producing new meanings and revealing forgotten or obscured meanings—we also invite you to consider how this moment has shifted the grammar of trauma-informed pedagogies and care.

Praxis Pause: Here is a shortlist that we have begun to create in our work. Are there ways that COVID grammar has shown up in your work? Are there ways that the language and practices of COVID gave you insight into making your work more trauma-informed?

1. **Contact tracing** tracks exposures and transmission of COVID-19. It reveals the potential impacts of our small encounters and the urgency of everyday collective care practices. It illuminates connections that might have otherwise been forgotten. Our use of contact tracing is further informed by Powell et al.'s (2014) theorization of "constellations" as a means to understand the "different ways of seeing any single configuration within that constellation, based on positionality and culture" (Act 1, Scene 2, para. 6). We engage "constellating" as a way for us each to draw upon our experiences with and embodiments of trauma to inform our relationships and pedagogical practices. We believe that our witnessing and desire to critically grapple with narratives of trauma and being traumatized within the contextual relationship of dominant academic narratives provides space for the potential of trauma-informed practices that dismantle the violence of the institution. As a pedagogy, we see contact tracing as a tool for revealing institutional harm and other traumatizing contexts and

illuminating the impacts of everyday trauma-informed care practices that may be illegible or invisible to the university. Instead of tracing the virus, we call upon contact tracing to track our care work, labor that has always been central to our work but invisible to the institution. Contact tracing may also allow us to make lineages of harm and lineages of kinship visible. Tracking and tracing these lineages creates a constellation that can become sites of learning and **building kinship networks**. We deepen these discussions through attention to "pods" below.

Praxis Pause: Map out your networks. Who are the people in your life with whom you could deepen your connection? What conversations are waiting to be found—with your friends, colleagues, and classrooms?

2. **Pods** (or COVID pods) were an early answer to creating small groups of households to share care responsibilities within shared safety measures. We see notions of feminist and crip-care webs in this idea of pods; the idea that communities should deliberately come together to share safety, needs, security, and resources. We collectively weave care webs that "shift our ideas of access and care … from an individual chore … to a collective responsibility that's maybe even deeply joyful" (Piepzna-Samarasinha, 2018, p. 17). This attention to trauma-informed pedagogies and other trauma-informed care practices as a constant, relational practice that opens up world-making possibilities shapes our discussion of trauma-informed care. Here, we turn to ourselves as an example of a care web pod through connection and action. We work across campus in student support, teaching undergraduate courses, and gender-specific resources and advocacy. Due to ongoing engagements of parenting, teaching, being students, and working part-time and full-time, we carved out time to go away together to write and create. We created a pod for transformative care within our writing retreat as we embodied and collectively engaged in trauma-informed practices that we illuminate within this chapter. Even in our contained writing retreat, the institution still informed our time together: due to our roles on campus, throughout our week, we fielded what felt like a constant stream of messages from students as they navigated the most recent COVID-19 surge. This moment reflects the broader care practices that we have cultivated and deepened during pandemic time. We have delivered groceries and baked goods to one another's doorsteps throughout the pandemic to mitigate potential harm. We honored the fullness of each other's emotions as we grieved the loss of loved ones. We reminded each other of our wholeness while navigating doctoral exams and institutional bureaucracy.

    Care webs, pods, and critical kinships in practice reveal possibilities for transformative trauma-informed practices within the university.

3. **Social distancing**: in a time before COVID-19, we may not have understood "social distancing" as an act of collective care and protection. What

might have once been read as a lack of care is now positioned as a potentially life-saving care act. This inverse meaning illuminates the new ways of interpreting our learning spaces and organizing our shared and individual access needs, including those related to trauma. **How might we create more livable institutions from the ruptures of the pandemic? How might we do this while holding space for the incredible loss—and trauma—that we continue to endure?** As what was possible in March 2020 is again deemed impossible (such as fully remote work for many on campus), it is urgent that we ensure these practices continue. Social distancing has been a way to protect our communities and ourselves from potential infection. What if we were to see the toxic institutional policies and practices for the infections that they are. **What would it look like to apply social distancing to these day-to-day institutional harms as an act of collective care and protection**?

4. **Quarantines** have become a normalized experience and element of our vocabulary. These quarantine periods do not account for the differential ways in which bodies are impacted by sickness and exposure. They are positioned as something to get through rather than something to learn from. We hear this in the messages to return to campus, to teach in person, in the ways we are being compelled (verbally, in practice, etc.) to forget (our traumas), to disembody, to just come to class. These messages actively deny the traumas of this moment.

We expand upon this initial discussion of COVID grammar through attention to **masks, mandates,** and **medicine** and their lessons for trauma-informed teaching and care within the university. We engage masks as a means of grappling with the limits and possibilities of interpersonal trauma-informed approaches including those that intervene within a university that continually harms those who do not or cannot conform to its norms and desires. Next, we consider the urgency and perils of practicing trauma-informed care within the university by discussing mandates. To close, we offer a reflection on medicine that reveals how trauma-informed and healing-centered approaches respond to the immediate violence of traumatic contexts, including systemic oppression, and how these approaches support us in creating worlds in which experiences of harm, oppression, and trauma are not inevitable.

Masks

Face coverings and masks became a new visual norm. They operate as a tool of safety and a means of communicating our commitments to community care. This section discusses the balance of masks as protection and, alternately, as a covering or hiding. We consider how our trauma-informed approaches mitigate harm and also help to obscure or "re-order" (Ferguson, 2012) institutional violence. We discuss the trauma-informed and healing-centered approaches that allow us to navigate this fraught institutional context.

Masks, as we have learned, protect the self against the virus, but importantly protect others from contracting the virus (or viruses) from us. Masks are a practice of community care. As with protective face coverings, moving through the university from a trauma-informed and healing-centered perspective serves as a constant, everyday care practice for ourselves and the community. Trauma-informed practices (examples of which we have offered throughout this piece and noted as "praxis pause") make the university more livable for those who do not or cannot conform to dominant constructions of the "good" student, scholar, professor, administrator. Trauma-informed approaches may not register as a skill; we have experienced how this work can be reduced to individuals who merely care. However, we position these skills as vital means of creating safer relations for ourselves and others in their interactions with us. Yet, in mitigating harm, we also strengthen the institution; for example, localized efforts and responses may ultimately damper dissent, calling for more overarching, systemic-level changes. We frequently question how to contend with internalized institutionality while enacting feminist work within the academy.

Praxis Pause: Carina offers a practice: "When I am experiencing a student who I perceive to be 'difficult' I tell myself that the first thought I have about that student is the narrative that white supremacist capitalist patriarchy needs me to believe about that student—but the second thought is the one I choose to act upon. The second thought is the caring one, which attempts to dismantle what white supremacy and patriarchy attempt to tell me about students." Following this practice is a way to intentionally challenge the assumptions systems of dominance have trained you to make. If a student is quiet, you can imagine them daydreaming of possibilities, processing information that contradicts what they have been taught, scanning the room for trust and safety, or maybe just not rested and healed enough today to have all eyes on them.

While we trouble an individualistic, pathologized understanding of trauma, we also account for how our presence as trauma-informed diversity workers is cited as evidence of the institution's care. The weight of being included in the institution, as Ahmed (2012) explores, compels us to responsibly leverage the institutional power and positionality that we do hold. We must work to realize connections between individual acts and broader institutional behaviors. When does our work shield students from institutional harm? **When does our work mask the workings of institutional violence? How do we move forward when, brutally, both things are so often true at once? Are masks enough?**

So much trauma-informed discourse ignores the university as a site of ongoing trauma. Trauma is presented as anomalous rather than systemic and resulting from the university's white supremacist, cis-heteropatriarchal foundations. In noting how the institution has contributed to the pandemic and, in the process, contributed to ongoing trauma, it becomes possible to see how the institution reflects and maintains interlocking systems of oppression. A university that does not account for its ongoing role in maintaining oppressive, traumatizing structures cannot be "trauma-informed." Just as the masks that have become a part of everyday lives lessen the impact of the COVID-19 virus, the interpersonal practices that we offer in this piece as sites of possibility lessen the impact of harm, but fundamentally are not enough. Without institutional intervention, harm will continue and expand. We need mandates.

Mandates

Mandates as Obstacle

While the language of mandates has come to hold new and deepened meanings in pandemic times, mandates have always existed within higher education—most notably through academic and professional norms that reflect and maintain interlocking systems of oppression. Mandates are value-aligned in that they reflect institutional investments and desires. At the pandemic's start, institutional mandates reflected a professed desire to protect those within the institution. As we write this at the start of 2022, these investments have returned to one of maintaining pre-pandemic normalcy. We are experiencing triple the highest number of daily cases from prior years, yet we are being told to have shorter quarantine days with less access to testing sites, masks, and work-from-home options. We feel we have no choice but to return, listen to these mandates, keep the lights on, keep calm, and move forward through the ongoing pandemic. We know that in our return, we contribute to institutional un-caring. These impossible situations create conditions in which harm and trauma to our body-minds are inevitable.

Praxis Pause: We recommend flexibility as a trauma-informed praxis. We declare our syllabi as living documents and subject to change. This has at times meant cutting readings or adapting assignments. We've noticed engagement increase and learning deepen when we've done so. A limitation of mandates is that they are prescriptive and assume everyone needs the same intervention. Flexibility reminds us there is a multitude of ways to meet a learning outcome.

A trauma-informed university needs to contend with how experiences of trauma inform those within the institution as well as with the university itself as a traumatizing entity. This is true of pandemic responses and more broadly. To this point, Byrd (2018) writes, "despite the liberatory intentions of many researchers, more often than not, academic knowledge is co-opted by the state to reproduce the palatability of state violence" (p. 94). To theorize about how an institution can perform or behave being trauma-informed might open more capacity for harm to occur. Just because an institution places mandates does not inherently make it safe. We must remain attuned to the possibility of further harm within that theorizing and those mandates.

Naming how academic and professional norms reflect white supremacy and other interlocking systems of oppression is interpreted as a deviation from academic norms of collegiality and rationality (Price, 2011, p. 5). But what is rational in a pandemic? To remain calm amid our current context/surroundings is irrational. We question *ourselves* in all this questioning (Ahmed, 2012). We might come to believe institutional stories. Were we seeing things that were not there? Are we reading too deep into what was said and "un-said" (Duncan, 2004)? These "institutional betrayals" are crushing, their weight accumulating as they stack upon one another (Freyd & Birrell, 2013). We are failed by institutional "un-caring" (Hedva, 2016). We are failed again by its gaslighting and its refusals to conceive of itself as traumatizing and a space in which white supremacist cis-heteropatriarchy is continually bolstered. We are cautioned with tenderness by others who worry that we will be harmed in naming the unnamed (Ahmed, 2012, 2017). White supremacist, capitalist, ableist, and other oppressive norms are naturalized—and rewarded—to such an extent that we question the harm we are experiencing and understand those wounds as evidence of our lack. But, how can we staunch a wound that we cannot see? Simultaneously, we must grapple with how we embody and reproduce institutional norms, including those that reflect white supremacist, masculinist, (settler) colonial, ableist, and other oppressive norms and desires. As we have written throughout this piece, trauma-informed institutional practices must account for the institution itself as a space in which systemic, institutional, and interpersonal traumas happen. In the next section, we consider how the wisdom of COVID time reveals the urgency of institutional trauma-informed practices.

Mandates as Opportunity

In pandemic time, we have come to know the limits of individual responses. Regardless of our individual care—the masks we wear, the experiences we sacrificed to protect ourselves and others—the virus continues to spread without substantial institutional responses. We might have bristled at a call for more institutional mandates *before*. As we are subject to an ongoing pandemic exacerbated by institutional failures, we better understand the urgency of institutional responses to trauma. It is not enough to relegate trauma-informed care to particular bodies, programs, or units. The pandemic has heightened our understanding that it is not possible to pretend that trauma is an anomalous experience limited to certain students, faculty, and others within the university. Trauma-informed care needs to be woven into the entirety of the institution. It is the only path forward. These approaches are urgent as we move through an ongoing mass trauma. They call us to locate our power—perhaps in **whisper networks** in which we share our experiences of harm within an institution that will not or cannot account for itself as traumatizing and oppressive or by **leveraging positions in which we have greater access to institutional power**.

This work needs to **stay messy and humble.** The crisis of the COVID-19 pandemic is situated within ongoing colonial and white supremacist disasters in which trauma is inevitable. These entangled emergencies demand creativity and innovation. They demand that our institutions operate with the level of care, commitment, and sustained engagement with trauma-informed frameworks they have asked of us as students, teachers, and practitioners within the university. We do not know what this other university will look and feel like. She is iterative and emerging. We find glimpses of her in our classrooms, in our conversations with the students we work with and support, and in the slow, careful collaboration through which we create this piece.

Praxis Pause: We welcome mistakes and failure in our slow, flexible collaborations. Like how we position trauma as a site of possibility, we suggest that failure can also be generative. In our work with students, we create spaces for mistakes and failures to deepen learning, growth, and development. What could be waiting for you and the students you teach when you engage failures as a site of possibility?

The next section considers the medicines that allow us to survive as we imagine and work toward worlds in which trauma is not an inevitable condition of life within the horrors of white supremacist cis-heteropatriarchy. **How do we move forward when we have witnessed what might be possible and borne witness to how these possibilities fall away again as the institutional "returns to normal?"** These medicines help us navigate the university as it exists; they help move us toward a more livable university in which whole-making healing and trauma-informed practices are possible.

Medicine

In the previous sections, we traced how institutional behaviors and mandates both have opportunities for failures and protections. This section offers ways to respond to or address institutional harm. Like any other harm, physical or medical, treatment is required. In the context of this work, medicine is about witnessing harm that has caused a break or rupture in an individual, in relationships, or in our trust in our institutions. In our medicine offerings, we think about the breaks and ruptures as needing medicine of **wholeness**. We draw upon Charlene Martinez and Dr Erich Pitcher (2021) in our discussions of wholeness. In conversation, Martinez and Pitcher explore what it means to be whole.

Erich: Charlene, what does wholeness mean to you?
Charlene: For me, wholeness is the ability to feel fully present to one's self, one's
community, and the world. Wholeness allows us to know our power and

> exercise our agency. Wholeness allows us to exhale and breathe deeply without anticipation of future anxiety or the remnants of past trauma.
>
> *Erich:* So, what is the opposite of wholeness?
>
> *Charlene:* The opposite of wholeness is not brokenness or a lack of suffering, but unattended to damage. (p. 127)

We can help one another apply salves that soothe our agitated wounds. In attending to our trauma—including trauma resulting from moving through the institution—we move toward wholeness. Even when our institutional encounters leave us feeling broken, Pitcher and Martinez remind us that that does not make us less whole. Still, we need the space, connection, and resources to feel present and restored to ourselves and others.

In *Medicine Stories*, Aurora Levins Morales (2019) asks readers to consider what is in their medicine bags. When approaching healing processes, what salves and medicines do you turn to? Writing of her own, Levins Morales describes "my personal medicine bag and tool kit have been gathered over a lifetime of activism" (p. 14). Recognizing that there are many different frameworks and tools available when considering trauma-informed practices of healing (e.g., Sara Ahmed's feminist killjoy toolkit (2017), Leah Lakshmi Piepzna-Samarasinha's "Chronically Ill Touring Artist Pro Tips" (2017)), we hope that our collective medicines shared in this piece can illuminate alternative frameworks to think through your approaches. In this section, we open our bag and offer the beginning of a care kit. We hope that readers will consider the supplies and ingredients that are not yet present and add them to their medicine bag or tool kit.

We have sprinkled our offerings throughout the chapter. We have offered ways that **creating kin, whisper networks**, and **care webs** become ways for us to connect in a way that brings opportunities that both subvert institutional harm and begin to heal our individual and collective wounds. Amid the institutional pull toward silence and compliance, care webs (Piepzna-Samarasinha, 2018) and critical connections offer the possibility of making wounds visible and helping one another in healing (Levins Morales, 2019). Levins Morales reminds us that what is broken can be made whole again. In whatever form your community takes, be it a whisper network or a care web, the stories we share of how we survive serve as "communal medicine" (Levins Morales, 2019, p. 50).

The work that we do in the present shapes the future for others. In *Emergent Strategies*, adrienne maree brown (2017) offers a vision in which the ways we enact and embody our beliefs in the present can reverberate into the future in the form of more "complex patterns and systems of change" (p. 2). In this way, we build communities and environments in which the conditions of oppression are no longer permissible or possible. Throughout this text, we have noted elements of our care kit by bolding elements and critical questions that serve as medicine in our work as trauma-informed teachers, practitioners, and scholars. We hope that they might be of use to you in your own communities or help you generate a practice of your own. A salve to soothe the agitation of institutional trauma and violence, a move toward honoring one another's wholeness.

Praxis Pause: We bring activities into our classrooms and workspaces that invite dreaming the futures we desire. We've created in-class "visionary fiction" (Imarisha & brown, 2015) exercises and assignments that invite students to archive their desired futures in 2050. For example, Cassandra Hall asks students to "imagine more livable futures for mothers and children most impacted by systems of oppression." Students have shared that these assignments have been sources of hope. "The future is not an escapist place to occupy. All is it is the inevitable result of what we do today, and the more we take it into our hands, imagine it as a place of justice and pleasure, the more the future knows we want it, and that we aren't letting go" (brown, p. 164)

(Not the) Conclusion

Trauma bends time—we reimagine the past, are anxious that our experiences of trauma will be re-articulated in the future, and struggle to stay in the present. As a trauma-informed work, our chapter bends time. We proposed our chapter pre-pandemic and created much of it amid the Omicron variant. We are living through a pandemic in which the impossible was made possible. We learned new ways to be together. We grieve the loss of what might have been as our institutions profess to return to normal. This chapter will be published and engaged in a future whose contours remain fuzzy and unformed. What world do you live in, dear reader? Instead of a conclusion, we offer an opening, the space in which you choose how to make meaning of this work and the stories that we shared with you, and perhaps, in the stories you have come to know about yourself.

Using COVID vocabularies, we have traced how the pandemic—a mass trauma and a disabling event—necessitates holistic, structural trauma-informed approaches. We can no longer assume that someone in the room might be traumatized when we are all (differentially) impacted by the traumas of the COVID-19 pandemic. No one leaves this moment unscathed. With attention to this context and the urgency of this moment, we modeled trauma-informed and healing-centered approaches that attend to damage, destabilize the oppressive conditions from which trauma emerges, and illuminate healing possibilities for trauma-informed pedagogies in higher education. We illustrate transformative approaches that allow us to grapple with trauma without affirming curative rhetorics that obscure the continual work of healing within ongoing oppressive and traumatic contexts.

We considered how we pull from our lived and embodied experiences of trauma to enact whole-making care within an uncaring institution. Through a discussion of masks as community care and institutional performances, mandates as nuanced and needed, and medicine as salves for immediate harm, we situate our work within the shifting world of the COVID-19 pandemic. We offered a guide that balances trauma-informed pedagogies' necessary complexity and messiness with the urgency of specific practices and approaches. Our intention is for a collective move toward skills that allow us to hold space for this complexity and mess. Through attention to how varied flows of trauma and care move through the university, we have revealed how seemingly disconnected experiences are imbricated within and shaped through interlocking systems of oppression, including white supremacy, colonialism, and ableism. To close, we move toward wholeness through attention to the lingering tensions that follow us into our work as trauma-informed scholars, teacher-learners, and practitioners. We name these tensions through a series of questions. In grappling with these tensions, we do not position trauma-informed work within uncaring institutions as impossible. Rather, we name them, hoping that contending with them in the present will enable us to create a more livable university.

Can the institution be saved? Our work fights for those who are harmed rather than for the institution. While our work is articulated within the university, we are most invested in mitigating and attending to the damage of historical and ongoing oppressive projects which are reflected within and nourished by existing university structures. As offered in our earlier reflections on the uses and limits of masks, we wear and advocate for masks to support those who are most vulnerable, rather than as a means of returning to the capitalist, white supremacist machine of *before*. We recognize that, as Clelia O. Rodríguez (2018) reminds us in *Decolonizing Academia*, "No assignment will ever capture the impact of the violent legacy of colonialism and other-isms" (p. 30). We account for the limits of individualized trauma-informed responses when they are not accompanied by trauma-informed efforts or shifts within broader university structures. We remember that our approaches may be co-opted and re-worked in ways that most benefit our traumatizing institutions. We do the work anyway. This is not the conclusion.

For whom is trauma-informed work expected or required? For whom are trauma-informed approaches seen as unnecessary or a distraction from other "important" work? Trauma-informed approaches require skill and call us to invest our emotional and other labor. From our varied positions within the university, we have witnessed how those with greater institutional power are absolved of their responsibilities to engage trauma-informed approaches. Instead, trauma-informed work is relegated to particular units, programs, and bodies. This work is demanded of us, even as it is devalued within institutional hierarchies. We are still grappling with these tensions and how they shape our lived experiences of trauma within the university. This is not the conclusion.

What is our accountability and agency within a university that continually harms and traumatizes? We are continually reminded of our complicity in maintaining university structures and how we have internalized and embodied institutionality. Our use of institutionality refers to how those within institutions maintain institutional norms and processes through their participation within them—even with the best intentions. For example, regardless of the flexibility and grace that we extend to students, we are still required to provide passing and failing grades at the close of the term. Each of us must contend with how our trauma-informed approaches and other work within the university are informed by our loyalties to succeed within university metrics, including our desires to complete our doctoral degrees and retain our professional positions. There are stories that we have not shared here, stories that we have relegated to drafts and brainstorming sessions for fear of institutional retribution. There are stories that we are not ready to tell (stories that we may never tell). We accept how this silence may allow institutional harm to continue and hold space for this tension. This is not the conclusion.

What if we never get to witness and experience a more livable university? In this chapter, we planted the seeds from which a more livable university—a university in which institutional harm is not inevitable—might grow. In planting these seeds, we refuse the limits of institutional possibilities and illuminate possibilities for trauma-informed institutional care work that attends to the systemic contexts from which our lived and embodied experiences of trauma emerge. Our work as traumatized people within a traumatizing institution is anchored in care for one another's souls and those of the students we teach, support, and otherwise care for. In planting these seeds, we reveal alternate possibilities for the university classroom and other institutional teaching-learning spaces and consider how they may operate as sites where we create and maintain critical kinship networks (Justice, 2018). We plant these seeds knowing that we may not witness the university that we conjure through our work in the present. We position our work as "science fictional behavior"—an approach that accounts for how "our actions and beliefs now, today, will shape the future, tomorrow, the next generations" (brown, 2017, p. 16). Like brown (2017), "we are excited by what we can create, we believe it is possible to create the next world" (p. 16). This is not the conclusion.

In planting seeds for a more livable university through our trauma-informed work in the present, we nourish kinships with those in the future and engage the time-bending truth of trauma as a condition of possibility rather than abject grief or loss. We find our closing story amidst these endless connections. Carina Buzo Tipton shared ideas about this project with academic and kinship sibling Robin Fifita and Robin's baby, Mahina Tupou Silioti. Robin casually and profoundly offered the quote, "The only path forward is through the past," a quote that she attributed to the Tongan philosopher, Okusitino Māhina. The only path forward is through the past. While a curative approach to this framing might argue that we should overcome and move past our trauma, we engage it to remind us that we can create the university that we desire through our work in the present.

This is not a conclusion—it is an invitation. We invite you to witness your trauma and the trauma of others within the institution. We invite you to reflect on how attending to the damage of these experiences might allow for a more trauma-informed and healing-centered future. Vitally, we are asking our institutions to join us in this work and to attend to their historical and ongoing complicity in oppressive and other traumatizing projects so that we can conjure the university that we desire.

References

Ahmed, S. (2012). *On being included: Racism and diversity in institutional life*. Duke University Press.
Ahmed, S. (2017). *Living a feminist life*. Duke University Press.
brown, A. M. (2017). *Emergent strategy: Shaping change, changing worlds*. AK Press.
Byrd, R. M. (2018). "Prison treated me way better than you": Reentry, perplexity, and the naturalization of mass imprisonment. In Abolition Collection (Eds.), *Abolishing carceral society* (pp. 91–115). Common Notions.
Carruthers, C. (2019). *Unapologetic: A black, queer, and feminist mandate for radical movements*. Beacon Press.
Combahee River Collective. (1977, April). *The Combahee River Collective statement*. https://www.blackpast.org/african-american-history/combahee-river-collective-statement-1977/.
Duncan, P. (2004). *Tell this silence: Asian American women and the politics of speech*. University of Iowa Press.
Freyd, J., & Birrell, P. (2013). *Blind to betrayal: Why we fool ourselves, we aren't being fooled*. Wiley.
Gumbs, A. P. (2020). *Undrowned: Black feminist lessons from marine mammals*. AK Press.
Hedva, J. (2016). Sick woman theory. *Mask Magazine*, 24. http://www.maskmagazine.com/not-again/struggle/sick-woman-theory
hooks, b. (1994). *Teaching to transgress: Education as the practice of freedom*. Routledge.
Imarisha, W. & brown, A. M. (Eds.). (2015). *Octavia's brood: Science fiction stories from social justice movements*. AK Press.
Justice, D. H. (2018). *Why indigenous literatures matter*. Wilfred Laurier University Press.
Levins Morales, A. (2019). *Medicine stories*. Duke University Press.
Morrigan, C. (2017). Trauma time: The queer temporalities of the traumatized mind. *Somatechnics*, 7(1), 50–58.
Piepzna-Samarasinha, L. L. (2018). *Care work: Dreaming disability justice*. Arsenal Pulp Press.
Pitcher, E. N., & Martinez, C. C. (2021). From here to there: Educating for wholeness. In N. Osei-Kofi, B. Boovy, & K. Furman (Eds.), *Transformative approaches to social justice education* (pp. 124–140). Routledge.
Powell, M., Levy, D., Riley-Mukavetz, A., Brooks-Gillies, M., Novotny, M., & Fisch-Ferguson, J. (2014). Our story begins here: Constellating cultural rhetorics. *Enculturation*. http://enculturation.net/our-story-begins-here
Price, M. (2011). *Mad at school: Rhetorics of mental disability and academic life*. University of Michigan Press.
Rodríguez, C. O. (2018). *Decolonizing academia: Poverty, oppression and pain*. Fernwood Publishing.

6
AFFECTIVE SOLIDARITY AND TRAUMA-INFORMED POSSIBILITIES

A Comparative Analysis of the Classroom and the Clinic[1]

Kriti Prasad and Pritha Prasad

When the COVID-19 pandemic abruptly forced classes online in Spring 2020, universities, recognizing both the anxiety and stress brought on by the pandemic as well as the grave threat it posed to the financial stability of the institution, performed a particular rhetoric of care. "Check-in" emails were sent urging students to take advantage of counseling and psychological services on campus. Instructors were told to increase the flexibility of their course policies and due dates. Administrators called for instructors to increase virtual communication and engagement with students. Nonetheless, the university continued to suffer materially from the effects of the pandemic: students, faculty, and staff contracted COVID-19 at alarming rates, vital adjunct and staff positions were eliminated to accommodate budgetary exigencies, and instructors—especially contingent and untenured faculty—experienced a perfect storm of burnout-inducing conditions as teaching and research responsibilities continued on alongside the increased institutional and curricular demands necessitated by the pandemic (Nagoski & Nagoski, 2019).

At the same time, public health experts began foreshadowing the collapse of the US healthcare system as ICUs across the nation neared capacity as a result of COVID-19. Burnout among healthcare workers has remained a common complication of increased electronic medical record burden, long, rigorous medical training, and chaotic workplace culture. The pandemic exacerbated these underlying problems, creating an "acute-on-chronic" health issue for healthcare workers and medical students. Physicians and nurses remained at the center of mass media discourse, yet nearly half of all healthcare workers, from doctors to medical assistants to housekeeping, have experienced COVID-related burnout (Prasad et al., 2021). With medical students, like university undergrads, receiving most of their curricula online, isolated from their peers

DOI: 10.4324/9781003260776-7

and community for much of the pandemic, ("COVID-19's Emotional Impact") and clinical students witnessing the consequences of COVID-19 on patients and providers firsthand, there has been a strikingly high rate of depression and suicidal ideation among students.[2] The medical learning environment has always been exploitative for medical students, but COVID-19 has further disrupted medical training by exposing soon-to-be physicians, and especially those who are multiply marginalized, to increased burnout-exacerbating and trauma-inducing conditions.

While educational and healthcare institutions grew increasingly unstable, we also witnessed across the nation a hyper-visible and widely discussed racial uprising in response to the anti-Black murders of George Floyd, Breonna Taylor, and Ahmaud Arbery (among many others); the violent murders of Asian and Asian American women in Atlanta in early 2021; and the May 2021 outbreak of deadly air strike and rocket attacks in Israeli-occupied Palestine after right-wing Jewish settlers in East Jerusalem violently raided, attacked, and attempted to displace Palestinian residents ("Israeli-Palestinian Tensions Erupt"). These events have irreversibly shaped the experiences of Black, Indigenous, and people of color (BIPOC) in the wake of a pandemic that has also been disproportionately deadly for communities of color, and especially poor and migrant communities without proper access to healthcare (Lopez et al., 2021). Indeed, Floyd's autopsy revealed that he himself had COVID-19 at the time of his death (Neuman, 2020). The statement, "I can't breathe," which Floyd cried out for eight minutes as he was murdered by white police officer Derek Chauvin, has since become a reminder of both state-sanctioned anti-Black violence[3] and the racial disparities that have exacerbated the deadly impacts of the pandemic.

We write this chapter as two sisters and women of color who each professionally occupy radically different corners of the university spectrum, but whose interdisciplinary collaboration in this project has made visible key intersections of trauma in culture, politics, higher education, and medicine at a unique moment in which such intersections are especially visible. Kriti is in her third year of medical school at the University of Minnesota in the middle of her clinical rotations. Pritha is an Assistant Professor of English at the University of Kansas. The majority of time we have spent in these positions has coincided with the pandemic. We have, therefore, often found ourselves discussing particular types of questions: How do pandemics, and both the "acute" and "slow" traumas[4] they necessitate, uniquely make visible the cracks in our institutions and dominant paradigms of pedagogy, healthcare, and academic knowledge-making? How does the witnessing of both immediate and distant traumas impact what *care-oriented* relationships look like in educational, clinical, and professional settings? How do abstract institutional rhetorics of "care" serve—or not serve—students, medical trainees, instructors, and healthcare workers? And finally: What does it mean to be *trauma-informed* in our pedagogical and professional relationships while suffering from shared, collective traumas ourselves?

It may seem difficult at first to imagine what a comparative analysis of the university and healthcare setting could possibly reveal about trauma-informed *pedagogy* in our current moment, but our work in this chapter shows that these two spaces are already deeply embedded. Educators are "mandatory reporters," who, according to US federal law, are required by virtue of their regular contact with vulnerable groups to report any suspected instances of abuse or neglect, civil rights violations, mental health crises, and sexual violence/harassment. Other mandatory reporting professions include physicians, social workers, healthcare workers, childcare professionals, law enforcement, and animal control officers, to name a few. Mandatory reporting, in spite of its potential to contribute to the ableist, racist, sexist, and classist profiling of students (Inguanta & Sciolla, 2021), is one of many ways that instructors, in ways not completely unlike healthcare workers, are continually placed in *care-oriented* relationships with their students. Whether they are or are not, this dynamic expects instructors to be intimately familiar with healthcare systems, psychiatric and mental health resources, and otherwise recognizing and interpreting expressions of trauma.

More acutely during the pandemic, anxieties surrounding sickness and contagion have become so central to experiences of teaching and learning that instructors are now often required by their institutions to hold the dual responsibility of delivering course material while also enacting public health *pedagogies* such as ensuring students wear masks, establishing safe distances between desks, and contact-tracing when students have exposed others to COVID-19. But it is important to mention that this heightened awareness of the body, sickness, and accessibility in the classroom has long persisted for some bodies, even before the pandemic. Disability studies scholars, activists, and disabled students have for decades called for a sustained focus on accessibility in the classroom and a deeper understanding of the inherent risks public classroom and campus spaces pose to those who are disabled, immunocompromised, and chronically ill (Lau, 2021).

We offer here a comparative, narrative-based inquiry into the transformative possibilities of trauma-informed pedagogical approaches in care-oriented settings—in this case, the classroom and the clinic. As Sara Ahmed argues (2004), truth-telling and narrative in response to trauma and historical justice can offer critical possibilities for exposure and recognition, particularly for those who have been historically colonized and enslaved (p. 200). However, we actively challenge the common definition of trauma in medical literature as being dictated by a singular "event" or a "sudden, expected, or non-normative" experience that "disrupts the individual's frame of reference" (McCann & Pearlman, 1990, p. 10). Instead, we view trauma as "a mode of being" (Schwab, 2010, p. 42) that is linked "to the formation of collective identity and the construction of collective memory" (Eyerman, 2004, p. 60), even if acute traumas may often be sparked by particular cultural, political, or embodied events. We therefore follow Anne Cvetkovich's seminal understanding of trauma (2003) that displaces "the dyadic and hierarchical relationships" that characterize clinical approaches to trauma between doctor and patient—and, we'd add, between teacher and student—by "opening that relationship out into the public sphere and expanding the repertoire for the expression of emotion" (Cvetkovich, 2003, p. 286). As we consider what trauma-informed *pedagogy* might look like, then, our understanding of "pedagogy" is also purposely expansive. Like critical pedagogy studies scholar Henry Giroux (2018), we define pedagogy as any political practice or "technology of power, language, and practice that produces and legitimates forms of moral and political regulation that construct and offer human beings particular views of themselves and the world" (Giroux, 2018, p. 226).

In what follows, we each offer first-person narratives of our experiences managing and negotiating collective, historical, and personal traumas throughout the pandemic as researchers/practitioners and, in Kriti's case, as a student/trainee. In centering our narratives across the classroom and clinic as the basis for pedagogical *theory*, we intentionally mobilize what women of color and Third World feminists conceptualize as "theory in the flesh."[5] In doing so, we also seek to enact a form of institutional rhetorical critique that, as Jennifer Sano-Franchini writes, considers "how institutions and bodies interplay in ways that affect human beings" (Cobos et al., 2018, p. 148). In our concluding section we reflect on how our narratives pose important questions about how trauma-informed pedagogy can and should look given the demands of our current moment in which the intersections between university classroom spaces and healthcare settings are especially—and uniquely—visible. We close by offering preliminary practical suggestions for care-oriented practitioners across the humanities and medicine.

Kriti

I saw my first patient with COVID-19 a month into my third year of medical school and a full 15 months after the start of the pandemic. My breath quickened in anticipation as I read the emergency physician's note: positive test two weeks prior, increased dyspnea, febrile, non-English-speaking male. I gingerly reached for my N95 mask, neatly tucked away in a crisp brown-paper bag, untouched and unused. My preceptor and I ventured down to the room and donned our pale-yellow gowns. With the help of an iPad interpreter distancing me from the patient, I collected all the necessary elements of his history, avoiding just one: code status.

I glanced expectantly at my preceptor, as she calmly, yet purposefully inquired: "In the event your heart stops beating, would you like us to push on your chest to keep you alive? And if you stop breathing, would you want us to put you on a breathing machine and do everything we can to save your life?" While she avoided the patient's gaze, waiting for the interpreter to relay what had been asked, my eyes met his as I anticipated his reply. I watched as a mixed sense of confusion and terror filled his face. Her voice quickened in response as she described the nature of her questions, attempting to reassure him that these were questions we ask all patients to assess their desires and needs. Each flicker of desperation that crossed his face was met with the same words my preceptor had likely spoken a hundred times over since last March. I watched as her form began to crumple in on itself, as the energy needed to insinuate he could die from this left her body.

I wrote the above vignette in August 2021, at the start of my third year of medical school and beginning of my clinical training. That day, I learned how to ask about code status. I also witnessed how two simple questions seemed to trigger a cocktail of pain, regret, exhaustion, desperation, and trauma for both my patient and my preceptor. And as I read it again, I feel the same tightness in my shoulders, the pulling sensation at the back of my jaw, the slight furrow in my brow.

These physical sensations are familiar to me, and similar to those that I have experienced many times over since starting my clinical rotations. I recall my first day on the trauma surgery service. Our team had admitted a 17-year-old Black patient with a collapsed lung secondary to a gunshot wound the night prior. As a temporary measure prior to surgery, a chest tube was placed to vacuum out the serosanguinous fluid from his lung. We visited him during rounds early in the morning around 6:30am, a typical time for surgery teaching teams to see their patients before starting their procedures for the day. He was alone in the room, tired and irritable after what was imaginably a painful and sleepless night with an early morning wake-up call from the surgery team. A resident on our team led the interview and suggested to the patient that the chest tube was not draining enough fluid and that we would need to pursue surgery that very same day. The patient objected, and in response, the surgery resident emphasized, "you could die if we don't operate." The patient called his dad on the phone to explain the situation, while the rest of our team discussed logistics around scheduling the procedure. The patient then pushed his phone toward us with a voice yelling on the other side. His father was exclaiming, "How can you tell a 17-year-old boy that he is going to die if you don't operate? Tell me—*are you trying to kill my son?*" I watched as the resident physician stumbled in response, attempting to explain what he said to the patient and why. It all came to a head in that moment: the ever-looming threat of state-sanctioned violence against Black bodies in the same city responsible for the high-profile deaths of George Floyd and Daunte Wright; the background of historical and community-based traumas associated with the healthcare system; and stringent COVID-19 visitor policies that limited the presence of loved ones at the bedside of their sick relatives. I wanted to speak, correct the path of this conversation and work toward restorative justice, yet felt acutely aware of my intersecting identities in this situation: a Brown, South Asian woman in the presence of an all-white surgery team and a third-year medical student in the company of resident physicians on my very first day on the service. I think about this day often—the harm I witnessed and my inability to speak up.

Beginning my clinical career in conditions that are eroding the waning resilience of our overworked, traumatized, and burned-out healthcare workforce has created significant cognitive dissonance. As I venture between specialties, instead of reflecting on which unique qualities of a field interest me most or what goals I hope to achieve in my future career, I find myself barely treading water in an ever-deepening pool of distressing thoughts: "How will we care for all the patients waiting in the emergency department tonight when there are no beds available? How can individual care make a difference if our systems and public health strategies consistently fail our patients? Did I make the right choice in pursuing medicine?" I get frustrated by these thoughts, knowing I am just three years into a certifiably long career in medicine. My ever-so-often daydreaming reaffirms a clear truth: if we do not actively work to transform our systems to address the trauma and stress exacerbated by this pandemic, we cannot possibly retain or sustain our future healthcare workforce.

As students and future physicians, we learn that bearing witness to suffering is unfortunately an inevitable consequence of caring for sick people. But bearing witness without intentionality or the space to process suffering or death, within a field dedicated to healing, is paradoxical. I recall a recent skills-based learning session for an emergency medicine rotation. Per the lab manual, we were told that we had the "rare opportunity" to work with "fresh cadavers" (recently dead bodies not yet fixed with formaldehyde) to practice critical life-saving procedures such as endotracheal intubation, chest tube placements, and intraosseous cannulations. When we reached the cadaver lab and changed into scrubs and PPE, we were told that, per course policy, we could only leave once throughout the lab to go to the bathroom. They emphasized that if we left the room a second time, it would count as an "absence" and we would not be able to enter the room to complete the lab. I was astounded by such a policy that required students to perform procedures on recently dead persons yet did not allow the space for students to leave the room if they need to take time to process. This was particularly shocking within the context of the pandemic's significant bereavement toll: each person who has died of COVID-19 has left nine loved ones in grief, with an even higher toll for marginalized communities (Verdery, 2020). When we started the session, neither instructor prefaced the session by mentioning the potential difficulties of working with a recently dead body or even describing who this person was in the context of their comorbidities/ultimate demise. The focus was solely on describing the equipment and learning how to conduct the procedures. Throughout the session, I observed each of my peers contend with our discomfort and then progressively dissociate out of self-preservation. I looked at our white, male instructors and the white female cadaver, on the table; was their inability to see the inherent trauma caused by this session a mere oversight? Was it a symptom of the dehumanization and compartmentalization embedded in medical school's hidden curriculum? Or was it an implicit disregard for the impact of a pandemic that has traumatized students, their families, and disproportionately impacted Black and brown people?

The continued assault of COVID-19 and its aftermath in the ever-present background of systemic racism, a worsening global climate crisis, and compounding economic recession will continue to drive rates of toxic stress among patients, providers, and trainees. But embedding an empathic understanding of toxic stress using trauma-informed frameworks can engender a long-overdue shift in how we provide care—an evolution from a deficit-, disease-based approach to a salutogenic one based in collective strength and valued relationships.

As I walk the halls of the hospital, a mere two years into what I hope to be a long career in medicine, I cannot help but wonder about the paradox we so willingly accept: we, as healthcare workers, are in this profession to help others, yet we are consistently subjected to conditions that directly undermine our health. To bear witness to patient suffering is an inescapable aspect of our profession, but to bear the burden with inadequate resources, desperate working conditions, and diminishing support for increasing counts of moral injury is simply untenable.

Pritha

It is January 2022 and I am meeting on Zoom with one of my PhD students of color who is currently preparing for her doctoral candidacy exams. "With everything going on," she says, a shorthand meant to refer to the COVID-19 pandemic and the litany of intersecting state-sanctioned racialized violences we have witnessed throughout the past three years, "it's hard to focus." I don't know how to respond. I myself am well into my third year of the six-year tenure clock in my first faculty job ever at a predominantly white institution, with two and a half of those years having coincided with the pandemic. I can't focus either, but I keep this to myself.

These conversations with my BIPOC students about "everything going on" make me think often about how the pandemic, in addition to anxieties about sickness and health, has also brought into sharp focus the deeply biopolitical, racialized operations of labor and the workplace. In the early days of the pandemic, rhetorics surrounding the "closing" of the economy in spring 2020 necessitated widespread public discussions weighing the value of human life against the value of the United States' political, economic, and educational institutions. It is no coincidence, Brittney Cooper points out, that the white conservative push to reopen the economy in May 2020 intensified after preliminary studies at the time had begun reporting that COVID-19 is disproportionately deadly for communities of color (qtd. in "Scholar Cites 'Politics of Death' Behind Choice to Reopen States"). Recalling Achille Mbembe, Cooper reads the rhetoric of reopening as a mode of necropolitics whereby the presumed value of the economy subsequently reinforces the expendability of particular lives (Mbembe, 2003)—in this case, poor, working-class, and racialized "essential workers." As an example: the US meatpacking industry's heavy reliance on largely non-white undocumented migrant workers and refugees has produced unique modes of precarity during the pandemic. In addition to being dangerous, high-pressure workplaces for non-English speaking migrants (Jabour, 2020), meatpacking plants have also been a hotspot for COVID-19 infection and transmission, a situation systematically exacerbated by employers' failures to provide public-health information in multiple languages, routine access to healthcare, and federal policies that pressure workers to continue working in unsafe conditions by denying pandemic unemployment benefits to those who are undocumented (Jabour, 2020).[6]

In the wake of overtly anti-Black and anti-Asian death and assaults,[7] the pandemic has also re/ignited historical racial traumas surrounding illness and contagion that have heightened the hypervisibility and alienation of particular bodies. Literary scholar Joey Kim, for example, recalls her perpetual feelings of embodied dispossession and unease at the start of the pandemic as an Asian American woman in the United States at a time when terms like "China virus," "Kung flu," and the "Wuhan virus" were circulating widely in mainstream media. From the moment the virus was thought to have originated from China, it became racialized in the global lexicon, an Orientalist phenomenon that indeed pre-dates the current moment and recalls both 19th-century Yellow Peril discourses that were used to justify European colonialism in China (Kim, 2020), and, eventually, 20th-century–era racist anxieties in the United States surrounding East Asia and East Asian immigrants.[8]

It is no wonder that BIPOC students and faculty have felt particularly traumatized by both the consistently looming threat of sickness and the heightened feeling of racial precarity in universities, spaces which have never been exempt from the very same state-sanctioned racialized violences, xenophobia, and white supremacy that proliferates "in the streets" (Kynard, 2015). Racism, as the CDC has reported, is itself a well-studied, documented *public health* issue (Office of Minority Health and Health Equity). Indeed, to live in a global pandemic is already to be hyper-aware of one's body and its vulnerability. As a brown-skinned South Asian woman living in a predominantly white college town, this feeling for me is intensified by the already complicated sense of un/belonging I feel in the United States. When I enter the university classroom to teach in-person in fall 2021 for the first time since before the pandemic, I notice how my students, mostly white, scrutinize my body and face as they struggle to place my ethnicity when I am wearing a mask. I can feel their surprise at my American accent on the first day. *But where is she really from?* I feel obligated to "come out" to students early on about my racial identity because the Cultural Rhetorics class I am teaching is about racism and coloniality. I want them to know of my affective investment in the material, of my ancestors' lived traumas under British colonialism.

But when I read my course evaluations following the fall 2021 semester, I see an especially upsetting comment from a white student who felt "silenced" in class. Out of fear of speaking over their classmates of color, this student writes that they did not feel "welcome to participate." Weaponizing the common perception of women of color in the academy as angry, difficult (Lin et al., 2006), the student accuses me of having "hate in [my] heart." It is probably lost on this student that their discomfort with being *decentered* is precisely proof of just how often they are *centered*. What is also striking, however, is that the student is willing to think critically about their whiteness in relation to the embodied experiences of their BIPOC classmates, but not of their whiteness in relation to their BIPOC *instructor*. This elision of my embodiment, furthered by the assumption that I have "hate in my heart," scripts me as devoid of any lived reality or racial trauma.

How can I emphasize "things done right" when nothing feels "right?" I desperately want to reveal these feelings to my students, but I don't feel I can. I often think back to my early training as an instructor during my teaching practicum when I was in graduate school. Early-career instructors are consistently told to minimize their embodiment and their affect at all times. "Try to stay calm and turn it into a teaching moment," I've been told when sharing about the racialized and gendered microaggressions I experienced from white students. "Use it to help them reason through the flaws in their thinking." I also think of the more recent example of my university's administrators' justifications for requiring all instructors to teach in-person during the pandemic. In August 2020, the Provost sent a campus-wide email urging instructional faculty to embrace in-person teaching fearlessly in spite of the threat of COVID-19, citing a quote from Nobel prize-winning physicist and chemist Marie Curie: "Nothing in life is to be *feared,* it is only to be understood" (B. Bichelmeyer, personal communication, August 31, 2020). Ironically, however, Curie herself died as a result of radiation-related anemia that resulted from her continual exposure to radiation throughout her decades of research (Grady, 1998). The Provost's praise of Curie's "fearlessness" celebrates her groundbreaking knowledge, yet renders her body invisible by disavowing the fatal dangers she faced in producing it.

Such processes of *disembodying* knowledge from its material and affective conditions are indeed central to dominant models of pedagogy, research, and labor in universities. As Linda Tuhiwai Smith (1999) argues, this is forwarded by ways that the Western, imperial academy valorizes researcher "objectivity" and "neutrality" (p. 56) and reinforces "the idea that research is a highly specialized skill" to be developed and supported at a distance from actual material communities and individuals (p. 125). Such an epistemology subsequently informs pedagogical approaches and paradigms that see affect, trauma, and embodied experience as inhibiting the transfer of knowledge rather than as a *generative* force towards trauma-informed pedagogy and intellectual knowledge-making.

As forces of racism, a global pandemic, institutional biopolitics, and ongoing difficulties in accessing resources for mental and emotional health in the university continue to enact a "slow violence" (Nixon, 2011, p. 2) upon multiply marginalized students, faculty, and staff, how might making *all* bodies and their affects intentionally visible in the institution allow us to see the classroom and its goals differently?

Toward Affective Solidarity and Trauma-Informed Pedagogy

We recognize that our focus on our experiences of the pandemic may suggest that the pandemic has been an exceptional moment of structural inequity, violence, and trauma. It is true that the pandemic, as Pritha notes, has brought into sharp focus the biopolitical operations of our economic, medical, and educational institutions, but the systems of oppression and exploitation that render racialized, gendered, disabled, and classed bodies vulnerable in the United States persisted long before COVID-19. At the same time, however, we hope our narratives demonstrate how the pandemic is more than a moment of crisis—it is also an assemblage that reveals "a series of dispersed but mutually implicated networks" (Puar, 2007, p. 128) that bring "into play within us and outside us populations, multiplicities, territories, becomings, affects, events" (Deleuze and Parnet, 2007, p. 51). In other words, it might be thought to function much like a looking glass through which we can see differently what has long been there: the racist collusion between healthcare and carceral institutions (Benjamin, 2016); the capitalist logics that govern even public, non-profit universities (Harney & Moten, 2013); the historical and contemporary targeting and scapegoating of BIPOC as symbols of sickness and contagion (Shah, 2001; Polk, 2020); and, as we both demonstrate, the trauma, exhaustion, and emotions that shape multiply-marginalized students, instructors, and practitioners' pedagogical and care-oriented experiences and practices.

Following Tanya Titchkosky's (2011) definition of embodiment as "an interpretive relation between self and the world" (p. 129), we argue that the trauma, emotions, and affects our narratives of pedagogy, the classroom, and institutionality underscore present possibilities for articulating a trauma-informed pedagogy that highlights how trauma can be used to form generative *relations* among instructors, students, and practitioners alike. While Margaret Price

(2011) rightly warns of the risks of treating trauma as a universally shared, rather than distinctly marginalizing experience (p. 51), we understand trauma as doing *both*, especially for those who suffer both from "acute" traumas triggered by specific events and actions as well as "slow" cultural and historical traumas that are shaped by racism, colonialism, heterosexism, ableism, etc. For this reason, we are intentional in suggesting that the trauma-informed pedagogical practices for which we advocate below are most specifically oriented toward multiply-marginalized instructors and students—and, in particular, women of color and BIPOC more broadly (including those who are disabled, queer, poor, and im/migrants). It is also worth mentioning that versions of the pedagogical practices for which we advocate are often already happening in the "backchannels" in various ways among students, faculty, and practitioners who share marginalized identities and experiences, such as the conversations that happen in faculty offices behind closed doors, stealthy text messages during departmental meetings, and other immediate and embodied survival strategies cultivated in the academy to work within and against white, masculinist institutional logics (Prasad, 2022). While many of these "backchannel pedagogies" must out of necessity remain hidden, how can we take *some* of the same impulses and translate them into structured classroom or clinical pedagogies?

Indeed, conveying or making knowledge as an educator or student who is multiply-marginalized has long been a uniquely embodied act, an observation that, though theorized at length by cultural studies and critical pedagogy studies scholars, has yet to be integrated as a central consideration in instructor-training curricula, course design, and assessment practices. Educators, as bell hooks notes, are trained in accordance with the philosophical context of Enlightenment and Western/European dualisms, which maintain an (artificial) binary between the body and the mind. This binary betrays the white, masculinist legacy of repression and denial that has historically shaped institutional spaces and forwards a view that "the public world of institutional learning [is] a site where the body [has] to be erased, go unnoticed" (hooks, 1994, 191). Sayantani DasGupta and Rita Charon (2004) illustrate how this logic is also pervasive in medical education, as students learn early in their medical training that "patients are predominantly defined by their bodies whereas physicians are defined by their scientific minds" (p. 352). More recently, scholars in disability studies, science and medical education, and critical pedagogy studies have followed up on this work, arguing, as Michalinos Zembylas (2016) does, that failing to understand how students'—and, we'd add, instructors'—embodied and emotional attachments "are strongly entangled with epistemological, cultural and historical circumstances, and material conditions" (p. 545) can seriously undermine possibilities for "affective solidarity" between instructors and students (p. 547).

Below, we offer three preliminary recommendations for multiply-marginalized instructors seeking to create possibilities both for "affective solidarity" with their multiply-marginalized students that both validate the immediacy and materiality of traumas marginalized students and faculty alike bring to the classroom as well as make space for future structural change. These recommendations are not exhaustive, but rather present a starting point for trauma-informed pedagogies in the wake of the national and global crises that continue to expose the long-standing cracks in our institutions.

Recommendation 1

Be explicit about embodiment, affect, and emotion in the classroom in addition to the structural and institutional forces that shape knowledge-making.

Discussions of the body and its vulnerability—whether it is racialized, gendered, disabled, or classed—should be validated as a deliberate frame through which to interrogate knowledge in the classroom. As Price notes, for example, even as our theories often "welcome emotion in the classroom," in practice "we still treat emotionality and intellectuality as adversaries" (p. 50). Charon similarly notes the paucity of attention given to the role of emotion in medical education, as the ability of clinicians to regulate emotions is often scripted as an important feature of professionalism—a fact that sends mixed messages to students about what to feel and how to express it (p. 38). In the university, Price understands this implied binary of emotion vs. professionalism as due largely to institutional cultures that establish strict distinctions between teachers and therapists, as instructors are often reminded not to try to "counsel" students, but instead refer them to more "appropriate" authorities on campus (Price, 2011, p. 50). Charon shows us in her study of emotions in medical education, however, that even "appropriate" authorities are urged to practice "emotional distance and detachment" as a matter of "professionalism" (p. 39). Price therefore raises some key questions: Why are we led to feel that it would be dangerous to explore the links between teaching and therapy—or, more broadly, emotion and professionalism? What ideologies are supported "by maintaining that divide so fiercely" (Price, p. 51)? And finally, we'd also add: What fuels the perception that the embodied knowledges, traumas, and affects students, instructors, and practitioner bring to the classroom or clinic cannot—or should not—be directly engaged as a basis for meaning-making and education?

The moments of embodied discomfort we both highlight in our narratives are directly perpetuated by institutional and dominant pedagogical imperatives to maintain a clear separation between intellectuality and trauma during historical moments of crisis and despair. Think, for example, of Kriti's reflection on the trauma invoked by working with a "fresh cadaver" in her anatomy class and her instructor's disavowal of students' embodied, lived realities during the pandemic. Or Pritha's discomfort with revealing to her students her personal and embodied investment in the course material as well as her struggle to contain her affective responses to students' microaggressions. At times like these, when the body seems to "get in the way" of knowledge-making, what would it look like to *let* it?

Even though we acknowledge that specific curricular and pedagogical recommendations for sustainably integrating questions of embodiment, affect, and emotion into the classroom might look different across subject areas and disciplines, we encourage instructors across humanities, medicine, and the social sciences to make room for structured, modeled vulnerability in the classroom among students and instructors alike and the mobilization of *lived experience* as a criterion of meaning (Hill Collins, 1990). Enacting these initiatives might mean: 1) making space and providing suitable frameworks for students and instructors to collectively link course material to subjective, lived experiences and memories; 2) encouraging students to reflect on subjective, lived experiences and memories of ongoing violences and crises like those that have persisted throughout the pandemic; and 3) actively presenting opportunities to reflect on the *specific* ways that learning, writing, teaching, and providing care are—first and foremost—acts that occur through, with, or in service of the body.

Recommendation 2

Allow for dwelling in discomfort rather than perpetually seeking resolution.

In the relatively small body of scholarship on trauma-informed teaching, it is common to see calls to create "safe spaces" for students in the classroom, especially during times of crisis (Glover & Jones, 2021). It has also become common for scholars to call instead for "brave" spaces (Wood, 2021). As Jill W. Wood writes, safe spaces are often extensions of privilege, while "brave spaces'" can bolster students' "resiliency around their vulnerabilities from trauma" (p. 34). We agree that no instructor, curriculum, or administration can ensure the safety of any space, especially when the means of enforcing safe spaces in any institution necessarily requires invoking policing and carceral institutions that, paradoxically, often pose the greatest threats to BIPOC's safety in the first place (Chávez, 2017). But we also oppose the notion of "brave" spaces for their implied emphasis on futurity, resilience, and resolution. As Gada Mahrouse (2021) importantly notes, disabled people and racial minorities—especially migrants and refugees—are often framed by discourses in the Global North as inherently displaying perseverance and bravery, a narrative that perpetuates ableist, xenophobic, and neoliberal/capitalist logics by suggesting that disability, nationality, and race are tragic conditions or flaws to be "overcome" (p. 174). This emphasis on resolution enacts a compulsory futurity that leaves little room for "nonlinear temporalities" or states like anger or trauma that unsettle futurity by being "unable or unwilling" to move on (Prasad, 2022). Making room for disruptive affects in the present is critical for revaluing the lived realities of BIPOC students and instructors who are too often told to forget, "forgive," or discipline their emotions (Prasad, 2022). As DasGupta adds

(2008), dwelling in discomfort is also key in clinical settings. In order to cultivate "narrative humility," clinicians and medical students must "acknowledge that our patients' stories are not objects we can comprehend or master, but rather dynamic entities we can approach and engage with, while simultaneously remaining open to their ambiguity and contradiction" (p. 981).

We'd like to clarify that by advocating for dwelling in discomfort, we do not mean that instructors, students, and practitioners should passively enable harm in pedagogical spaces. To the contrary, we suggest an approach that actively acknowledges harms when they occur. As our own narratives in this chapter illustrate, instructors, students, or practitioners witness or experience harm in classroom or clinical settings and are led to feel time and time again—according to institutional norms or sheer propriety—as though these situations should be quickly resolved or even disavowed. This often occurs through a shift to abstraction or distance (i.e., "let's be positive," "let's focus on the bigger picture," "turn it into a teaching moment") or through appeals to rationality (i.e., "let's calm down," "let's take a step back," "let's think logically"). We suggest that instructors might begin to resist these Western, Eurocentric logics by *actively integrating* curricular elements that encourage students to reflect upon harms, traumas, tensions, or emotions they've witnessed or experienced in the classroom or clinic, making it a point to put systems in place for students to do so without fear of retaliation from instructors. These curricular elements might look like: 1) regular journaling or freewriting assignments about trauma in the classroom or clinic that are never graded or read by instructors or other students; 2) structured class discussions about the ways that dominant educational and medical institutions are, for many, spaces of past and ongoing trauma; 3) establishing frameworks that emphasize the importance of simply processing as an end goal rather than resolution; 4) providing training for instructors to intervene during situations of harm or discomfort in ways that do not enact distancing moves, appeals to rationality, or compulsory resolution; and 5) recognizing and interrogating the ways that discomfort and tension can be deeply generative for situated, nuanced knowledge-making and care-giving across contexts and disciplines.

Recommendation 3

Enable students to take ownership of classroom/curricula by actively collaborating with them to design courses, pedagogical practices, and standards of "care" in the institution.

There exists a broad range of work in the interdisciplinary field of critical pedagogy studies and medical education on the importance of integrating students' perspectives and feedback into course design, grading, and assessment. For example, rhetoric and writing studies scholar Asao Inoue (2015), in his work on anti-racist assessment practices, argues for contract grading practices that make visible the mutual labor of both students and instructors as well as instructor–student collaboration in the composing of evaluation rubrics (p. 132). These mutual, collaborative practices urge structural and institutional critiques by enabling students to understand how to read and recognize the politics of grading and assessment and their impacts. Educational coproduction frameworks acknowledge that education is a service that marries the expertise of both students and instructors in the context of their community and society writ large (Gregoire et al., 2021). Proponents of humanities-based approaches to medicine and narrative medicine importantly expand beyond coproduction frameworks, stressing how interdisciplinary collaboration across providers, students, medical education programs, and patients establish modes of care that mobilize "reciprocal influence." Simply put, instructors, clinicians, and medical students "need to be *open* to the possibility that the care encounter with patients (and colleagues) will be mutually transformative" (Weiss & Swede, 2016, p. 224). In both disciplinary contexts, encouraging collaborative pedagogies and reciprocally designed classroom and clinical curricula can help critically demystify the systemic operations of the educational, intellectual, medical, and political institutions that are often responsible for inflicting acute and "slow" traumas on students, instructors, and practitioners.

While our recommendation to enable students to take ownership of the classroom by collaborating with instructors on curricula and pedagogy may not at first seem related to the notion of responding to *trauma*, our narratives each highlight the ways that lack of transparency and mutual, collaborative dialogue in pedagogical/clinical settings have directly created conditions that have perpetuated harm. Think, for example, of Kriti's reflection on her anatomy course's policy that counts students as "absent" if they leave the classroom to process their emotions when working with a dead body, or the instructors' failure to describe to students who the deceased person was in the context of their comorbidities/death. In this instance, students' traumas were furthered by the intellectual distancing of "objects" of learning—in this case, a dead person's body—as well as a lack of contextualization or mutual dialogue among students and instructors course policies that count students as "absent" if they leave to process their emotions. One might also recall Pritha's reflection on her students' inability to consider their whiteness in relation to her as their BIPOC instructor, even when they are able to consider their whiteness in relation to their BIPOC classmates. Pritha, here, is seen as operating external to the classroom, fundamentally distanced from the bodies of "real" students impacted by "real" racisms. The radically different pedagogical settings and experiences highlighted in our narratives suggest that encouraging a culture of collaboration among students and instructors in course design, curriculum, and pedagogy can allow students and instructors to see how they are *both* implicated in pedagogy. In particular, such a culture can intentionally make visible the embodied needs and experiences of students and instructors alike as they are shaped or limited by dominant institutions and practices of knowledge-making. These initiatives can in turn make space for students and instructors to build collaborative communities through shared experiences and intellectual/professional goals.

Again, while specific recommendations for realizing these goals in the classroom necessarily vary across disciplines, we encourage the following concrete practices: 1) instructors and students should openly and systematically reflect upon their labor—intellectual, pedagogical, emotional, and embodied—in engaging with or teaching course material; 2) instructors should regularly discuss pedagogical and curricular choices openly with students, remaining mutually flexible and modifying course objectives and policies when necessary in order to best serve the diverse range of students in each course; and 3) students and instructors should actively and routinely collaborate on broad-scale program development and scholarship/research (as we both have in this chapter, based on our respective and distinct positionalities as student and instructor).

The COVID-19 pandemic, historical and current structural violences on multiply-marginalized people, and the widespread failure of institutional rhetorics of "care" suggest that pedagogical practices across the humanities, social sciences, and medicine, are uniquely embodied and inextricably tied to our greater sociopolitical contexts. We believe strongly that trauma-informed pedagogical frameworks may not—and should not—take the form of a simplified checklist or quantifiable learning outcomes. But we hope that this chapter will at least provide a starting point for multiply-marginalized instructors, students, and practitioners to employ affective solidarity to work toward responsive and flexible trauma-informed practices. As both an explanation and intervention, we *ourselves* model—through our "theory in the flesh," interdisciplinary, cross-rank inquiry, and our own affective solidarity with one another as women of color with shared lived experiences—future possibilities of trauma-informed pedagogy and research for molding both collective understanding and structural change.

Notes

1 Author note: we have no conflict of interest to disclose.
2 Medical students report alarming rates of depression (27%) and suicidal ideation (11%) that are significantly higher than the general population (Rotenstein et al., 2016).
3 It is important to point out that the phrase "I can't breathe," as uttered by Floyd in his last moments, also strikingly recalls the 2014 murder of Eric Garner by white police officer Daniel Pantaleo in which Garner cried the same exact words just moments before his death (Vinograd, 2021).
4 Our usage of the term "slow trauma" builds from Rob Nixon's definition of "slow violence," which he defines as violence "that occurs gradually and out of sight, a violence of delayed destruction that is dispersed across time and space" (Nixon, 2011, p. 2).

5 See the foundational women-of-color feminist text *This Bridge Called My Back* (Moraga & Anzaldua, 1983) for an overview and demonstration of "theory in the flesh" by editors Gloria Anzaldua and Cherrie Moraga, as well as many other women-of-color feminists, Third World feminists, and Black feminist thinkers.
6 Most recently, in 2022, one might also consider the ableist and racist rhetoric surrounding Omicron, a presumed milder COVID-19 strain that, as of the moment I am writing, accounts for the majority of COVID-19 infections in the United States. On January 7, 2022, CDC director Dr. Rochelle Walensky noted the "encouraging" news that 75% of recent COVID-19 deaths have occurred in those with four or more comorbidities—people "who were unwell to begin with" (qtd. in Dickinson). This narrative perpetuates the ableist and necropolitical notion that disabled people are expendable because they are "unwell," or, in Mbembe's words, in a state of "living dead" (2003, p. 40). What's more, Walensky's statement exhibits a profound ignorance of the ways that histories of colonialism and enslavement have contributed to many of the very same comorbidities in poor Black and immigrant communities that are linked to the risk of serious illness or death as a result of COVID-19 (Khazanchi et al., 2020).
7 On March 16, 2021, white man Robert Aaron Long killed eight people at three massage parlors in Atlanta: Delaina Ashley Haun, Paul Andre Michels, Xiaojie Tan, Daoyou Feng, Hyun Jung Grant, Suncha Kim, Soon Chung Park, and Yong Ae Yu. Six of the eight people murdered were Asian women. Long told police after he committed the murders that he had a "sexual addiction" and needed to eliminate his "temptation" (Hagen, 2021). However, given the historical timing, it is impossible not to read this act of violence as also inextricably linked to the increased anti-Asian rhetorics that have surrounded COVID-19.
8 See Nayan Shah's *Contagious Divides* (2001) for an expanded discussion of these histories in relation to the 20th-century tuberculosis epidemic in San Francisco that directly perpetuated white anxieties surrounding East Asian—and specifically, Chinese—immigrants.

References

Ahmed, S. (2004). *The Cultural Politics of Emotion*. Routledge.
Benjamin, R. (2016). "Catching Our Breath: Critical Race STS and the Carceral Imagination." *Engage Science, Technology, and Society*, 2, pp. 145–156.
Charon, R. (2017). *The Principles and Practice of Narrative Medicine*. Oxford University Press.
Chávez, K. R. (2017). "From Sanctuary to a Queer Politics of Fugitivity." *QED: A Journal in GLBTQ Worldmaking*, 4(2), pp. 63–70. https://doi.org/10.14321/qed.4.2.0063.
Cobos, C., et al. (2018). "Interfacing Cultural Rhetorics: A History and a Call." *Rhetoric Review*, 37(2), pp. 139–154. https://doi.org/10.1080/07350198.2018.1424470.
"COVID-19's Emotional Impact: Medical Students Cope with Isolation." *AAMC*. https://www.aamc.org/news-insights/covid-19-s-emotional-impact-medical-students-cope-isolation. Accessed 22 January 2022.
Cvetkovich, A. (2003). *An Archive of Feelings: Trauma, Sexuality, and Lesbian Public Cultures*. Duke UP.
DasGupta, S. (2008). "Narrative Humility." *The Lancet*, 371(9617), pp. 980–981. https://doi.org/10.1016/S0140-6736(08)60440-7.

DasGupta, S. and Charon, R. (2004). "Personal Illness Narratives: Using Reflective Writing to Teach Empathy." *Academic Medicine: Journal of the Association of American Medical Colleges*, 79(4), pp. 351–356. https://doi.org/10.1097/00001888-200404000-00013.

Deleuze, G. and Parnet, C.C. (2007). *Dialogues II*. Columbia University Press.

Dickinson, T. (2022). "CDC Director Slammed for Comments Devaluing Disabled Americans." *Rolling Stone*. https://www.rollingstone.com/politics/politics-news/cdc-disability-rochelle-walensky-encouraging-death-1282179/.

Eyerman, R. (2004). "Cultural Trauma: Slavery and the Formation of African American Identity." In *Cultural Trauma and Collective Identity*, book co-authored by Jeffrey C. Alexander, Bernard Giesen, Neil J. Smelser, and Piotr Sztompka. University of California, pp. 60–111.

Giroux, H. (2018). *Pedagogy and the Politics of Hope: Theory, Culture, and Schooling: A Critical Reader*. Routledge.

Glover, L. and Jones, J. (2021). "COVID-19 Pandemic and Trauma-Informed Teaching with African American College Students: A Narrative Experience of Students at an HBCU in the Southeast." In J. Carello and P. Thompson (Eds.), *Lessons from the Pandemic: Trauma-Informed Approaches to College, Crisis, Change* (pp. 73–81). Springer International.

Grady, D. (1998). "A Glow in the Dark, and a Lesson in Scientific Peril." *The New York Times*. https://www.nytimes.com/1998/10/06/science/a-glow-in-the-dark-and-a-lesson-in-scientific-peril.html.

Gregoire, B., Trager, L. and Blum, J. (2021). "Coproduction in Medical Education during the COVID-19 Pandemic: Critical Components of Successful Curricular Reform." *International Journal of Quality in Health Care*, 33(Supplement 2), pp. ii65–70. https://doi.org/10.1093/intqhc/mzab126.

Hagan, L. (2021). "'Sex Addiction' Cited as Spurring Spa Shooting, but Most Killed Were of Asian Descent." *NPR.Org*. https://www.npr.org/2021/03/17/978288270/shooter-claimed-sex-addiction-as-his-reason-but-most-victims-were-of-asian-desce. Accessed 18 May 2021.

Harney, S. and Moten, F. (2013). *The Undercommons: Fugitive Planning & Black Study*. Minor Compositions.

Hill Collins, P. (1990). *Black Feminist Thought: Knowledge, Consciousness, and the Politics of Empowerment*. Hyman.

hooks, b. (1994). *Teaching to Transgress: Education as the Practice of Freedom*. Routledge.

Inguanta, G. and Sciolla, C. (2021). "Time Doesn't Heal All Wounds: A Call to End Mandated Reporting Laws." *Columbia Social Work Review*, 19(1), pp. 116–137. https://doi.org/10.52214/cswr.v19i1.7403.

Inoue, A.B. (2015). *Antiracist Writing Assessment Ecologies: Teaching and Assessing Writing for a Socially Just Future*. Parlor Press LLC.

"Israeli-Palestinian Tensions Erupt into Open Conflict." *Vox*, 17 May 2021. https://www.vox.com/22440330/israel-palestine-gaza-airstrikes-hamas-updates-2021.

Jabour, A. (2020). "Immigrant Workers Have Borne the Brunt of Covid-19 Outbreaks at Meatpacking Plants." *Washington Post*. https://www.washingtonpost.com/outlook/2020/05/22/immigrant-workers-have-born-brunt-covid-19-outbreaks-meatpacking-plants/. Accessed 13 March 2022.

Khazanchi, R., Evans, C.T. and Marcelin, J.R. (2020)."Racism, Not Race, Drives Inequity Across the COVID-19 Continuum." *JAMA Network Open*, 3(9), p. e2019933. https://doi.org/10.1001/jamanetworkopen.2020.19933.

Kim, J. (2020). "Orientalism in the Age of COVID-19." *Los Angeles Review of Books*. https://lareviewofbooks.org/short-takes/orientalism-age-covid-19/.

Kynard, C. (2015). "Teaching While Black: Witnessing and Countering Disciplinary Whiteness, Racial Violence, and University Race-Management." *Literacy in Composition Studies*, 3(1), pp. 1–20.

Lau, T.C.W. (2021). "Access from Afar: Cultivating Inclusive, Flexible Classrooms after COVID-19." *Nineteenth-Century Gender Studies*, 17(1).

Lin, A., et al. (2006). "Theorizing Experiences of Asian Women Faculty in Second and Foreign-Language Teacher Education." In G. Li and G. H. Beckett (Eds.), *"Strangers" of the Academy: Asian Women Scholars in Higher Education* (pp. 56–84). Stylus Publishing, LLC.

Lopez, L.III, Hart, L.H. and Katz, M.H. (2021). "Racial and Ethnic Health Disparities Related to COVID-19." *JAMA*, 325(8), pp. 719–720. https://doi.org/10.1001/jama.2020.26443.

Mahrouse, G. (2021). "Producing the Figure of the 'Super-Refugee' Through Discourses of Success, Exceptionalism, Ableism, and Inspiration." In T. Phu and V. Nguyen (Eds.), *Refugee States: Critical Refugee Studies in Canada* (pp. 173–193). University of Toronto Press.

Mbembé, A. (2003). "Necropolitics." *Public Culture*, 15(1), pp. 11–40.

McCann, L.I. and Pearlman, L.A. (1990). *Psychological Trauma and the Adult Survivor: Theory, Therapy, and Transformation*. Brunner-Routledge.

Moraga, C. and Anzaldua, G. (1983). *This Bridge Called My Back: Writings by Radical Women of Color*. Kitchen Table, Women of Color Press.

Nagoski, E. and Nagoski, A. (2019). *Burnout: The Secret to Unlocking the Stress Cycle*. Random House Publishing Group.

Neuman, S. (2020). "Medical Examiner's Autopsy Reveals George Floyd Had Positive Test for Coronavirus." *NPR.Org*. https://www.npr.org/sections/live-updates-protests-for-racial-justice/2020/06/04/869278494/medical-examiners-autopsy-reveals-george-floyd-had-positive-test-for-coronavirus.

Nixon, R. (2011). *Slow Violence and the Environmentalism of the Poor*. Harvard University Press.

Office of Minority Health and Health Equity (OMHHE). (2021). "Racism and Health." *Centers for Disease Control and Prevention*. https://www.cdc.gov/healthequity/racism-disparities/director-commentary.html.

Polk, K.O. (2020). *Contagions of Empire: Scientific Racism, Sexuality, and Black Military Workers Abroad, 1898–1948*. UNC Press Books.

Prasad, K., et al. (2021). "Prevalence and Correlates of Stress and Burnout among U.S. Healthcare Workers during the COVID-19 Pandemic: A National Cross-Sectional Survey Study." *eClinicalMedicine*, 35, p. 100879. https://doi.org/10.1016/j.eclinm.2021.100879.

Prasad, P. (2022). "Backchannel Pedagogies: Unsettling Racial Teaching Moments and White Futurity." *Present Tense: A Journal of Rhetoric in Society*, 9(2). https://www.presenttensejournal.org/volume-9/backchannel-pedagogies-unsettling-racial-teaching-moments-and-white-futurity/.

Price, M. (2011). *Mad at School: Rhetorics of Mental Disability and Academic Life*. University of Michigan Press.

Puar, J.K. (2007). *Terrorist Assemblages: Homonationalism in Queer Times*. Duke University Press.

Rotenstein, L.S., et al. (2016). "Prevalence of Depression, Depressive Symptoms, and Suicidal Ideation Among Medical Students: A Systematic Review and Meta-analysis." *JAMA*, 316(21), pp. 2214–2236. https://doi.org/10.1001/jama.2016.17324.

"Scholar Cites 'Politics of Death' Behind Choice to Reopen States." *MSNBC*, 2 May 2020. https://www.msnbc.com/am-joy/watch/coronavirus-outcomes-worse-for-people-of-color-as-states-reopen-82945093590.

Schwab, G. (2010). *Haunting Legacies: Violent Histories and Transgenerational Trauma*. Columbia UP.

Shah, N. (2001). *Contagious Divides: Epidemics and Race in San Francisco's Chinatown*. University of California Press.

Smith, L.T. (1999). *Decolonizing Methodologies: Research and Indigenous Peoples*. Zed Books.

Titchkosky, T. (2011). *The Question of Access: Disability, Space, Meaning*. University of Toronto Press.

Verdery, A.M., et al. (2020). "Tracking the Reach of COVID-19 Kin Loss with a Bereavement Multiplier Applied to the United States." *Proceedings of the National Academy of Sciences of the United States of America*, 117(30), pp. 17695–17701. https://doi.org/10.1073/pnas.2007476117.

Vinograd, C. (2014). "'I Can't Breathe': Garner Decision Protests Hit Fifth Day." *NBC News*. https://www.nbcnews.com/news/us-news/i-cant-breathe-garner-decision-protests-hit-fifth-day-n263476. Accessed 17 February 2021.

Weiss, T. and Swede, M.J. (2016). "Transforming Preprofessional Health Education Through Relationship-Centered Care and Narrative Medicine." *Teaching and Learning in Medicine*. https://www.tandfonline.com/doi/full/10.1080/10401334.2016.1159566.

Wood, J.M. (2021). "Teaching Students at the Margins: A Feminist Trauma-Informed Care Pedagogy." In J. Carello and P. Thompson (Eds.), *Lessons from the Pandemic: Trauma-Informed Approaches to College, Crisis, Change* (pp. 23–39). Springer International.

Zembylas, M. (2016). "Making Sense of the Complex Entanglement Between Emotion and Pedagogy: Contributions of the Affective Turn." *Cultural Studies of Science Education*, 11(3), pp. 539–550.

7
TRAUMA-INFORMED MINDFULNESS MEDITATION IN THE COLLEGE CLASSROOM

Ernest Stromberg

The origins of this chapter go back more than a decade. After many years teaching in a variety of institutions of higher education, I noticed that an increasing number of my students were suffering from a variety of mental health challenges, ranging from chronic anxiety and depression to full-blown schizophrenia. My awareness was, in part, informed by the increasing number of students who self-disclosed their condition—as an aside, this increase in the number of students willing to self-disclose their mental health challenges is something that we might take as positive evidence of the gradual and ongoing de-stigmatization of mental health disorders. Nevertheless, the impression grew that more of my students than in the past were suffering. Ensuing hallway conversations with colleagues indicated that I was not alone with these observations. Indeed, a glance at the research nationally reveals an alarming increase in the demands for mental health services on college campuses. More recently, the American Psychological Association notes that "In 2019, nearly 90% of [university and college] counseling center directors reported an increase in students seeking services" (Abrams, 2020).

Given the increasing anecdotal, observational, and research-based evidence that more students enrolled in our classes were suffering from some form of a health disorder, the question arose of what role, if any, as their professor, did I have in supporting their wellness. That is, beyond effectively teaching the content of my classes, in what ways might I create a learning environment that not only did no harm but might actually serve in promoting the students' wellness and pathways toward healing? These questions continued to churn and spurred me to engage in additional conversations with colleagues from across our campus. One conversation evolved into a discussion with a colleague from the sciences. We shared how our own experiences and practices of formal

DOI: 10.4324/9781003260776-8

meditation had supported us through challenging circumstances and assisted us in maintaining a degree of emotional equilibrium. This conversation raised the question about the potential benefits of meditation for our students.

The research in the field of psychology from approximately the past 20 years is quite compelling in support of the mental health benefits to be derived from mindfulness meditation. Studies on mindfulness-based cognitive therapy (MBCT) have found it to be effective in preventing relapses of acute depression in those who have suffered three or more depressive episodes in their life and that "MBCT is at least comparable to other forms of first-line maintenance treatments" (Shamblaw & Segal, 2022). Furthermore, recent research suggests that mindfulness-based stress reduction (MBSR) may be particularly efficacious in treating the symptoms of PSTD (Goldsmith, Gerhart, & Chesney, 2014). In their study, Goldsmith, Gerhart, and Chesney (2014) found that their "data, combined with previous studies of mindfulness-based interventions for participants exposed to trauma, suggest that individuals with posttraumatic stress can benefit from mindfulness-based stress reduction."

Informed by this research, the colleague and I co-authored an intra-institutional grant in 2017 to provide mindfulness-based stress reduction training to faculty from across the campus. In our grant, we noted that research, such as the studies cited above, demonstrates that practicing mindfulness meditation results in better mental health outcomes for practitioners. We argued that mental health disorders, especially those associated with PTSD such as anxiety and depression, reduce student resilience, impair academic achievement, and contribute to student attrition. We requested funding for the trainings on the hypothesis that improved mental health outcomes among students would contribute to their academic success and improve campus graduation rates.

In the ensuing four years since implementation, and as a condition of the grant, I begin each class that I teach with five to ten minutes of guided meditation. I keep the sessions brief for several reasons. One is that all of my courses, obviously, have content and specific learning outcomes to address. Thus, in service both to the stated curriculum and the students' expectations, I believe that ten minutes is the maximum amount of time in an hour-and-twenty-minute class period appropriate to dedicate to meditation. My second rationale for the time limit is that the meditation practice in my class is ultimately an introduction, an opportunity for students to dip a toe in the water of meditation and to get at least a hint of what the experience of meditation feels like and to observe any potential benefits. And finally, in light of the slight but real risk that some students may experience adverse effects from meditation, the shorter time period has been associated with a reduced risk of adverse responses. In addition to keeping the sessions brief, I do not require students to participate in the meditation practice (I will say more, shortly, about the optional aspect and the time limitation as elements of a trauma-informed approach). I inform students that meditating is not required and their meditating or not mediating will have no influence on their grade. For the students who choose not to meditate, I ask that they simply sit quietly so as not to distract the students who do choose to meditate—of course simply sitting quietly for five minutes is an aspect of meditation and may allow students to accrue some of the same benefits as the students who do meditate.

In order to assess students' experiences and responses to the meditation practices I administered an anonymous online survey. Because students—especially at my institution, where many students are first-generation students and employed—are busy and feeling stressed for time toward the end of the semester, I kept the survey relatively brief. Beyond asking what year they were in attending California State University, Monterey Bay (CSUMB), I did not ask for any identifying information. In future iterations of the survey, information on gender, race/ethnicity, and age may be included to further understand the benefits and limitations of the meditation practice along demographic lines. I asked students the following questions: Prior to taking this class, did you have any meditation experience? Independent of this class, do you have a regular meditation practice? When given the opportunity and guidance to practice mindfulness meditation at the start of each class session, do you participate in the meditation? If you responded "No" to the previous question, please briefly share the reasons for why you choose not to practice the meditation offered as part of the class. If you responded "No" to the question on participating in the daily meditations, is there anything the class instructor might have done differently that would have resulted in your participating in the meditation practice each class? If you responded "Yes" to the question on participating in the daily meditations, please briefly explain why you have chosen to meditate. If you are participating in our mediations, have you also started practicing meditation outside of our class meetings? If you responded "Yes" to the question on participating in our meditations, how beneficial would you say the meditation has been in terms of helping you to manage any stress or anxiety you experience? If you responded "Yes" to the question on participating in our meditations, to what extent would you say the meditation has been helpful in terms of your academic success (completing assignments, studying, performance on exams, participating in classes, etc.)? And I ended the survey with an open-ended opportunity for students to provide additional comments.

In the two sets of surveys compiled during the academic year 2021–2022, the majority of respondents were upper-division juniors or seniors (70% in fall 2021 and 80% in spring 2022). In both semesters, 60% to 70% indicated they had prior experiences with meditation. However, only around 10% of the student respondents indicated that they had a regular meditation practice independent of our class. In terms of their participation in our brief classroom meditations, in the fall of 2021, 53% indicated they consistently meditated; 39% indicated that they "sometimes" participated; and 8% indicated that they did not participate in the meditation. To the same question, the spring 2022 semester students provided the following responses: 72% indicated they did regularly participate in the meditations; 14% indicated they "sometimes" participated; and 14% indicated they did not participate.

Over the course of the academic year, approximately two-thirds of the students who responded indicated that they participated in the meditation and less than 15% indicated that they consistently did not meditate. Before discussing the affirmative responses, I want to examine some of the reasons provided for not meditating. A number of students indicated something to the effect of, "my mind wanders too much, so I have … decided meditation doesn't work for me." The students who provided this type of response reflect, at least in part, that, as the instructor, I did not adequately explain that the purpose of meditation is to notice your thoughts as thoughts, rather than stopping your thoughts. Unfortunately, there remains a popular though inaccurate notion that the purpose of mediation is to still your thoughts. There is also the possibility, and I will discuss this further under "trauma-informed approaches to meditation," that while meditating, some of the students were overwhelmed by the volume of thoughts they were noticing. The act of pausing to notice and experience their thoughts free from distraction may have been an unpleasant experience.

In addition to those students indicating that they did not meditate because they could not quiet their thoughts, others shared that they did not meditate because they found it "hard to get comfortable in a class environment" and "I prefer a more private space to meditate." These and similar observations make sense as it clearly remains unusual to sit and meditate in a college class not specifically focused on meditation. This is why it remains imperative to provide the time to mediate as an option and to minimize the pressure students may feel to participate.

Before discussing the feedback from the students who elected to participate in the meditation sessions either all or some of the time, I need to note that in introducing the practice I shared with the students highlights from recent research on the potential benefits to be derived from mindfulness meditation. I informed them that the integration of brief periods of meditation was in support of the grant we had received, provided them with some information on the work of Jon Kabat-Zinn and his mindfulness-based stress reduction program, and gave them overviews of some of the findings from the field of psychology on the mental health benefits associated with meditation. I let the students know that I and other colleagues on our campus were incorporating meditation into our classes as a means to support their mental and emotional well-being and, by extension, their academic success. I mention the evidence and arguments made to justify the inclusion of meditation in the class for two reasons. I wanted to model for them curricular decision-making based on research, evidence, and good reasoning. The efficacy of my persuasive efforts may indicate why so many of the students were willing to participate; they found the evidence and arguments in support of meditation compelling. In terms of the students' self-reporting of the benefits they experienced from meditating, there may be a degree of the "placebo effect" operating. In other words, my students were informed that the meditation would benefit their mental well-being and with that expectation in mind, they experienced the meditation as beneficial. Regardless, I take the students' self-reporting of the benefits they derived as additional support for me to continue offering the meditation.

In the qualitative responses, to the question of why they chose to participate in the meditation, many students offered responses along this vein: "it helps to release the stress." Students responded that it helped with anxiety, stress, focus, and their ability to relax. As one student asserted, "it's healthy for your mind and body." Many of the students stated that they found the meditation helped them to be focused and more attentive in class: "getting the five mins to meditate really helped me actually be there focused and listening." While some students may have experienced the placebo effect—"our professor made it sound like a cool experience and I felt like it would also improve my anxiety and stress"—overall, all the students who responded indicated that they found the meditation to be beneficial. Furthermore, of the students who indicated that they participated in the class time meditations, more that 50% indicated that they had started meditating on their own, outside of our class. Additionally, all of the respondents who indicated they participated in the meditation found the meditation to be "Somewhat" (55% in the fall and 69% in the spring) or "Very" (45% in the fall and 31% in the spring) beneficial in helping them "manage any stress or anxiety" they experienced. In terms of contributing to their academic success, of those who participated in the meditation, 24% in the fall and 35% in the spring found it "Very helpful"; 57% in the fall and 53% in the spring found it "Somewhat helpful"; and 17% in the fall and 12% in the spring were "Not sure" if it was helpful. In sum, the majority of the students in my classes elected to participate in the meditations and all of the students found it beneficial to their mental health and the majority believed it contributed to their academic success.

While the academic research and my own experiences support introducing students to mindfulness meditation, there are concerns to be addressed and precautionary measures to take in order to assure that meditation is introduced and integrated in a trauma-informed manner. As scholars and practitioners in both psychology and medicine know, therapeutic interventions—including pharmaceuticals, exercise, and therapy—while generally associated with positive health outcomes may also produce unintended adverse side effects for some individuals. Recent scholarship on the potential adverse effects of meditation has revealed that many people do experience some unwanted and unpleasant effect as a result of meditating (Goldberg et al., 2021; Crane, Miller, & Kuyken, 2019; Britton, 2019). According to Goldberg et al. (2021), "Anxiety, traumatic reexperiencing, and emotional sensitivity were the most common" meditation-related adverse effects. However, Goldberg et al. (2021) also found that respondents "reporting [meditation-related adverse effects] were equally glad to have practiced meditation as those not reporting" any adverse effects as a result of their meditation practice. The findings to this point suggest that while many individuals who practice meditation do experience some unpleasant or adverse effects, the majority find the benefits they experience as a result of meditation outweigh the negative effects. The research indicates that most adverse effects experienced as a response to meditation are relatively mild and not long-term. However, there are exceptions, with some people experiencing more extreme effects, such as an amplification of their anxiety and a restimulation of their traumatic experiences.

Given that meditation, analogously to other therapeutic interventions, may in some instances result in adverse experiences, it is vital for anyone planning to integrate meditation into their pedagogy to do so in a trauma-informed way in order to mitigate, to the extent possible, any negative outcomes. The research on the potential for adverse effects from medication has also yielded insights into ways to reduce, if not completely eliminate, the risks.

Trauma-Informed Mindfulness Meditation

As meditation and particularly mindfulness meditation has grown in popularity as a therapeutic treatment for a range of mental health issues, concerns have arisen regarding the potential for adverse effects. As noted above, researchers have found that some practitioners of mediation do experience negative outcomes in response to meditation. While most of the adverse effects reported are relatively mild and short-term, some people, especially those with a history of adverse childhood experiences (ACE) or those with PTSD, may experience more severe adverse effects (Goldberg et al., 2021).

To integrate mindfulness mediation into one's class in a trauma-informed, or what David A. Treleaven calls a trauma-sensitive manner, several elements and protocols need to be acknowledged and followed. The first and arguably the most important consideration is to acknowledge that the classroom is not, by definition, a therapeutic setting and as instructors we are not operating in the role of therapist. While aspects of our curriculum, whether it be in the humanities, social sciences, arts, or sciences, are transformative and even potentially healing for students, our classes are not offered as therapy and few of us have the requisite training to offer therapy. That noted, we nevertheless can in good conscience introduce students to mindfulness meditation as a resource in support of their overall wellness and by extension their academic success. Additionally, as noted above, most students are already familiar with the idea of mindfulness and many of them will have tried meditating at some point in their lives.

A trauma-informed approach requires that we fully disclose what we know about meditation and the reasons behind dedicating a small portion of class time to meditation. To this end, I share with students overviews of the research on the benefits of meditation to practitioners' mental and physical health. I provide them with information, including videos, on the work of Jon Kabat Zinn and his development of the mindfulness-based stress reduction program (MBSR). Additionally, as noted above, it must be clear to students that participating in the meditation is entirely optional. The evidence is compelling that even a few minutes of meditation are beneficial, and meditation is not a requirement of the class. Judith Herman (1997), referencing the *Comprehensive Textbook of Psychiatry*, notes, "the common denominator of psychological trauma is a feeling of … 'helplessness, [and] loss of control'" (p. 33). Given that college classes come with a set of rules and requirements, a trauma-informed integration of meditation emphasizes that students have a choice and control over whether they meditate or not. Additionally, the message needs to be clearly conveyed and reenforced that students may discontinue meditating at any time without a sense of shame or concern about repercussions.

A trauma-informed approach also requires transparency about the potential, however minimal, chance of adverse effects resulting from meditation. As Miguel Farias and Catherine Wikholm assert,

> Key considerations for clinicians contemplating referring patients to mindfulness interventions include past experiences of meditative techniques, providing information as to the range of effects that may occur, ensuring that the individual has support in place to help them to manage difficult experiences should they occur, and giving them a choice.
>
> *(2016)*

Drawing from Farias and Wikholm's advice for clinicians to the non-clinical classroom setting, a trauma-informed approach requires that we inform students of potential adverse responses, provide information on the available campus mental health resources, and emphasize that participating in the meditation is optional. In essence, the first requirement of a trauma-informed approach is to provide information, including the research supported potential benefits of meditation and the potential for adverse reactions.

In his groundbreaking book, *Trauma-Sensitive Mindfulness*, David A. Treleaven (2018) argues that a trauma-sensitive approach to meditation attends to what he calls the "four Rs": "*realizing* the pervasive impact of trauma, *recognizing* symptoms … *responding* … skillfully … [and] preventing *retraumatization*" (pp. 12–13). As college instructors rather than psychological therapists, I would slightly modify his list of Rs. It is crucial that if we are to integrate mindfulness meditation into our courses in a trauma-informed manner, we recognize the high likelihood that some members of our class have experienced trauma and may even currently suffer from PTSD. While it risks requiring too much of instructors not trained as therapists to recognize symptoms of PTSD—which may be subtle and which students may be looking to conceal—we can, however, in establishing the context for meditating in the class, speak openly about trauma and the reality that some members of the class have likely experienced trauma. While noting that research has affirmed that many trauma survivors participating in mediation as an aspect of their therapy have "exhibited significantly decreased levels of posttraumatic stress symptoms, depressive symptoms, and anxious attachment" (Kelly & Garland, 2015), for some trauma survivors the practice of meditation may allow unwanted memories, thoughts, and feelings to arise and risk retraumatizing them. Students should be encouraged to inventory their own history around trauma and, if they elect to meditate, to assess if the experience is unpleasant or distressing. Encouraging students to make informed decisions regarding their participation or non-participation in the meditation reduces the likelihood of adverse effects, especially retraumatization. Should a student inform us of any challenge, it is crucial that we respond skillfully, granting the student agency and providing them with information about the resources available to them.

Additionally, Treleaven (2018) suggests that within meditation practice, trauma survivors be taught and encouraged to "apply the brakes" as needed. Among his suggestion for applying the metaphorical breaks are the following: "Open one's eyes during meditation practice … Take a few slow, deep breaths … [and] [e]ngage in shorter practice periods" (p. 107). As instructors inviting students to briefly meditate in a classroom context, a trauma-informed approach would note that closing one's eyes is not required for meditation, that some practices explicitly advise meditation with eyes open and gaze lowered. Anyone not comfortable closing their eyes in a room full of relative strangers should be encouraged to keep their eyes open. Similarly, we can encourage students who notice increased levels of anxiety to consider consciously taking slower, deeper breaths as deeper breaths have been associated with activating the relaxation response. Additionally, keeping the meditation sessions short (five to ten minutes) is a way of slowly easing students into the experience before the need to "apply the brakes" even arises.

Many mindfulness meditation practices direct participants to focus on their breath as an anchor to the present moment. However, Treleaven argues that for some trauma survivors, the breath itself may be triggering or restimulating. A trauma-informed approach to mindfulness meditation would teach students multiple ways to anchor their attention to the present moment. While paying attention to the breath may be a safe and effective anchor for most people, inviting people to pay attention to specific parts of their body (or body scans) may be one way. For others, attending to external sounds may provide an effective anchor. In the introduction to mindfulness meditation I offer through our short sessions of each class, the emphasis is on returning attention to the present moments. While in a longer mindfulness training context or in a therapeutic context, instruction to notice particular thoughts may be applicable, in the context of my classes the emphasis is simply on working to be a bit more present.

In sum, a trauma-informed approach to integrating mindfulness meditation into the classroom requires that we be fully transparent about the purpose and potential adverse effects of meditation. We allow students control over their participation and minimize any pressure to participate in the mediation. We support students in the choice to discontinue meditating if they experience significant adverse effects. We introduce trauma-sensitive approaches, including having eyes open and the use of deep breathing to activate the parasympathetic nervous system. And we need to be sensitively responsive to students if they disclose adverse effects or disclose any of their own mental health challenges.

Conclusion

In this chapter, I have argued for the integration of mindfulness meditation as a means to support the emotional wellness of our students, particularly students suffering from the effects of traumatic experiences. The evidence is compelling and continues to grow that for most people, meditation provides psychological and physiological benefits. Within the context of an academic class, devoting a brief period to a practice that contributes to student wellness and reduces stress and anxiety, will ultimately contribute to student resilience and academic success. However, to fully realize the benefits of the integration of meditation into the curriculum, the meditation practice must be introduced and facilitated in a trauma-sensitive or trauma-informed manner. This means providing a clear rationale for the meditation, a disclosure of potential adverse reactions to meditation, and an emphasis on the optional nature of the meditation practice.

In closing, I want to share advice I was given by two faculty mentor figures. The first was the assertion that "teaching is a relational art." To cultivate a successful learning environment depends on cultivating healthy and productive relationships between students and instructors. Similarly, trauma expert Judith Herman asserts that recovery from trauma "can take place only within the context of relationships" (2015, p. 133). Thus, a trauma-informed pedagogy recognizes and prioritizes the development of safe, respectful, and trusting relationships between students and instructors. The second advice I received was that to teach well, in addition to knowing your subject matter, "students must know that you love them." We express this love by demonstrating that we are there to support their goals, we respect them as individuals, and we care about their well-being. A trauma-informed approach to teaching effectively conveys to all students that they are truly cared for and that as instructors we have their best interests at heart. I will end with observations made by my students:

> I now look at meditation as something to use in my arsenal of techniques when I need a break from the stressors of life. It has been nice to sit and

think about certain areas of my body that need attention when the day to day routines make it seem as if they don't. I cried a couple times which I think should be normal.

I truly believe it is such a great idea to incorporate the integration of mindfulness-based meditation practice within this class and so many more. I think it's a compassionate decision to do for the students and the instructor, especially after such a difficult time we've all gone through/are still going through … I truly observed a change within my attitude after meditating, especially when I was struggling. Thank you.

I really did enjoy the mindful meditation. It was brief but effective and I would love other courses to follow the structure.

I really enjoyed meditation before class, it shows us students that are [sic] mental health is valued by instructors and that although academics are important the well-being of students is more important than anything.

I think it's a great way to concentrate before starting our discussions, it's a chance for the class to take a collective breath, and I'm grateful for learning healthy breathing techniques and mediation that I will continue to practice after this class ends! Thank you, professor :)

References

Abrams, Z. (2020). A crunch at college counseling centers: These mental health centers were overloaded even before COVID-19. What happens now as students return to school as budgets are cut? *American Psychological Association: Education and Covid 19*, *51*(6). https://www.apa.org/monitor/2020/09/crunch-college-counseling

Baer, R., Crane, C., Miller, E., & Willem, K. (2019). Doing no harm in mindfulness-based programs: Conceptual issues and empirical findings. *Clinical Psychology Review*, *71*, 101–114. https://doi.org/10.1016/j.cpr.2019.01.001

Britton, W. B. (2019). Can mindfulness be too much of a good thing? The value of a middle way. *Current Opinion in Psychology*, *28*. https://www.sciencedirect.com/science/article/pii/S2352250X18301453

David, T. A. (2018). *Trauma sensitive mindfulness: Practices for safe and transformative healing.* W.W. Norton & Company.

Farias, M., & Wikholm, C. (2016). Has the science of mindfulness lost its mind? *BJPsych Bulletinl*, *40*(6), 329–332. https://doi.org/10.1192/pb.bp.116.053686

Goldberg, S. B., Lam, S. U., Britton, W. B., & Davidson, R. J. (2021). Prevalence of meditation related adverse effects in a population-based sample in the United States. *Psychotherapy Research*. https://doi-org.csumb.idm.oclc.org/10.1080/10503307.2021.1933646

Goldsmith, R. E., Gerhart, J. I., Chesney, S. A., Burns, J. W., Kleinman, B., & Hood, M. M. (2014). Mindfulness-based stress reduction for posttraumatic stress symptoms: Building acceptance and decreasing shame. *Journal of Evidence-Based Complementary & Alternative Medicine*, *19*(4), 227–234. https://doi-org.csumb.idm.oclc.org/10.1177/2156587214533703

Herman, J. (1997). *Trauma and recovery: The aftermath of violence—From domestic abuse to political terror.* Basic Books.

Kelly, A., & Garland, E. L. (2016). Trauma-informed mindfulness-base stress reduction for female survivors of interpersonal violence: Results from a stage I RCT. *Journal of Clinical Psychology, 72*(4), 311–328. https://doi-org.csumb.idm.oclc.org/10.1002/jclp.eee73

Shamblaw, A. L., & Segal, Z. (2022). Mindfulness meditation in the long-term improvement of mood disorders: Contributions by Canadian researchers. *Canadian Journal of Behavioural Science./Revue Canadienne des Sciences du Comportement, 54*(2), 142–151. https://doi-org.csumb.idm.oclc.org/10.1037/cbs0000286

8
EXAMINING AUTHORITY THROUGH TRAUMA

Reflections From Student to Teacher

Angela Moore

Much has been written on the topic of authority and the student–teacher relationship in higher education: from how to establish authority as an educator, to how to inspire students to question and challenge authority, to how to imagine authority functioning within the context of a democratic classroom (Freire, 1968; Giroux, 1986; Llewellyn & Llewellyn, 2015; Pace & Hemmings, 2007; Roberts-Miller, 2004; Shor, 1996). In addition to formal scholarship, I think it's fair to say there is also a lot of "lore" exchanged around the topic of authority, which, in my experience, has been predominantly centered on advice about how to establish and maintain authority in the classroom, and how to avoid (if possible) and manage (if not) the occurrence of any "authority issues." In this chapter, I argue that trauma-informed pedagogies should be included in our discussions of authority in higher education and aim to highlight the benefits that both students and teachers stand to gain from this inclusion.

Before going any further, I'd like to define "authority-related traumas" as any traumatic experiences that involve authority figures. Research reveals that it is unfortunately common for people to experience trauma at the hands of authority figures, such as parents, guardians, or elders. It has been reported that "nearly 14 percent of children have been repeatedly maltreated by a caregiver, including nearly 4 percent who were physically abused"—respectively roughly one in seven, and one in 25 children (Finkelhor et al., 2013). Research on the experiences of marginalized groups also points to a trend of trauma perpetuated by authority figures such as police officers, judges, politicians, and teachers (Lange & Young, 2019; Varghese et al., 2018), which means authority-related traumas are likely far more common than indicated by the numbers above, which represent only caregiver-related traumas. As such, a significant portion of our students and colleagues are likely to have experienced some

DOI: 10.4324/9781003260776-9

sort of authority-related trauma in their lives. Furthermore, this category of trauma, because it is related to authority, is specifically important to consider when we examine the concept of classroom authority and the student–teacher relationship.

In this chapter, I aim to begin a conversation about the impacts authority-related traumas may have on both students and teachers, as well as highlight pedagogical moves that may make classrooms more inclusive for those with histories of authority-related trauma. To do this, I read several of my own experiences as both a student and a teacher through a lens of trauma-informed pedagogy and critical pedagogy. It is relevant to disclose here that I have a history of authority-related trauma related to both my stepparents and to police officers, and as such, am offering my experiences as a starting point to this conversation. In doing so, I do not wish to assert that my thoughts or experiences are representative of anyone else with a history of authority-related trauma, as traumatic experiences, as well as responses to them, can be wildly diverse.

Undergraduate Student Experiences: Pieties, Unconditional Positive Regard, and Offerings

First, it is important to note that the authority-related traumas I experienced led me to associate the concept of "authority" with things like "rejection" and "danger" so strongly in my mind that those associations might be better referred to as *pieties*. A "piety," as defined by Kenneth Burke, is an association between two or more concepts or ideas that a person believes is natural, inherent, and important: a "sense of what properly goes with what" that we believe is *true and real* to a pious extent (Burke, 1954, p. 74).

A bit of background: when I was in high school, my mom, my favorite parent and the only parent I felt accepted by, was arrested (by police officers) and I was left to live with other parental figures who didn't want me there and regularly told me so. They seemed to associate me with my mom and looked down on me as a problem. I began to believe all authority figures would look down on me as such, and this piety played an important role in shaping how I understood teachers. More specifically: it felt as if there was an invisible signal that radiated out from me telling all authority figures that I was somehow suspicious. As an undergraduate, I remember hearing my peers discuss meetings with professors, or going to study halls, or using any number of university resources, and feeling an overwhelming sense that these resources were simply not meant for me, the suspicious one. That I'd need to figure it out on my own because of who I was.

This brings me to my first major point: expressing unconditional positive regard for a student with authority-related traumas may have valuable and lasting impacts. The first time I met with one of my professors in office hours, it was because I had messed up on a paper so badly that it couldn't be graded, and "professor conference required for resubmission" was written in red ink at the bottom of the last page. I went into the professor's office fidgeting with anxiety, ready to be called out as a failure who didn't belong, but that's not what happened. The professor was not only helpful but *interested in* and *supportive of* what I had to say, *and* she helped me get to a point where I felt good about rewriting the paper. I had failed, but she didn't treat me like a failure; this was my first memorable experience with unconditional positive regard (read: positive regard despite errors and faults) in a higher education setting. That moment challenged the stability of my "authority = danger and rejection" piety and was pivotal in my educational career. That professor became my "in" into higher ed and is the main reason I had the confidence to go on to grad school.

Another move that challenged my "authority = danger and rejection" piety was when professors demonstrated a willingness to question tradition and authority. I call these demonstrations "offerings." One example of this kind of offering I remember is a mini-lecture from one of my professors on the concept of procrastination. In this discussion, the professor invited us to question procrastination, see both the ups and downs of it, and revealed that professors regularly procrastinate, too. In the moment, I remember this disclosure feeling both surprising and comforting, and in hindsight, I think that's because it was an offering: she was offering up something supposedly sacred to teachers (the mantra: don't procrastinate) and showing us that it was okay to question it. In other words, she was modeling that it was safe to question authority and tradition. Other versions of this offering have come in the form of teachers asking to be called by their first name, using grade contracts, or modeling critical questioning of authoritative sources.

To summarize this discussion of my undergraduate experiences, I'd like to say two things. First, authority-based traumas may lead to pieties that make it difficult for students to reach out to teachers or use campus resources, and second, there are moves that can work against these pieties, such as intentional displays of unconditional positive regard and offerings that create a safe space for questioning authority.

Graduate Student/Instructor Experiences: Vertical and Horizonal Advice

Most of the advice I received related to classroom authority as a graduate student and graduate instructor falls into two categories: vertically oriented advice and horizontally oriented advice. By vertically oriented advice, I mean that which comes from more hierarchical understandings of the student–teacher relationship, such as the "banking model," which positions students as empty banks waiting for the knowledgeable teacher to "deposit" pieces of information into their minds (Friere, 1968, p. 72). By horizontally oriented advice, I mean that which comes from more collaborative and dialogic understandings of the student–teacher relationship, where power is decentered and teacher and student are conceived of more collaboratively, or rather, horizontally oriented toward one another: on the same plane but coming from different positions (Bryson & Bennet-Anyikwa, 2003; Friere, 1968; George, 2001; Llewllyn & Llewllyn, 2015; Luke, 1996; Shor, 1996; Rose, 1989). It is probably not surprising that the more vertically oriented advice tended to make me feel uncomfortable, like an outsider in higher education, while the horizontally oriented advice, which is often advocated by feminist and critical pedagogies, made me feel more included.

One of the trends in vertical authority advice I encountered was being warned that I would need to put extra work into establishing and maintaining authority because of my identities (short, female, queer, young, new to teaching). This advice often triggered my "fight or flight" response. And I should clarify right away that I don't think this is entirely bad advice (teachers who represent marginalized identities face different classroom issues than teachers who do not). However, if my pieties about "authority = rejection and danger" impacted my relationships with teachers as a student, they have just as greatly impacted my relationship with students *as a teacher.* What made me uncomfortable wasn't just this prediction of an uphill "authority" battle for me, but also that I desperately didn't want to understand myself as an "authority figure" (authority still meant—and still means—rejection and danger for me deep down, so thinking about myself as an authority figure means thinking about myself as someone who might make students feel rejected and unsafe). However, it's also worth noting the hierarchical understandings of relationships embedded in this advice. Because of my identities, I ranked *lower* in terms of how much students were predicted to respect me, and as such, I was supposed to put *more* effort into establishing authority (and I really, *really* didn't want to do that). I'm not saying the advice I was given about marginalized identities having more difficulties with conduct issues is wrong or unhelpful, but rather that, because of my pieties, this advice felt like a double punishment: not only was I being told that students are likely to not respect me because of who I am, but I was also being told that as the solution, I need to grapple *more* with this concept of authority that feels unsafe for me.

I refer to another kind of "vertical" advice I was commonly given as "disguise yourself as an authority figure" advice. This kind of advice generally included suggestions of ways to present myself so that students would understand me more as an authority figure: advice about what to call myself or how to look or dress differently so as to gain more student respect. For example, as a graduate student/instructor, I was strongly advised to have students call me "Ms. Moore" rather than by my first name, and once had a professor/mentor suggest that wearing high heels might help me avoid future authority issues. This advice about high heels, while undoubtedly problematic and ableist, is also potentially valid on some level when we consider the role implicit bias plays in how humans (including students) interpret others. That is, looking and dressing differently may actually change how some students react to a teacher, so, in some ways, perhaps this advice could have been useful; had I appeared taller or more traditionally feminine or more formal, students may have reacted differently to me, just like they may have reacted differently if I had asked them to call me by my last name. However, this kind of advice also has elements of hierarchy that are quite uncomfortable (similar to high heels). The implication here, to me, was that if I dressed in a way that made me uncomfortable or went by a name that made me uncomfortable, I could come across as someone different than who I really am (taller; more feminine; more formal; older) and who registers as higher on the "presumed authority scale" or the "deserves respect scale" than the real-me does. It made me feel as though how much students would respect me was based on how much I was willing to conform to arbitrary traditional standards that are uncomfortable to me. In other words: it made me feel as though students would only respect me insofar as I pretended to *not be me*, because otherwise, I ranked too low in respectability. Needless to say, this kind of advice has never felt good, or very useful for me.

Now let's turn to the advice that was not only more helpful to me in figuring out how to approach my classes, but also much better feeling; this advice, even though it wasn't always immediately obvious at the time, was usually advice about *boundaries*, which is really another way of saying *horizontally oriented understandings of relationships*. Here's one example: a professor and mentor of mine once suggested that I start out the semester by adhering slightly more strictly to the rules and deadlines outlined in my syllabus than felt intuitive for me, so that I was in a position to ease up on those throughout the semester (instead of starting too lax and needing to get stricter over time). His reasoning was this: loose guidelines and rules in the beginning can feel unstable for students, but also getting stricter throughout the semester feels like a punishment for students, while easing up throughout the semester feels like a reward. He explained how this can change the way students experience their relationship with the teacher and the class. This advice—although not phrased in terms of boundaries, was really about boundaries. He was suggesting that I clearly establish and maintain my boundaries early on, and if I ever become more relaxed with those boundaries, to do so after having established a relationship with students. His reasoning (how this would impact my relationship with students) was actually very in-line with trauma-informed approaches, which place a considerable focus on developing positive relationships with consistent, predictable boundaries. The only slight discrepancy between his advice and that advanced by trauma-informed approaches is that trauma-informed approaches typically recommend maintaining boundaries *consistently and transparently* rather than changing them in any meaningful way over time (Thomas et al., 2019).

Another example of helpful, horizontal advice I received came from a fellow (more advanced) graduate student. She recommended (and I'm not sure where this advice originated) that as teachers, we imagine that we have a backpack containing all our worries and concerns about students and teaching, and that we pick a physical line/place that we cross each day where we let ourselves set that backpack down and allow ourselves to stop worrying about our students for at least a little while, every day. She reassured us that our invisible backpacks full of cares would always be there for us to pick up again the next day, but that it was important for us to draw a line (a physical representation of a boundary) and essentially say "my boundary is that I can care about my students and be in work mode this much, but I cannot give any more than that." I think another thing that is important here is the horizontal imagery: the idea of crossing a physical line or boundary that says "I've given enough today."

To summarize this section: as someone with authority-related traumas, I struggled with the notion that I should expect authority issues because of my identities, and even more so with the vertical kinds of advice I was given about how to appear more authoritative. I found advice that centered more on the ideas of boundaries and expectations, or horizontal relationships, much more useful, but also much less triggering and therefore, far more comfortable in practice.

New Faculty Experiences: Trauma-Informed Cornerstones

I didn't encounter scholarship on trauma-informed approaches to pedagogy until after graduate school, as a new full-time teaching faculty member at a big university. The more I read about trauma and trauma-informed approaches, the more all the experiences described above began to make sense, and the more I began to develop a theoretical approach to "authority" and the "student–teacher relationship" that felt both practical and in-line with my pedagogical goals and values. I encountered two specific pieces of advice that I think together make wonderful cornerstones for any approach to classroom management (both should be familiar from earlier discussions):

1. Establish and maintain clear, intentional boundaries (Brunzell et al., 2019; Davidson, 2017, p. 12; Morgan et al., 2015)
2. Practice unconditional positive regard (Brunzell et al., 2019; Thomas et al., 2019)

The first cornerstone, *establish and maintain clear, intentional boundaries*, means thoughtfully coming to conclusions about how much you can give to and expect from students. Some examples of boundary-setting include explaining what students need to do to get a certain grade, or when students can expect the teacher be in office hours or available through email. We all engage in boundary setting when we create our class policies, so the general idea of boundary setting is likely familiar. However, I think for all of us, but especially newer teachers, it is helpful to think about assignments, classroom policies, and specifically about authority and the student–teacher relationship in terms of boundaries and expectations, and to know that being thoughtful, clear, and consistent about boundaries and expectations is one way to make classrooms feel more navigable, predictable, and safer for both students and teachers.

The second cornerstone, *maintain unconditional positive regard*, states that we should make it clear that we view our students with positive regard, no matter what is happening in terms of their grade or class performance. That means, if we are questioning a student about a possible plagiarism case or asking a student about an assignment they didn't turn in, we should take the time to make it clear that we still view the student positively and still want them to succeed, even if we may be disappointed in their actions or disagree with their choices. We should not act as though the quality of a student's class performance will change the fact that we want the student to grow and succeed. Many times, issues with class performance involve boundaries crossed or expectations not met, and we can respond to those issues by reiterating those boundaries and expectations, along with the repercussions for not meeting or respecting those, but all the while *still maintaining unconditional positive regard for the student*. For example, saying something along the lines of: "Dear Student, I'm writing because x behavior goes against our class conduct policy. I'd like for you to be able to stay in our class, so I need to ask you to refrain from engaging in such behavior going forward (if you, too, would like to stay in our class). If it happens again, I will have to follow through with the consequences outlined in our conduct policy. I appreciate your understanding and hope to see you in class on Monday. Wishing you the best." When we infuse these moments of "boundary crossing" or "repercussions" with unconditional positive regard, we model a "growth mindset," and push back against the idea that "messing up" means a student doesn't belong, which may be an important message for many students, and perhaps especially those with authority-related traumas. And to go back to that first undergraduate story I shared, the move of intentionally communicating unconditional positive regard may also help to push back against any self-sabotaging pieties related to authority that students may have.

An important part of maintaining *unconditional positive regard* is trying not to mirror or reflect student's emotions back at them when students are getting frustrated or upset, and instead trying to maintain a kind of emotional calm (Brunzell et al., 2019). Relatedly, another important part of *unconditional positive regard* is remembering that students have a whole life outside of our classes, and that a lot of their behaviors stem from other parts of their lives—not always from their experiences in our classrooms (Thomas et al., 2019, p. 17). That is to say: it's important to remember that student behavior and ability to produce work is *often* not about us. This, in itself, is also a kind of boundary: a boundary that says, "I will try to remember that students' engagement with my class is not always or solely about me and that I don't control the other influences in their lives impacting their behavior in my class." I don't mean to say that we should assume all student behavior is irrelevant to our teaching, nor that we should ignore trends in student behavior that may provide insight into how to improve our classes. What I do mean to say is simply that it is easier to maintain unconditional positive regard for students when we try to keep in mind the various influences in their day-to-day lives.

I also want to be sure to recognize that this unconditional positive regard task is, in some ways, a lot to ask, especially for teachers with marginalized identities who may be regularly faced with students who question their very right to stand at the front of a classroom. I want to be clear that unconditional positive regard is only practical or effective when paired with careful, consistent boundary-setting and maintenance, and recommend that when students knowingly and repeatedly cross boundaries, teachers bring in administrators to help figure out and enact the next steps, and that administrators support teachers in maintaining their boundaries. If a student refuses to respect reasonable, clearly defined and articulated boundaries in a classroom, it should not be on the teacher alone to figure out how to resolve that boundary issue.

These two cornerstones have been the most comfortable and practical pieces of advice I've encountered related to the student–teacher relationship: they have guided me through numerous difficult student interactions and helped me make decisions I feel confident in. They are also compatible with feminist and critical pedagogies and the shift toward more dialogic/horizontal (and less hierarchical/vertical) relationships with students.

Here's one example of how these cornerstones aided me in a difficult classroom situation: I had a student choose a surprising topic for an assignment that was extremely hurtful to certain, specific identities. I decided that, based on my boundaries, I needed to tell this student I did not want them to proceed with that topic and it was not going to be possible to get a passing grade with that topic. As I did so, I explained my boundaries and expectations based on both my class conduct policy and the assignment requirements. The student initially questioned my decision and tried to make a case for their topic choice. I reiterated my boundaries and expectations (that the student change topics or face a failing grade) but maintained a positive air of support and tried to help the student think of other topics they might be interested in. I reassured the student that I wanted them to be able to succeed in our class, and that was one of the reasons I was urging them so strongly to change topics. The student shortly thereafter agreed to switch topics and we were able to continue having a respectful relationship in class. I am not implying that I handled the situation perfectly, nor that the two cornerstones discussed above will be helpful in every difficult student situation. Instead, I share this example to illustrate how those cornerstones can work as one possible heuristic for figuring out how to approach difficult student situations.

Conclusion

In conclusion, I'd like to argue that authority is not as stable a concept as some of our pedagogies make it out to be. Different people have different pieties related to the concept of authority, which means that, in any given classroom, authority means a handful of different things to different people, and likely stirs up many different feelings. I tend to associate authority with the idea of rejection and danger and so, for a long time, I distanced myself from authority figures. However, I also have students who express discomfort with calling me by my first name, and their reasoning usually has something to do with how they very much want to show respect for authority, or in other words: something to do with their own pieties about authority. It is important for us all to understand that these pieties related to authority play a special role in shaping classroom experiences for many of us (students and teachers alike), and to respect that some of those pieties may also be deeply connected to experiences of trauma.

Furthermore, I'd like to argue that trauma-informed research yields useful advice about establishing positive student–teacher relationships, or rather, useful advice about how to approach this thing we call classroom "authority." I believe that two of the most useful pieces of advice or *cornerstones* from trauma-informed research, at least in terms of helping educators navigate the student–teacher relationship and "authority," seem to be: establishing and maintaining clear, consistent boundaries, and maintaining unconditional positive regard. These two pieces of advice are particularly useful in that they are:

1. Practically applicable for new teachers because they provide heuristics for navigating difficult interactions.
2. Likely to be less troublesome and anxiety-inducing for new teachers who come from a background involving authority-related trauma, specifically because these pieces of advice are based on horizontally, rather than vertically, oriented understandings of relationships.
3. Helpful for providing teachers tools that may prevent burnout and other stress-related side effects, like *secondary traumatization* and *retraumatization*, specifically by emphasizing skills like emotional regulation and boundary-setting (Carello & Butler, 2015).
4. Likely to help facilitate a safe and stable classroom for students, and in so doing, also model positive relationships for students.

Below, I expand upon each of these four points.

First, the two cornerstones discussed above are very practically applicable for new teachers in that they provide heuristics for behavior. As can be seen from my difficult encounter discussed above (which I don't think is a particularly uncommon situation) these two pieces of advice provided me with a way to navigate my responses. Advice on what name to have students call me, or what to wear or look like, was not helpful to me in this moment because it did not provide instructions on what to *do* (could establishing authority through titles and dress earlier in the semester have prevented this situation? It's possible but seems unlikely). The advice I received from trauma-informed approaches directed me to think about my boundaries and ask myself questions like: Was I willing to let a student write about this topic or did that cross a boundary? What boundary did it cross? What would be the resulting action if the student chose to continue crossing that boundary? And finally: How do I make sure to express unconditional positive regard while communicating that boundary? These heuristic questions guided me through the situation, and the outcome (at least in this instance) was positive.

Second, these two cornerstones are likely to be less troublesome and anxiety-inducing for new teachers who come from a background involving authority-related trauma. Remember: because of my pieties, the task of even talking about "establishing authority" in the classroom made me feel uncomfortable at best and triggered at worst. There were moments discussing authority in my graduate pedagogy classes where I could feel my whole body turn red with shame and anger and an intense feeling that I didn't belong and needed to run away to a safer place. The more horizontal and boundary-focused advice I encountered felt more inviting and applicable for me, and based on conversations I've had with colleagues, I'm not alone in that experience.

This brings me to my third point: I believe these cornerstones are helpful in that they provide teachers tools that may reduce burnout, stress, and other side effects, like *secondary traumatization* and *retraumatization*, specifically by emphasizing skills like emotional regulation and boundary-setting (Carello & Butler, 2015). Secondary traumatization is defined as trauma-like symptoms that occur from bearing witness to someone else's trauma, like reading a student journal about something terrible they've been through, while retraumatization is defined as the experience of having previous traumas brought back up by a stimulus, for example: a student who had experienced abusive parents being retraumatized by reading a book about abusive parents (Carello & Butler, 2014, p. 156). In a recent article in the *Review of Research in Education*, Shelley M. Thomas et al. (2019) compile an interdisciplinary review of research related to trauma-informed education practices between 1998 to 2018. One of the implications they draw from their research is the "importance of organizational support to promote staff well-being" (p. 447). They point out that "while self-care is noted ... as a critical element for educators who are exposed daily to students dealing with trauma and adversity, putting the full onus on individual staff members to support their well-being ... is not sufficient" (Thomas et al., 2019, p. 477). Providing information about and advocating for trauma-informed approaches to classroom management is one way that departments and colleges can support educators in their journey to self-care, as these approaches tend to focus on positive relationship skills like boundary-setting and emotional regulation: skills that are specifically known to be useful for reducing things like secondary traumatization, retraumatization, and burnout (Brunzell et al., 2019; Carello & Butler, 2015). In other words: by training teachers on trauma-informed approaches and *supporting teachers in implementing them*, administrators stand to help improve the overall well-being of teachers and potentially reduce burnout.

The last point I'd like to make circles back to the experience of students: the more teachers incorporate trauma-informed research into their approach to the student–teacher relationship and "authority," the more we increase the chances that teachers will be able to facilitate safe and stable classrooms for students, and specifically for students with histories of trauma. We also, in this process, have the chance to model positive relationship skills both for students and ourselves. I've always thought of education, and humanities education specifically, as being very "relational," that is, being in part concerned with teaching how to question, understand, and approach our *relationships* to the people and world around us. These two cornerstones not only stand to facilitate positive relationships within the classroom, but also to model positive relationships so that both students and teachers can recognize and strive for those relationships outside the classroom as well.

Qualifications/Limitations

I'd like to take a moment to clarify a few things before ending this chapter. First, I do not want to argue here that we should abandon the frameworks of power and authority in our pedagogical discussions of classroom management. Despite the fact that I (and others) may find them triggering at times, these conversations are still incredibly important. Teachers of different marginalized identities *do* experience disrespect and boundary-pushing often at higher rates than teachers of less-marginalized identities. This is something important to discuss, be aware of, and attend to as best we can as colleagues. In arguing that we begin to approach this conversation from a trauma-informed lens, I am not arguing that we leave behind critical inquiries into how power and authority function in the classroom, but rather that we add trauma-informed approaches to them.

Second, I'd like to note that I do not intend, in this chapter, to argue that teachers should feel responsible for playing the role of therapists. In fact, I think it is important to remember that, as teachers, although we take on a lot of emotional labor, we are *not* therapists and should not feel responsible for providing the services a therapist would provide (Carello & Butler, 2015). In arguing that we approach the student–teacher relationship through a lens of trauma-informed, positive psychology, I am not arguing that classrooms should be seen as therapists' offices, but rather that classrooms should be *safe,* not only because it might stand to make the classroom a more healing space, but also because students learn more and more effectively in safe environments (Dorman et al., 2006). As noted above, I also believe the two cornerstones discussed in this chapter stand to improve the emotional workload and regulation of teachers, which is partly why I find them to be so useful.

Finally, I'd like to note that these two cornerstones represent only a small part of trauma-informed discussions on pedagogy. There are a great many more insights out there in trauma-informed research, and many more still to be articulated.

References

Brunzell, T., Stokes, H., & Waters, L. (2019). Shifting teacher practice in trauma-affected classrooms: Practice pedagogy strategies within a trauma-informed positive education model. *School Mental Health*, *11*(3), 600–614.

Bryson, B. J., & Bennet-Anyikwa, V. A. (2003). The teaching and learning experience: Deconstructing and creating space using a feminist pedagogy. *Race, Gender and Class*, *10*(2), 131–146.

Burke, K. (1954). *Permanence & change: An anatomy of purpose*. Hermes Publications.

Carello, J., & Butler, L. D. (2014). Potentially perilous pedagogies: Teaching trauma is not the same as trauma-informed teaching. *Journal of Trauma and Dissociation*, *15*(2), 153–168.

Carello, J., & Butler, L. D. (2015). Practicing what we teach: Trauma-informed educational practice. *Journal of Teaching in Social Work*, *35*(3), 262–278.

Davidson, S. (2017). *Trauma-informed practices for post-secondary education: A guide*. Education Northwest. https://educationnorthwest.org/sites/default/files/resources/trauma-informed-practices-postsecondary-508.pdf.

Dorman, J. P., Aldridge, J. M., & Fraser, B. J. (2006). Using students' assessment of classroom environment to develop a typology of secondary school classrooms. *International Education Journal*, *7*, 906–915.

Finkelhor, D., Turner, H. A., Shattuck, A., & Hamby, S. L. (2013). Violence, crime, and abuse exposure in a national sample of children and youth: An update. *JAMA Pediatrics*, *167*(7), 614–621. http://www.unh.edu/ccrc/pdf/cv283.pdf.

Freire, P., Ramos, M. B., & Macedo, D. (1968/2014). *Pedagogy of the oppressed* (Ramos, Trans.; Thirtieth Anniversary Edition). Bloomsbury.

George, A. (2001). Critical pedagogy: Dreaming of democracy. In G. Tate, A. Rupiper Taggart, & K. Schick (Eds.), *A guide to composition pedagogies* (pp. 93–112). Oxford University Press.

Giroux, H. A. (1986). Authority, intellectuals, and the politics of practical learning. *Teachers College Record*, *88*(1), 22–40.

Lange, E., & Young, S. (2019). Gender-based violence as difficult knowledge: Pedagogies for rebalancing the masculine and the feminine. *International Journal of Lifelong Education*, *38*(3), 301–326.

Llewellyn, K. R., & Llewllyn, J. J. (2015). A restorative approach to learning: Relational theory as feminist pedagogy in universities. In T. P. Light, J. Nicholas, & R. Bondy (Eds.), *Feminist pedagogy in higher education: Critical theory and practice* (pp. 11–31). Wilfred Laurier University Press.

Luke, C. (1996). Feminist pedagogy theory: Reflections on power and authority. *Educational Theory, 46*(3), 283–302.
Morgan, A., Pendergast, D., Brown, R., & Heck, D. (2015). Relational ways of being an educator: Trauma-informed practice supporting disenfranchised young people. *International Journal of Inclusive Education, 19*(10), 1037–1051.
Pace, J. L., & Hemmings, A. (2007). Understanding authority in classrooms: A review of theory, ideology, and research. *Review of Educational Research, 77*(1), 4–27. https://doi.org/10.3102/003465430298489
Roberts-Miller, P. (2004). *Deliberate conflict: Argument, political theory, and composition classes.* Southern Illinois University Press.
Rose, M. (1989). *Lives on the boundary: The struggles and achievements of America's underprepared.* Free Press.
Shor, I. (1996). *When students have power: Negotiating authority in a critical pedagogy.* University of Chicago Press.
Thomas, M. S., Crosby, S., & Vanderhaar, J. (2019). Trauma-informed practices in schools across two decades: An interdisciplinary review of research. *Review of Research in Education, 43*(1), 422–452. https://doi.org/10.3102/0091732X18821123.
Varghese, R., Quiros, L., & Berger, R. (2018). Reflective practices for engaging in trauma-informed culturally competent supervision. *Smith College Studies in Social Work, 88*(2), 135–151.

SECTION II
Reading and Writing to Recover and Heal

9
TRAUMA TOGETHER
Rethinking Collaborative Learning

Brynn Fitzsimmons

It's Fall 2015, and I'm a junior-year undergraduate student in a mandatory English major course. I'm about to spend yet another break at yet another doctor, collecting weird blood-test results and chronic illness diagnoses, none of which fully explain years of worsening symptoms that are, among other things, the reason I'm in English classes rather than music classes I like far better but can physically no longer put in practice hours for. The slow loss of the instruments I love has been a series of traumas, guilt, doctors telling me I'm "psychosomatic," and religious leaders telling me I just need to pray more, God is testing me, or can heal me but chooses not to. Before class starts, I say something about the upcoming break, and how I hope "the doctors can figure out what's wrong with me," and the professor stops, looks at me, and tells me that while he hopes the doctors would help me feel better, there is nothing wrong *with me*. It's the first time anyone draws that distinction for me, between my illness and my own sense of worth.

The class period starts, and we turn to peer review. My groupmates ask more about my chronic illness; I tell them I'm in pain all the time. After a few more questions about my health, our conversation turns to the upcoming paper deadline, and they ask about my grade in the class. When I tell them I have an A in the class, one of my group members tells me I deserve to be in pain because I am "so good at everything else." That student will continue to make similar comments throughout the rest of my undergraduate program, at times threatening to do things to intentionally trigger my chronic pain. I won't talk about being chronically ill in a classroom space again until I am through my undergraduate and master's and well into a PhD program, and I'll never give details about doctors, diagnoses, or specific symptoms in a classroom again.

DOI: 10.4324/9781003260776-11

This story is, as the rest of this chapter will be, at the intersection of trauma and disability. What stands out to me about this specific story seven years later, as a graduate student and writing instructor who often assigns these kinds of peer review activities, is that my professor's pedagogical approach *to me* was *not* the problem; it followed, in many ways, guidelines for trauma-informed professor/student interactions. In fact, since I wouldn't encounter disability studies scholars and activists until graduate school, his response was actually one of the first times I heard someone directly tell me that my chronically ill, disabled body was *not* the problem. In that way, his momentary response proved both reparative and protective, in all the ways I think many teachers within trauma-informed pedagogy hope their relationship with students can be (Davidson, 2017). And yet, despite my professor's deeply kind pedagogy, what I remember most from that class was how my classmates responded, and there wasn't really a pedagogy to address that.

Collaborative learning activities, like the ones my classmates and I were engaged in, are useful pedagogical tools that can support active learning and a host of other effective, inclusive teaching practices, acknowledging that learning is fundamentally relational (Brufee, 1984). Critical pedagogical traditions ranging from Freire and hooks understand pedagogy as, among other things, relational—starting with and prioritizing the relationships among students and the knowledges they co-produce together rather than knowledge the teacher delivers to students (Freire, 1970; hooks, 1994). In addition, Avery et al. note the assumption that relationships are key to healing from trauma is implicit to trauma-informed approaches to teaching and learning (2021). Collaborative learning also offers a host of social, psychological, and academic benefits ranging from modeling dialogue among diverse perspectives to promoting critical thinking skills and trust within the classroom (Laal & Ghodsi, 2012).

And yet, that supportive, challenging, inquiry-based sense of community isn't what happened for me. It also isn't what happens for many students who experience harm through classroom microaggressions, which can cause or stimulate traumatic stress and trauma (Nadal, 2018). That is, relationships are sometimes at odds with *safety*—another pillar of trauma-informed approaches (Avery et al., 2021). Carello and Butler argue that "individual safety must be ensured through efforts to minimize the possibilities for inadvertent retraumatization, secondary traumatization, or wholly new traumatizations," and that this creation of safety is a far more trauma-informed practice than, for example, seeming to tackle questions of trauma "directly" by asking students to discuss or write specifically about trauma (2014, p. 156). As my story illustrates, though, addressing questions of safety and how we create it must extend beyond teacher–student interactions and take student–student interactions— particularly within collaborative learning—seriously as well.

Here I follow transformative justice scholars like Kim (2018) in understanding that creating safety does *not* mean assuming we can design a pedagogy that prevents harm—but rather that we can design one that addresses and repairs harm when it does occur, that repairing harm is a relational process that centers the needs of those harmed, and that those processes happen in *relationship*. While TIP offers a number of ways for teachers to understand their relationship to students through a trauma-informed lens (e.g., Brunzell et al., 2016), there has been comparatively little focus on building relationships and fostering trauma-informed interaction *among students*.

Tayles (2021) discusses how trauma-informed pedagogy can function as access and universal design, since trauma-informed pedagogy is often a move to help students with trauma *access* our classrooms—to feel safe enough to engage or learn (SAMHSA, 2014). As Dolmage notes, though, universal design requires "greater communal shaping" of our pedagogy (2017, p. 131); it requires collaboration. While I agree with Tayles' assertion that trauma-informed pedagogy can be a kind of access, a teacher enacting a trauma-informed pedagogy also did not make the classroom accessible to me, and it's not going to make it accessible to many students like me. Rather, I want to explore what might happen, especially to collaborative learning activities, if we understand "access" in the way disability justice advocates use that word, rather than simply "access" in the sense of ensuring our students who have trauma can still access our content. Specifically, I wonder how collaborative learning might help reposition trauma-informed approaches as the liberatory access Mia Mingus discusses: not just "access to the same crappy system that everybody else has" but rather a "move towards what a just world would look like for us all," (2013, n.p.). Disability justice is also *interdependent* (Sins Invalid, 2015), as

> thinking about how do we build relationships and how do we build in such a way that really pushes back against the myth of independence and this myth that we can and should be able to do everything on our own.
> *(Mingus, 2013, n.p.)*

This recasts access as an ongoing process "that we intentionally create collectively, instead of individually" (Piepzna-Samarasinha, 2020, n.p.).

Importantly, an emphasis on both interdependence and transformative approaches is also part of much of the guidance within trauma-informed approaches as well as collaborative learning. For example, SAMHSA's frequently cited 2014 overview of trauma-informed approaches notes that "In order to maximize the impact of these efforts [to address trauma], they need to be provided in an organizational or community context that is trauma-informed, that is, based on the knowledge and understanding of trauma and its far-reaching implications" (p. 2). That is, trauma-informed approaches require us to rethink the entire system *and* prioritize community, including the importance of things like peer support and "mutual self-help" among "peers," which, for the purposes of their discussion, is "individuals with lived experiences of trauma" (SAMHSA, 2014, p. 9). SAMHSA also notes the importance of survivors of trauma in understanding what trauma-informed approaches might look like. Trauma-informed teaching scholar Carello cites "collaboration and mutuality" as one of the principles of trauma-informed teaching and learning (2020, n.p.), while trauma scholars like Herman note that community recognition of a survivor's trauma is a "precondition for the restitution of a sense of a meaningful world," and that "recognition and restitution (as responses from the broader community) ... are necessary to rebuild the survivor's sense of order and justice" (1992, p. 70). That is, healing from trauma is *interdependent*. Collaborative learning is likewise interdependent, with Laal and Ghodsi noting "clearly perceived positive interdependence" as one of the conditions for successful collaborative learning, which they also note carries, among other benefits, the ability to "develop a social support system for learners" and "reduc(e) anxiety" (2012, p. 497). Although I predominantly think about these questions in the context of the writing courses I teach, reducing student anxiety has been discussed as crucial particularly for large classes in STEM fields, where student anxiety around evaluation and class discussion can prove a barrier to learning—but where strategies like active learning, which offers students "more control over their performance in the course because they (believe) that active learning enhanced their knowledge," can decrease anxiety and improve classroom climate (Downing et al., 2020, p. 11).

In the remainder of this chapter, I walk through trauma-informed approaches to several collaborative learning activities (classroom agreements, reflection, group discussion, peer review, and group projects) that focus on fostering interdependence and access as both learning strategies and a trauma-informed practice of creating safety in the classroom. They all assume as part of their design that interdependent access-making is something students, including students who have survived trauma, are often *already* doing for/with each other, and something instructors can facilitate spaces for them to practice doing. All of these assignments take seriously Carello and Butler's recommendations that trauma-informed practice focus on creating "emotional safety" (including, when appropriate, how an understanding of theories of trauma can and should inform classroom interactions) rather than trying to prompt or force disclosure or discussion of trauma (2014). That is, I'm asking how trauma-informed pedagogy can help students experience and create safety for/with each other in collaborative learning, rather than expecting they will somehow do therapeutic work. To accomplish this, these assignments rely, directly or indirectly, on disability justice's conceptions of collective, liberatory access (e.g., an effort to *create different spaces* rather than simply ensure students who have access to the classroom as status quo), and interdependence (via practices that make visible the ways in which how we show up in class isn't and can't be individual). I hope to emphasize ways of fostering peer support and collective access-making (or what SAMHSA might call "mutual self-help") among students, because I understand "access" in the disability justice sense as foundational to safety (Ho, 2021; Wong et al., 2018).

Of course, what access looks like varies from person to person, based on their needs, their experiences (including prior experiences of trauma), and the situations in which they find themselves (such as our classrooms). Following the COVID-19 pandemic, we've all had discussions on our campuses and in our departments about what a "new normal" looks like after an arguably collective trauma. The value of moves like flexible design, which can, among other benefits, alleviate student anxiety (see Mohammed et al.'s [2021] discussion of student anxiety in large online science courses, for example), have been recognized across fields, but I am interested here in more than that. I hope they offer spaces for students—particularly students who are themselves survivors of trauma—to remake ways of being with each other, and I hope those ways of access-making goes far beyond a 16-week semester. I hope they support the rest of the work of disability justice in our classrooms, which includes (but is not limited to) getting beyond seeing access as a series of accommodations we have to make and considering access—of which trauma-informed pedagogy is a part—as a move toward worlds we want to build.

Setting the Stage: Classroom Agreements

From the beginning of the semester, I want students to understand that they bring the embodied knowledge on which the class and its policies (especially around access) can and should be built. Dolmage notes this type of collectivity as crucial to universal design, which "is finally a matter of social justice—the importance of including everyone in the discussions that create space" (2017, p. 143). This assertion—that we need to include everyone in discussions of what universal design looks like—is also supported in trauma research like SAMHSA's noting the importance of peer intervention and support. This intersection tells me that a trauma-informed syllabus has to be more than edits to policies I make before the semester starts. Rather, students find that we build the table we'll meet at together. To create classroom agreements (which eventually become part of my syllabus, offering students input in the setup of the course right from the start), I will generally use a series of prompts like this one:

- Write about a time you felt listened to, deeply heard, or understood. What made you feel that way? What specific details let you know that you were heard/understood? How did you experience that in your head, your feelings, or your body?
- Write about a time you felt deeply *mis*understood or unheard. What showed you that you were not being understood? How did you experience that event in your mind, emotions, or body (either while it was happening or after the fact)?

- In one word, phrase, or sentence, what *demonstrated* the difference between you being listened to versus not? What made one experience feel like "listening" or "understanding" and the other not? Please put this on the whiteboard (or in the chat).

With these questions, I aim to give space for (and a private space for) students' difficult experiences without requiring them to talk or write *about* trauma, which can potentially be retraumatizing (Carello & Butler, 2014). I am also, however, asking them to identify how they want to feel—what kind of life they want to make (Herman, 1992), at least in the space of the class. This is an effort at making space for what Herman (1992) calls "reconnection" after trauma, which can take the form of creating a sense of reality, of the self, of relationships, of beliefs—or beginning to imagine the just world (or, at least a small piece of it) for all of us that Mingus discusses (2013). Rather than continuing on, however, I will ask students to reread what they wrote, and then discuss questions like the following in small groups. In general, I ask students to spend a few minutes on one question (taking notes in a shared Google document) and then switch to another question when the timer goes off. Questions for a writing-heavy course include:

- *How* do we want to listen to each other in this class (and/or the voices we read or watch throughout the semester) in this class? What do we want to have *characterize* our listening?
- What other guidelines would help us create a good classroom environment?
- What principles will help us discuss and disagree with each other productively?
- How should we review/give feedback on each other's work?
- How should we address issues or conflict in class?

Creating guidelines together is always tied to an articulation of a course philosophy that includes a belief that student learning, how they access spaces and content for it, and how they practice or use it is necessarily tied up not just in what *they* or *I* bring to the class, but rather what their classmates bring—in the type of collective access we create for/with each other. The questions here reflect, in some ways, the content of the class; as I'll discuss below, peer feedback is a large component of collaboration in a writing course like this one, and so it is an explicit part of classroom guidelines. However, the general topics—how we will listen, collaborate, address conflict, and engage with each other in class—show up across courses. Small classes might allow the instructor to talk with students one-on-one about these topics, while large classes might use the creation of classroom guidelines as a way to set the tone for semester-long discussion groups.

Embodied Knowledge and Recognizing Wholeness: Reflective Writing

Research on embodiment and trauma is growing, and frequently cited texts within trauma research, such as Herman's *Trauma and Recovery* (1992) and Van Der Kolk's *The Body Keeps the Score* (2014), note the extensive links between practices of safe embodiment and being able to ground oneself following traumatic experiences. Within trauma-informed pedagogies, efforts around promoting embodiment have ranged from including grounding practices like meditation and guided mindfulness practices in the classroom to movement activities grounded in contemplative practices (see Barbezat & Bush, 2013). However, while practicing awareness of one's body is certainly a valuable goal, a sense of safety in a space isn't an individual practice; it's a collaborative one. Audre Lorde saying "our feelings are our most genuine paths to knowledge" wasn't just about individual self-reflection; it was about the beginning of "new visions, how we begin to posit a future nourished by the past" (2004, p. 91). Feeling deeply *and with other people* was the foundation of social protest and change, Lorde argued (2004). They are how we "move together" (Sins Invalid, 2015, n.p.)—with our feelings, with our experiences, with our bodies—and is how get to a world "where no body/mind is left behind."

Thus, in asking students to practice an awareness of their bodyminds (Price 240), I find it important to *also* frame these practices as collective rather than individual—as interdependent in a way we have to *do* something about. On the first day of class, for example, I always ask students to privately journal or email me, telling me about themselves (including asking questions such as whether their name is different than what is in the learning management system (LMS), as is often true for trans and gender-nonconforming students, asking for their pronouns, and asking whether they want me to use their preferred name/pronouns in front of class). However, I also ask students to collaborate—via discussion and synchronous work in a Google document—on first-day-of-class activities like this one:

Please discuss the following questions and write down your answers in the Google document (or on the whiteboard behind you).

- What does "success" mean in class? What does it look like, or how would you measure it?
- What things help you succeed in class? Please be as specific as possible.
- What is "class participation?" What are the different ways of participating and which do you prefer?
- What makes a classroom or class space feel comfortable, enjoyable, or low- stress?
- What causes stress, anxiety, or annoyance for you in a class?

On an immediate level, this activity allows me to get a sense for the access needs of the class—not just in the formal accommodation sense, but rather in a much broader sense, one that tries to encompass students' bodyminds—the ways physical, mental, and emotional needs intersect, the ways students may bring with them the anxiety or (traumatic) stress classrooms caused them in the past, etc. Sins Invalid (2015) calls this "recognizing wholeness," understanding that "People have inherent worth outside of commodity relations and capitalist notions of productivity. Each person is full of history and life experience" (n.p.). It's also a way of asking students to recognize what influences how they and their classmates move through the space, which may include trauma. Recognizing trauma is, of course, one of SAMHSA's key recommendations for a trauma-informed approach (2014). By asking students to do this activity as part of the first-day activity and making the activity impossible to complete individually, I hope to ground the course practices in a model of both embodied and interdependent access-making for all bodyminds, including those impacted by trauma. However, I'm also aiming to make educational norms (like "class participation") things we can discuss, make explicit, and negotiate together—something scholars of antiracist pedagogy like Asao Inoue note as particularly important to combatting systemic injustice in the classroom (2015). While other disciplinary or course contexts might emphasize different parts of the classroom experience in these sorts of situations, reflection and discussion that recognizes students as whole people with many experiences (perhaps including trauma) from which they can both interrogate the classroom space and work together to build a new one can be an important, justice-oriented framing of the course—what Freire called problem-posing education (Inoue, 2015).

Reflective writing is also a way of doing the "thinking about thinking," metacognitive part of learning (see Silver et al., 2013). While I do use reflective writing as a metacognitive activity that takes place after high-stakes writing activities (these will be discussed later), my students also *start* most class periods by journaling briefly about the reading assigned for that day. On a teacher–student level, this practice allows students to gather their thoughts (or skim the reading if they didn't have time to read it before class) and have something prepared to say in class discussion, rather than having to figure out how to articulate their thoughts on the spot (which often proves extremely stressful for many students, especially neurodivergent students). Although reflective writing perhaps lends itself more easily to a writing class, then, it can be a useful activity for helping students ground and better access the course discussion regardless of the course subject matter.

Generally, my prompt is an open-ended question that asks students to connect something from the reading to their own experience and/or feelings. If I ask about feelings, I will always follow a request for students to write about their feelings with a question of where that feeling is located in the body—a small practice aimed at working against the disembodiment and depersonalization that often comes along with chronic stress and trauma (Van der Kolk, 2014).[1] However, this fairly common writing classroom practice also becomes a practice of recognizing wholeness and building interdependence through practices such as asking students to return to their journals, following group (and sometimes full-class) discussion, to engage with these questions:

- Reread what you wrote in response to today's prompt, and then think through your group discussion. How did class and/or your group's discussion challenge your thinking, add to it, or change your mind on some things?
- What is one idea from another group member (not the instructor) that you would like to remember? How does it relate to your own ideas?

Notably, neither of these questions are "about" trauma, and they don't even ask about embodied experiences or emotions in the way some of the individual journaling prompts do. However, what these prompts *do* aim at is creating a classroom practice where we understand our own learning and perspective as happening in relationship, and we understand our own experience of the class as necessarily tied up in everyone else's experiences, not just the content of the course, what each individual thinks about it, or what the teacher has to say about it. In this way, I aim to build on the syllabus' foundation of the course as something we make access to together to help students understand and practice meaning-making itself as a collaborative practice—one they do, importantly, with each other more so than with me (as will, of course, be true outside of and after the course). In other words, negotiating (access to) a course and meaning-making itself is interdependent.

Showing Up for Each Other: Peer Review

Peer review[2] as a pedagogical tool generally involves asking students to share vulnerable material; at the very least, students are sharing rough drafts of their work, submitting their projects to the scrutiny of their peers. This fact alone tells me peer review deserves careful attention in a trauma-informed approach, since sharing unfinished work—especially writing, although peer review need not be limited to writing—can easily prove stressful or even triggering for students who have had previous negative experiences with having their work evaluated (either by teachers or peers). Canagarajah also describes how asking students to share their work in this way can foster a more interactive classroom and, importantly, support an epistemology that posits knowledge and meaning as "co-constructed" (2014, p. 33). That is, as discussed in the previous section, the knowledge and experiences students bring to a given class or activity should inform that activity. Yancey further notes that "inviting students to write about their own experience validates that experience" (2014, p. 326).

Although neither Canagarajah nor Yancey are discussing trauma-informed pedagogy, the process of listening and mutual validation and encouragement they describe are quite similar to the support Herman notes as crucial to recovering from trauma: being able to reach out to and trust others for support, especially "protection, emotional support, or practical help" (1992, p. 162). While peer review fundamentally aims to be "practical help" (at least for the assignment), it takes more careful framing to think about it as also, for example, asking students to emotionally support each other in the writing process (as well as in the discussion of experiences they might write about or discuss in the course of peer review).

Building on the agreements for how we will listen to and support each other that we created for the syllabus, then, I generally talk with students before peer review about what supportive feedback looks like, why it matters, and what different needs are present around writing feedback within our class. When asking students to review each other's work, I draw on Trupiano's set of peer-review questions, which aim to discourage students from simply focusing on grammar and focus instead on what the author is "trying to say" and what the reader "would like to hear more about" (2006, p. 193). While these questions focus mostly on the writing itself, the question about what the writer is trying to say as well as the question of the tone seem to imply some concern for the intent or context for the piece—something that becomes particularly important if a writer has in some way narrated their trauma in their writing. In addition to these questions, however, I also ask students to engage in the reflections they turn in to me:

- What did you learn about your classmates through reading/viewing their projects today?
- How did your responses today help your classmates feel heard, encouraged, and supported in doing their best work?
- What would you like to change or improve about how you do peer review next time?

Like the earlier reflection assignments, there's a dual purpose here. On one hand, it allows me to gauge the usefulness of the peer review more holistically than trying to overhear conversations as I walk around the room (something that, due to an injury, I often couldn't do while teaching my Fall 2021 classes). It also, however, asks students to consider how they are or are not showing up in relationship with other students—what role they are or aren't playing in creating encounters in peer review that help *and support* their classmates as whole people. The assignment assumes this collective access as part of the expected work of the activity.

However, in spite of my attempt to frame questions that asked students to think about how they (could improve how they) engage with and support their classmates, many of their responses in these reflections centered on grades, preparedness, and conformity to assignment/rubric—not necessarily on how they were interacting with each other as whole people. In future iterations of this prompt, I hope to rewrite the questions toward this focus (e.g., trying to remove the implication of a performance evaluation in the last one) as well as do additional in-class discussion and scaffolding around what it might look like to balance an impending deadline (since papers are often due not too long after peer review) with recognizing and appropriately responding to the vulnerability and opportunity for connection and/or relationship that often happens in peer review.

Group Projects: Defining Access

Like many of the smaller-scale collaborative activities discussed here, group projects envisioned as opportunities for creating collective access can help students practice connection, identifying and asking for what they need, and negotiating autonomy in relationship—all skills that are important in navigating trauma, traumatic or chronic stress, or experiences informed by (the trauma of) systematized oppression, including as it exists within educational spaces. What is particularly exciting to me is that group projects might be more explicitly framed as projects of creating access. In my Fall 2021 courses, the last two of the four projects were group projects.[3] The course was organized this way because I hoped students would see group work—in which I asked students to articulate many of their own goals (including some around grading), work distribution, and access needs—as the point toward which the course was ultimately headed. Although I've discussed creating safety as a trauma-informed goal throughout this chapter, it's worth revisiting here, because group work is, as many of my students express every time I assign a group project (or even just ask questions about what causes students anxiety), a major source of anxiety for many students. This is part of why I tend to negotiate grading criteria and even parts of assignments *with* groups, asking them to tell me what they want to be graded on.[4] This aims to return a measure of autonomy (although it is important for teachers to, as Inoue notes, be transparent about where and to what extent this is true) to students and undo classroom hierarchies—both of which are important for antiracist pedagogies (Inoue, 2015) as well as trauma-informed ones (SAMHSA, 2014).

As part of this process, however, I ask students to make decisions about how they will be evaluated, not just for themselves individually but together with a group. Although the grading discussion is in some ways still a question of the teacher–student relationship, discussing grading with student *groups* aims to make the process less hierarchical and individual and more interdependent by asking students to negotiate (with as much autonomy as a course in which I'm still the person entering their grades allows) grades for themselves but with each other. Inoue has also discussed the ways in which grading systems are often a form of racist violence, especially in the context of the grading of writing, where our standards for "good writing" often have far more to do with white language supremacy than with communicative effectiveness (2015). His labor-based contract grading approach already assumes a kind of collectivity within the class, and thus can easily support the trauma-informed interventions mentioned here. In particular, groups might negotiate their labor (and how it will be assessed) together via a discussion (facilitated by the instructor, perhaps in a small-group conference) of the ways in which labor looks very different for different bodyminds, and neurodivergence as well as how experiences like trauma and traumatic stress might significantly alter what one's "labor" looks like. This is, of course, with the ultimate aim of working with students to create an agreement or grading contract that is also universally designed—a practice that both returns more power to students in the context of that specific project *and* aims to give them practice creating collective access for/with each other that can extend beyond the class (and/or beyond the part of the class over which the instructor has direct supervision; the vast majority of a group project, of course, also falls outside this field of vision).

I also ask students to create proposals and reflections similar to Jody Shipka's Statement of Goals and Choices, which uses students' own analysis of their work to guide the instructor's reading and/or grading of that work (2011)—something particularly important for grading multimodal projects (and, arguably, other types of projects that may not fit the norms of one's discipline or classroom). Asking for these kinds of statements is a small way, I think, for students to be the authority on their own experiences (which Herman and many others note as important for trauma survivors as well [1992]). In the proposal, students are asked to talk about their goals, who they're imagining as their audience (that is, who they expect will be accessing their work), how they will meet their goals, and how they will be dividing their labor. This document is what I generally discuss with them in group conferences (which I will discuss in a moment), but it also serves as a starting point for them to think about how the different needs in their group in terms of labor, and makes visible the ways in which the project itself is interdependent (that is, even if they are each doing individual parts of the project, they *also* have to tell me how all those individual parts are working together, and how they are planning to be accountable to each other for that).

Group conferences are also important. When I met with students, I asked them to walk me through what they were already doing. While I answered questions about the assignment guidelines, deadlines, and related concerns, I often returned to some variation of, "What do you need from me at this point?" (something my community partner also asked when meeting with student groups). Although students were encouraged to talk to me individually if they encountered issues within their group or needed individual support, it felt important, during these projects, to also ask them to think about what they needed *together*—how access could be collective and was interdependent. This practice was also an effort to undo the hierarchy of the classroom by positioning myself as a support for however they were conceptualizing and negotiating a project they were experts on far more than me. This worked particularly well in the service-learning group project, where students were both experts on their projects *and* were the only ones with all the information on what it was supposed to look like (when meeting with me, they were the ones with the guidance from the community partner regarding their project, which I could then support them in addressing; when they met with the community partner, they were experts in the course and the assignment guidelines).

Conclusion

As Goggin and Goggin point out, at points "writing *during* trauma is unavoidable" (2006, p. 39). If that is true, then writing, working, speaking, and learning *together* during trauma is likewise unavoidable. Part of student success in group projects, activities, and composing must be an inclusion and development of strategies for engaging with and/or *through* one's own trauma and/or the trauma of classmates. This is perhaps even more visibly true in the context of the COVID-19 pandemic. While the pandemic has both been traumatic for many and has demonstrated the ways in which the status quo is (and has always been) traumatically stressful for many, it's worth noting, I think, that this was SAMHSA's description of the need for system-wide changes toward trauma-informed approaches not in 2020, but in 2014: "the pervasive and harmful impact of traumatic events on individuals, families and communities and the unintended but similarly widespread re-traumatizing of individuals within our public institutions and service systems, makes it necessary to rethink doing 'business as usual'" (3). That is, our "business as usual" has always been *debilitating* (Puar, 2017).

But Mia Mingus says, "access is love," (2018, n.p.) and Chela Sandoval calls "love" the hermeneutic of social change, the "revolutionary maneuvers toward decolonized being" (2013, p. 140) that undo systems that are, among other things, systemically (re)traumatizing. Making access, then, is the work of trauma-informed pedagogy, but it's also how we love and honor each other well when the semester ends, and we all go home, and what should have been three weeks of respite turns into an Omicron outbreak and talk about whose bodyminds are fundamentally disposable (Hubrig, 2022). It's in those cases, I hope, that my students have practiced "access is love" not just as a way we navigate the impacts of trauma to get through a college course, but rather as a way we work against the debilitating, ableist norms that got us here to begin with. If trauma really does heal in safety and relationship (Herman, 1992), when our nervous system can finally register that we're safe (Van der Kolk, 2014), when we have the stability and the resources to get the support we need when we need it, in the community in which we need it, on terms we have set for ourselves (Ben-Moshe, 2020; Mingus, 2013) then what we mean, I think, by trauma-informed pedagogy is that we think (access-as-)*love* heals trauma, or at least is how we all live together, with it.

Notes

1 In the Fall 2021 semester, creating journal prompts that asked students to pause and connect with their emotions and embodied, emplaced presence was deeply aided by teaching Robin Wall Kimmerer's *Braiding Sweetgrass* (2013), which was my university's 2021–2022 Common Book. Kimmerer's description and style was often already modeling the mindfulness practices my journaling prompts often aim to get students to engage with, and students responded enthusiastically to her text in their journals.
2 Although this section will focus on peer-review worksheets and reflection activities, there is also a more immediate level of trauma response that should be scaffolded for in peer review as well. Especially if you expect the type of writing students are doing to be personal or possibly revealing of traumatic events (as is often the case in many of the personal essays assigned in first-year writing courses, for example) it's important to let students know when and how they should approach you about something they may read from another student that is concerning (e.g., if another student mentions assault, self-harm/suicide, or thoughts of violence). Because peer review often comes before students turn in a paper, the first eyes on a piece of writing are likely another student's, and thus, students need to know both how to be the first responses a classmate might receive as well as how and when to approach you with concerns about safety in relation to a classmate's trauma and/or level of reactivity. These concerns can be reflected on materials you hand to students but should be brought up verbally in class as well.
3 Students' third project, per departmental curriculum, required them to collaborate on a multigenre campaign. For one class, who partnered with Kansas City citizen journalism project Independent Media Association, this took the form of a service-learning partnership in which students took livestream citizen journalist news coverage and created social media recaps, articles, email summaries, and other pieces. In the other class, students chose an office on campus (the mental health center, the access center, etc.) and created a public-facing campaign that aligned with that office's goals and message. Students' fourth project required them to take their third project and revise it in some substantive way—for a different audience, into different genres, or some other change that required them to re-vision the project. Both sets of projects included substantial reflective writing (drawn from Shipka's Statement of Goals and Choices [2011]).
4 With 100-level students, it was useful to discuss grading criteria from a sample list (e.g., standard grading criteria I might use if I was writing them myself), rather than starting with a blank slate, which my students, at least, told me was overwhelmingly open. There are, of course, a variety of models for this, ranging from Shipka's Statement of Goals and Choices (2011) for grading multimodal projects to Inoue's labor-based grading model to collaborative rubric creation.

References

Avery, J., Morris, H., Galvin, E., Misso, M., Savaglio, M., & Skouteris, H. (2021). Systematic review of school-wide trauma-informed approaches. *Journal of Child and Adolescent Trauma, 14*(3). https://doi.org/10.1007/s40653-020-00321-1

Barbezat, D. P., & Bush, M. (2013). *Contemplative practices in higher education: Powerful methods to transform teaching and learning.* John Wiley & Sons.

Ben-Moshe, L. (2020). *Decarcerating disability: Deinstitutionalization and prison abolition.* University of Minnesota Press.

Bruffee, K. A. (1984). Collaborative learning and the "conversation of mankind." *College English, 46*(7), 635–652. https://doi.org/10.2307/376924

Brunzell, T., Stokes, H., & Waters, L. (2016). Trauma-informed flexible learning: Classrooms that strengthen regulatory abilities. *International Journal of Child, Youth & Family Studies; Victoria, 7*(2), 218–239. http://doi.org/10.18357/ijcyfs72201615719

Canagarajah, S. (2014). ESL composition as a literate art of the contact zone. In D. Coxwell-Teague & R. F. Lunsford (Eds.), *First-year composition: From theory to practice* (pp. 27–48). Parlor Press.

Carello, J. (2020, April). Trauma-informed teaching & learning principles. *Trauma-informed teaching blog.* https://traumainformedteachingblog.files.wordpress.com/2020/04/titl-general-principles-3.20.pdf

Carello, J., & Butler, L. D. (2014). Potentially perilous pedagogies: Teaching trauma is not the same as trauma-informed teaching. *Journal of Trauma and Dissociation, 15*(2), 153–168. https://doi.org/10.1080/15299732.2014.867571

Davidson, S. (2017). Trauma-informed practices for postsecondary education: A guide. *Education Northwest, 28.*

Dolmage, J. (2017). *Academic ableism: Disability and higher education.* University of Michigan Press.

Downing, V. R., Cooper, K. M., Cala, J. M., Gin, L. E., & Brownell, S. E. (2020). Fear of negative evaluation and student anxiety in community college active-learning science courses. *CBE—Life Sciences Education, 19*(2), ar20. https://doi.org/10.1187/cbe.19-09-0186

Freire, P. (2000). *Pedagogy of the oppressed* (30th anniversary ed.). Continuum.

Goggin, P. N., & Goggin, M. D. (2006). Presence in absence: Discourses and teaching (in, on, and about) trauma. In S. Borrowman (Ed.), *Trauma and the teaching of writing* (pp. 29–52). SUNY Press.

Herman, J. L. (1992). *Trauma and recovery: The aftermath of violence-from domestic abuse to political terror.* Basic Books.

hooks, bell. (1994). *Teaching to transgress: Education as the practice of freedom.* Routledge.

Ho, S. (2021, July 26). *Moving from survival.* Disability Visibility Project. https://disabilityvisibilityproject.com/2021/07/25/moving-from-survival/

Hubrig, A. (2022, January 26). *Disabled deaths are not your "encouraging news": Resisting the cruel eugenics of comorbidity rhetoric.* Disability Visibility Project. https://disabilityvisibilityproject.com/2022/01/26/disabled-deaths-are-not-your-encouraging-news/

Inoue, A. B. (2015). *Antiracist writing assessment ecologies: Teaching and assessing writing for a socially just future.* Parlor Press LLC.

Kim, M. E. (2018). From carceral feminism to transformative justice: Women-of-color feminism and alternatives to incarceration. *Journal of Ethnic and Cultural Diversity in Social Work, 27*(3), 219–233. https://doi.org/10.1080/15313204.2018.1474827

Kimmerer, R. W. (2013). *Braiding Sweetgrass: Indigenous wisdom, scientific knowledge and the teachings of Plants.* Milkweed Editions.

Laal, M., & Ghodsi, S. M. (2012). Benefits of collaborative learning. *Procedia - Social and Behavioral Sciences, 31,* 486–490. https://doi.org/10.1016/j.sbspro.2011.12.091

Lorde, A. (2004). *Conversations with Audre Lorde.* University Press of Mississippi.

Mingus, M. (2013, November 30). Beyond access: Mia Mingus on disability justice. *EquitableEducation.Ca*. https://EquitableEducation.ca/2013/mia-mingus-disability-justice

Mingus, M. (2018, October 26). *"Disability Justice" is simply another term for love*. Disability intersectionality summit. YouTube. Retrieved from https://www.youtube.com/watch?v=lm21KpsNk1s

Mohammed, T. F., Nadile, E. M., Busch, C. A., Brister, D., Brownell, S. E., Claiborne, C. T., Edwards, B. A., Wolf, J. G., Lunt, C., Tran, M., Vargas, C., Walker, K. M., Warkina, T. D., Witt, M. L., Zheng, Y., & Cooper, K. M. (2021). Aspects of large-enrollment online college science courses that exacerbate and alleviate student anxiety. *CBE—Life Sciences Education*, 20(4), ar69. https://doi.org/10.1187/cbe.21-05-0132

Nadal, K. L. (2018). *Microaggressions and traumatic stress: Theory, research, and clinical treatment*. American Psychological Association.

Piepzna-Samarasinha, L. L. (2020, October). Creating collective access: Crip made brilliance in detroit and beyond. *Allied Media*. https://alliedmedia.org/wp-content/uploads/2020/10/creating_collective_access.pdf

Puar, J. K. (2017). *The right to maim: Debility, capacity, disability*. Duke University Press Books.

Sandoval, C. (2013). *Methodology of the oppressed*. University of Minnesota Press.

Shipka, J. (2011). *Toward a composition made whole*. University of Pittsburgh Pre.

Silver, N., Kaplan, M., LaVaque-Manty, D., & Meizlish, D. (Eds.). (2013). *Using reflection and metacognition to improve student learning: Across the disciplines, across the academy*. Stylus Publishing.

Sins Invalid. (2015, September 17). 10 principles of disability justice. *Sins Invalid: An unshamed claim to beauty in the face of invisibility*. https://www.sinsinvalid.org/blog/10-principles-of-disability-justice

SAMHSA. (2014). *SAMHSA's concept of trauma and guidance for a trauma-informed approach*. https://calio.dspacedirect.org/handle/11212/1971

Tayles, M. (2021). Trauma-informed writing pedagogy: Ways to support student writers affected by trauma and traumatic stress. *Teaching English in the Two-Year College*, 48(3), 295–313.

Trupiano, C. (2006). Best classroom practices. In A. Horning & A. Becker (Eds.), *Revision: History, theory, and practice*. Parlor Press, 177–196.

Van Der Kolk, B. (2014). *The body keeps the score: Mind, brain and body in the transformation of trauma*. Penguin Books Limited.

Wong, A., Ho, S., & Mingus, M. (2018). Places to start. *Disability & Intersectionality Summit*. Retrieved January 29, 2022, from https://www.disabilityintersectionalitysummit.com/places-to-start/

Yancey, K. B. (2014). Attempting the impossible: Designing a first-year composition course. In D. Coxwell-Teague & R. F. Lunsford (Eds.), *First-year composition: From theory to practice* (pp. 321–347). Parlor Press.

10
INSIGHTS IN TRAUMA-INFORMED PEDAGOGY FROM THE FIELD OF BIBLIOTHERAPY, LITERARY TRAUMA STUDIES AND CREATIVE WRITING

Katarina Båth

Throughout time humans have used poetry and literature to cope with and process trauma, and to voice resistance toward different forms of trauma-inflicting oppression. From Aristotle's concept of *catharsis* (the purification and purgation of emotions through art) to famous statements such as Audre Lorde's "your silence will not protect you," there is a prevailing insight that if we turn our wounds into literary art, these literary works can also in various ways assist us and others with healing, liberation, political resistance and change in relation to the trauma.[1]

Since fiction and poetry have the ability to touch us deeply, and access layers of our unconscious, it can both engage, shatter and transform us as readers as well as writers. In this sense, literature has always had a close connection to trauma, long before the PTSD diagnosis and the field of literary trauma studies emerged in the 1990s. As J. Roger Kurtz points out, in his introduction to *Trauma and Literature* (2018), "the concept of trauma has asserted its relevance especially in literary settings," because "wounds, like words, require interpretation."[2]

However, since the 1990s, the increased awareness of trauma in society is reflected not only in contemporary fiction, it has also become a critical concept that shapes how we interpret and understand literature nowadays.[3] Literary trauma studies are, as presented in the *Routledge Companion to Literature and Trauma* (2020), "a rapidly evolving field," and judging by the increased number of publications on trauma, trauma has indeed become, as Lucy Bond and Stef Craps state in *Trauma: New Critical Idiom* (2020) "a catchword of our time."[4] Along with many other publications from recent years, these works testify that we live in both a traumatized and a trauma-obsessed time.

DOI: 10.4324/9781003260776-12

Since trauma has become more recognized, both as a diagnosis and as a critical concept within the fields of literature and cultural studies, the contexts in which different historical and fictional depictions of trauma and trauma theory are taught – and where student's own traumas might be triggered in the educational setting – have increased. This places new demands on trauma-informed pedagogy and the issue of risk and ethics in teaching trauma has been raised. In their article "Potentially Perilous Pedagogies: Teaching Trauma Is Not the Same as Trauma-Informed Teaching" (2014) Janice Carello and Lisa D. Butler (2014) raise concerns that within nonclinical disciplines such as literary trauma studies and creative writing, some instructors might promote potentially risky pedagogical practices involving trauma exposure and disclosure. They do not mean that we, who teach in the humanities, should refrain from teaching about trauma, but they point to the potential risk of retraumatization and secondary traumatization in educational practices where students are exposed to (possibly traumatizing) material. They, therefore, differentiate teaching about trauma from trauma-informed teaching and urge educators to adopt a "safety first" approach in their teaching.[5]

My own research and teaching practice is situated within the field of comparative literature, more precisely psychoanalytic literary criticism and literary trauma studies. I'm also interested in how literature and creative writing can be used for healing purposes, which has led me, as a literary scholar, to pay attention to the field of bibliotherapy, i.e., the use of literature to improve mental health, which is a growing practice in many parts of the world.[6] In another article I attempt to bring together insights from the more applied field of bibliotherapy practice with literary trauma theory.[7]

In this chapter I will draw from existent bibliotherapy research findings, my own teaching practice from a course held in literary trauma studies, and experiences from a creative writing course where some of the participants, but not all, used creative writing to work through different forms of traumatic experiences. My contribution to this anthology thus addresses three related and distinct practices where trauma-informed pedagogy is relevant in different ways:

1) Bibliotherapeutic practice: this is a setting where the literature read and used might or might not depict traumatic events, but there is an established therapeutic purpose to the activity. Bibliotherapy can be both clinical and non-clinical.
2) In a literary trauma-studies course I taught, the focus was on teaching trauma, i.e., reading literary representations of trauma and literary trauma theory. There was no explicit focus on how reading this material would affect the students psychologically, even though personal reactions of course came up in seminar discussions and in some of the students' individual papers.
3) A creative writing course where some of the participants, on their own initiative, wrote about different traumatic experiences to obtain the potential

healing that may come from this, although writing about trauma was not a pronounced purpose of the course.

I will present these three settings briefly and ask: What would constitute a trauma-informed pedagogy in these related, but also different contexts? In answering this question, I will address some of the concerns raised by Carello and Butler (2014), but also criticize some of their views, with help from educational theorist Gert J.J. Biesta (2013). In the literary trauma tradition within which I work, central theorists are, among others, Cathy Caruth (1995), Shoshana Felman and Dori Laub (1992). Carello and Butler call them "proponents of deconstructive trauma theory" and criticize some of their views.[8] Some of my outlook, therefore, differ from Carello and Butler's, and hopefully this will contribute to variate and complicate the understanding of what trauma-informed pedagogy might be in different settings. At the end of this chapter, I will also list how the insights from my research, teaching and creative- writing experience can be applied in a broader pedagogical setting.

Trauma-Informed Pedagogy in the Field of Bibliotherapy

The broad definition of bibliotherapy is "the use of literature to promote mental health," but depending on the setting, target group, working method and the material, the procedures vary. As Liz Brewster points out in her introduction "Bibliotherapy: A Critical History," "there have been many interpretations of what constitutes bibliotherapy, who should deliver it and how it should be delivered."[9] But the broader purpose, or value of engaging in literature and art, is in this context argued for in terms of being something that bestows on us redemption of pain or mental well-being. And this is not necessarily done by avoiding literature about difficult or painful experiences.

In the Nordic countries *kirjallisuusterapia* (literature therapy) has its longest tradition in Finland. Juhani Ihanus (2004) describes how regular literature therapy groups were initiated in Finland in the late 1970s and the first European organization for bibliotherapy was established in Finland in 1981.[10] Nowadays, bibliotherapy in Finland takes place in educational institutions, libraries, nursing homes, in mental health work and clinical work contexts and various care institutions.[11]

The "Finnish model" of bibliotherapy has traditionally had a focus on expressive and creative writing. The patient/participant is to be aided to find, and use, healing words. Ihanus has a long experience working with this kind of literature therapy, and in the above-mentioned anthology he describes how he views literature therapy as a kind of "word art therapy." It is supposed to be a "word adventure," a process where finding "the healing words" and "opening up new worlds of experience" is key. Ihanus also says that language can give structure to painful experiences, and he emphasizes the sensual, bodily dimension of language. The transforming power of literary language lies in its ability to say more than what is consciously communicated. The unconscious speaks through poetic images, metaphors, symbols.[12]

Finnish bibliotherapist and literary scholar Päivi Kosonen has added to Ihanus' description of creative word art therapy in a series of articles where she stresses the importance not just of creative writing but also of reading in bibliotherapeutic settings. The bibliotherapy contexts she describes are often about "identity work," where reading helps the participants get in touch with and put painful memories into words. You need a "reflective other," an educated discussion partner for this, i.e., the bibliotherapist, and often the bibliotherapy consists of group work sessions, but literature, the reading material, also "brings its own 'otherness' into play" in these sessions.[13] Kosonen also emphasizes "that literary fiction, poetry and poetic language can offer us expressive material, particularly when we are dealing with the most difficult human experiences that we encounter [...] that are difficult to put into words, such as early experiences of trauma."[14] So the idea here is that literary, poetic language has a special ability to touch unconscious, possibly traumatized, dimensions of our psyche. That is, the literary material "taught," or engaged in, is supposed to activate hidden psychic wounds for the session to have a therapeutic effect.

Within the field of bibliotherapy there is an established, psychoanalytic theory of how a bibliotherapeutic process works therapeutically. In Carolyn Shrodes' pioneer dissertation *Bibliotherapy. A Theoretical and Clinical-Experimental Study* (1949) the dynamic interaction between reader and literature was described by Shrodes as a psychoanalytic process with three stages: 1) identification, 2) catharsis, 2) insight. You are supposed to identify with a literary character or scene or story and, through this identification, experience an outpouring of emotions that will create *catharsis* and bring you to some sort of insight or redemption with regard to your own traumatic experience. This psychoanalytical understanding of bibliotherapy continues to be influential, even though it has evolved since Shrodes first developed it. In many contemporary guides to bibliotherapeutic method today, Arleen McCarty-Hynes and Mary Hynes-Berry's four-stage interactive process, where the stages are identification, selection, presentation and follow-up, is referred to.[15]

To present a general model of how literature can assist in working through trauma is, of course, in some ways a simplification. Humans react differently to literary texts and literary texts aren't all the same. As Elizabeth/Liz Brewster has pointed out, there is sometimes a gap between the intentions and expectations of those who arrange bibliotherapy sessions and the participants' experience of it.[16] Therefore, what has been called a user-centered perspective, has become more prominent within the field of bibliotherapy in the last decade.[17] This user-centered research has broadened the psychoanalytical descriptions of what constitutes a bibliotherapeutic process.[18]

Researchers such as Brewster and Swedish literary scholar Cecilia Pettersson (2018) have instead focused on the participants' experiences. Through interview studies they have shown how, for example, escapism – the possibility of shifting focus from one's own problem or trauma to other impressions of the literary work, and life in general – can also have therapeutic value. The social context of the reading group has also been shown to be an important part of a successful bibliotherapeutic process.[19]

Pettersson describes in *Biblioterapi* (2020) how non-clinical, so-called creative, interactive bibliotherapeutic reading circles have become more common during the last decade in Sweden. Often, these study circles are arranged by a library or a study association and directed toward individuals with a specific problem: drug abuse, or having lost a loved one to suicide, or elderly people who need to break out of social isolation.[20]

The bibliotherapy leaders I have interviewed said that even though the choice of text is important, it is the specific person and the social dimensions of the group that are in the foreground and govern the choice of reading material.[21] In *Poetry Therapy: Theory and Practice* (2003) Nicholas Mazza describes it like this: "in poetry therapy the focus is on the person, not the poem" and "[c]lients are not asked to identify the 'true' meaning of a poem, but rather the personal meaning."[22] In this sense, you can say it is a prerequisite that the bibliotherapy leader has trauma-awareness and a keen sense of the participants' eventual trauma-history as a starting point. The activity is also not educational in a standard way, but aims for healing and self-development.

Still, the bibliotherapeutic process has this stage of *identification* (mentioned above, in Schrodes' model) where you are supposed to recognize yourself in the read work and relate to your own traumatic experience. In a sense, this contradicts Carello and Butler's warning that "retraumatization and secondary traumatization" is a risk if you are exposed to (potentially triggering) material.[23] On the one hand, what they draw attention to might be a valid risk in a bibliotherapeutic setting: for instance, Emily T. Troscianko's research has shown that reading fiction about eating disorders triggered negative reactions in readers suffering from the same condition.[24] But there are also many other cases where reading about traumas similar to those from which you have suffered have proven helpful. To mention a few notable examples: clinical psychiatrist Jonathan Shay's work where he used Homer's *Iliad* and *Odyssey* to treat combat trauma suffered by Vietnam veterans, which is recounted in his works *Achilles in Vietnam: Combat Trauma and the Undoing of Character* (1994) and *Odysseus in America: Combat Trauma and the Trials of Homecoming* (2002). Another example is a project in Sweden resulting in the anthology *Du, jag, vi* (2016) where bibliotherapist Pia Bergström worked with youths (aged 16 to 20) who had a parent sentenced to time in prison and who were helped by reading the biography of the daughter of a well-known, long-term–sentenced Swedish criminal.[25]

Astrid Lindgren's beloved children's novel *Bröderna Lejonhjärta* [*The Brothers Lionheart*] (1973), about two brothers who face terminal illness and eventually take their own lives, is often read and treasured in palliative care units in children's hospitals.[26]

So, what insights about trauma-informed pedagogy can we draw from the field of bibliotherapy, where literature is used with a pronounced therapeutic purpose?

On the one hand, literary, poetic language can touch us more deeply, on unconscious levels, and an educator who uses literary depictions of traumatic events must, therefore, be sensitive to the participants' reactions and eventual personal traumas that might be triggered. This is in line with Carello and Butler's warnings, and the turn toward what is called a "user-centered perspective" within the field of bibliotherapy speaks to the importance of this.

On the other hand, the fact that many bibliotherapists work with "recognition" and use fiction and poetry's ability to access unconscious, hidden wounds, testifies to the fact that the reading of traumatic, upsetting literature can lead to healing, liberation, a sort of *catharsis*, and make us feel less lonely.

Teaching Trauma, Literature and the Ethics of Reading

The course I taught at the Department of Literature, Åbo Akademi University, Finland 2020–2021, Literature, Trauma and the Ethics of Reading, was an elective supplementary course for third- and fourth-year students with accomplished ground-level courses. The aim of the course was to give an overview of the field of literary trauma studies and discuss literary works with depictions of different forms of trauma. The syllabus consisted of theoretical as well as literary texts, both novels and poems.[27] The seminar had a textual focus, and the students' own possible traumas were not something that I explicitly addressed or took into account. My teaching assignment was as a literary scholar; I am not a trained therapist. That demarcation is important to remember.

At the same time, it's rarely that simple. As all teachers in the field of humanities know, you can never completely exclude your own person from the interpretations you make. Reading about the Holocaust, war, racism or sexual abuse will affect students with different backgrounds differently.

Some of the students tended to draw more explicit parallels to their own experiences from the traumas depicted in the literature. There were also students in the group who on a few occasions expressed that "this was difficult to read" or "unpleasant."

This, in combination with the prevailing "wound culture" of sensation and clickbait on the internet, made it important to include a discussion about the ethics of reading trauma narratives in the course outline.[28] We talked, among other things, about appropriation and the risk of leveling, if you too hastily compare different traumas or identify with the victims of a certain trauma without acknowledging that you are not the victim. This is something Carello and Butler also draw attention to, but within the field of literary trauma studies there is awareness and an ongoing discussion of this.[29]

In the course I taught, there was occasionally something of a tendency in the discussions to consider trauma as content in a way that became simplistic in a problematic way. When trauma was viewed as content, the discussion stopped at roughly identifying the trauma as explanation for the main characters' behaviors and plotlines. Literary critic Parul Sehgal's essay "The Case Against the Trauma Plot" (2021) has described this tendency. Sehgal argues that in a time of streamlined storytelling, the trauma plot has become too dominant and "synonymous with backstory" and character. In a fictional character's traumatic past lies the explanation to their personality and an air of victimhood that will give them moral authority. "The trauma plot flattens, distorts, reduces character to symptom, and, in turn, instructs and insists upon its moral authority," writes Sehgal.[30]

In my seminar discussions, I could sometimes notice the effects of this contemporary commodification of trauma. The fact that we are surrounded by simplified, clichéd images of trauma can make it tempting to use the critical concept of trauma in a similar way, as a sort of prefabricated explanatory model that simplifies and nails down, rather than opens up, the literary work to more dimensions for interpretation. Still, Sehgal's critique is, as I see it, mostly a critique against boring, uninspired craftsmanship. Stories that are casually created, and which simplistically equate trauma with identity, are expressions of a contemporary *zeitgeist* where the wound has become something you can capitalize on.

Our seminar discussions became more rewarding when focused on language and aspects of literary form. In the creation, or the creative interpretation, of a novel or poem, even if it embodies a difficult trauma, there is also always room to develop ingenuity, joy of language and reversal of perspectives – if you develop the attention to detail and form and images. If a work is crafted – and read – with a willingness to explore the unknown, it can make us more sensitive to which voices we ourselves participate in silencing.

The course was in comparative literature, so trauma-informed pedagogy in this context was about the following: 1) awareness of the fact that students could react negatively and strongly to certain works, 2) include a discussion of the ethics of reading trauma narratives and 3) maintain attentive focus on literary language and textual form and create awareness of the risk of reducing trauma to a simplified model of explanation. If you are aware of these risks, literary interpretation of trauma adds something to the clinical, psychoanalytic study of trauma.

I also want to add that if you, as do Carello and Butler, focus on the risks of teaching trauma within the fields of comparative literature and creative writing, it is easy to forget what the interdisciplinary perspective adds. Many clinical psychoanalysts find it enriching that literary scholars have developed their own relationship to psychoanalytical texts. To really *read*, as we read as literary scholars, is rarely included in psychoanalysts' training. There are psychology students who study literature on the side because the literary tradition concerning psychoanalytic theory gives them a deepened understanding of the psychoanalytic theory texts. It is a theory about language, representation, temporality, body and soul.

Working Through Trauma in a Creative Writing Course

In 2020 I participated in a one-year creative writing course in Finland. Course leaders were Finnish–Swedish authors Monika Fagerholm and Mia Franck. The participants were 14 people from different backgrounds and of different ages. You applied to the course with a work sample of the manuscript you wanted to work on during the course year. Some of us wanted to process more personal, more-or-less traumatic memories through our manuscripts, but there were also participants who just wanted to finish a planned novel, play or collection of short stories. Thus, there was no stated purpose or course requirement to deal with personal, traumatic experiences through creative writing.

Initially, my own desire to write came from a puzzling relationship that had activated a childhood trauma in me and had me doubt my own perception of reality. So, initially, my reason for writing was a search for clarity in "what actually happened." But during the process, a phase came where I realized that turning it all into fiction was a way for me – by attention to detail – to free myself from the trauma-induced perception of reality I had been stuck in.

Herbert Marcuse has written that "The truth of art lies in its ability to break the monopoly of the present reality (i.e. the monopoly of those who have established it) on defining what is real."[31] Creating my own fictive version of what I had perceived as hurtful became a way to distance myself from the angry and fearful perception of reality that had kept me prisoner. It became important not so much to create my own truth, in order to "win" over a perceived perpetrator, but rather to have the courage to recreate the trust and the love that had been damaged by the experience (and by the childhood trauma activated), and to integrate this love into my writing in order to let go of the experience. In that, lay a more profound sense of healing and a protest to inner judges that had made me feel angry and ashamed of what had happened. Before I joined the writing course, I had processed the traumatic experience in therapy, but creating a novel from it still had therapeutic value.

Feminist psychoanalyst Jessica Benjamin has explored the relationship between intrapsychic and intersubjective love. In *Like Subjects, Love Objects* (1993) she discusses how the integration of the ideal is a vital component in therapeutic processes, and how it can take different forms. In a therapeutic context, erotic transference can be a way to work through painful attachment patterns. Transference is the psychological term for "re-enactments of a patient's early life impulses and fantasies that emerge during the process of analysis and that replace a protagonist from the patient's past life with the person of the therapist."[32] Benjamin describes how therapeutic transference in a non-patriarchal culture can be about creating a "space to become absorbed with internal rhythms rather than reacting to the outside."[33] This description – creating a space for internal rhythms rather than being reactive – resonates well with my experience of how the creative writing process had a liberating, healing effect. The literary world I brought into existence became the space where I could channel a bruised desire and become creative, instead of reactive, to perceived abuse.

On the course, I befriended a woman who suffered trauma from an incident that had occurred several years earlier. She was a professional journalist in her mid- to late thirties, and we talked about her experience writing fiction about her trauma.[34]

Four years prior to applying to the course, Amanda experienced word-loss, and went into exposure therapy. All she could remember of the incident that had brought this about were torn fragments, and an important part of the therapy was therefore to process the trauma so that it became a story, with a clear narrative: beginning, middle and end. When she struggled to talk about what happened, her psychologist suggested that she first write down her memories. The written text felt further away than oral retelling, so taking the path over written text made it possible for her to retell what happened in therapy. This gave her the idea that if she could approach the whole course of events by writing them down, it would be a way not only to step into the trauma but also to step out of it again. Amanda stresses that she had not been able simply to join the creative writing course and start writing about the trauma on her own; clinical therapy was a prerequisite that gave her the overall framework of what happened and the basic conditions to start telling others about her experience.

Starting the creative writing course, the first challenge was to gain the courage to talk about the trauma in a new context, in front of people she didn't know. It was difficult at first. "The shame engraved in you is irrational, your psyche has suppressed the incident to protect you mentally, and to go against this survival mechanism isn't easy. But rationally, you know that it is the shame and the silence that kills you, not your words." On the course, quite quickly after the initial presentation of our different projects, the focus became creative writing as craft, i.e., techniques of literary depiction. To focus on literary technique made it easier to talk about the trauma. Amanda found the text-focus of the course liberating. The discussions with the supervisor were about attentiveness to language; finding the best way to convey what happened in words. She was relieved there were no kind of awkward "oh, how awful" mood during the discussions.

The next phase in the process came a little way into the writing process, when she realized that she could take control of the narrative and own it. "When it happened, I was totally powerless, but as a writer of my text I have power." To let this settle in the body was not a linear process; there were steps back and forth where she faced inner fear and resistance. "The paralyzing negativity comes back to haunt you every now and then, but slowly you chart a path towards a brighter way of being and recreate the story so that you can accept the trauma, live with it." In this way, the writing process had similarities with the healing process during therapy. In therapy, she worked with imaginary exposure, with restarts for the different stages of what happened. Every time she entered a new stage, resistance hit her. "It has been the same experience with writing. You think you are back at zero when the backlash hits you but that is not the case."

The main benefits from writing about trauma in a creative writing course were, for Amanda, broader and more in-depth insights in how the trauma affected not only herself and her relationships but how society in general reinforces shame in victims. She kept quiet for so long. Exploring how an oppressive culture forces victims to internalize shame has given her a better understanding of why she kept quiet for so long. The writing project became a space to resist that shame. There are scenes in her novel where she stands up for herself; writing those became an exercise in drawing the line and establishing her boundaries. "The fact that I speak out in different scenes of victim blaming in my novel has made me more confident that I will be able to do so also in reality, in the future." Writing the novel also made her more aware of how important language and word-choice are. This has made her more careful with how she talks about the trauma.

Depicting the trauma through creative writing was an "incredibly valuable" but not risk-free process for Amanda: to turn a traumatic experience into a literary text is to take a risk – "The risk of having it bruised or misunderstood" by the readers, as Audre Lorde put it.[35] Your readers can misunderstand or react in ways that can hurt you. If your text is met with fear, or disengaged detachment, it is, of course, painful; similar to when Amanda occasionally has told people about what happened to her and they couldn't handle it and reacted with aloofness. But writing about the trauma has made her better at managing the trauma. "It is still there, but the fact that I have now revisited what happened on my own, written about it, talked about it in a new context, makes it easier to endure and relate to."

Social psychologist James W. Pennebaker has, in several studies, shown that people writing about their traumas reported increased psychological well-being. In *Writing to Heal: A Guided Journal for Recovering from Trauma & Emotional Upheaval* (2004), Pennebaker describes how creative writing can transform a person suffering from trauma and how a number of studies testify to the benefits of expressive writing for people suffering from trauma.[36] The process described in Pennebaker's guided journal has similarities to Amanda's and my own experiences of how writing about our respective traumas changed our perspectives. Pennebaker mentions some risks, important to be aware of. Among these is that since the trauma might upset you, put aside writing about what upsets you too much. Be aware of the risk of overanalyzing and navel-gazing. If after several days of writing you do not make progress, you should change your approach. Keep your writing private or only for those who you want to read it. Pennebaker also mentions potential life changes, which of course, are never risk-free. "By reducing your inner conflicts, you may affect the course of your life and the lives of others in unintended ways."[37] To be trauma-informed in the context of creative writing is to be aware of this.

Conclusions and Applications for a Broader Pedagogical Context

This chapter has shown three educational contexts where trauma, literature and creative writing being taught in different ways. In dialogue with Carello and Butler, I have tried to highlight what trauma-informed pedagogy might mean in these contexts. From the field of bibliotherapy, which are. Perhaps, more of a care setting than a strictly educational one, we learned of the importance of putting the participants' needs first, and we let their reactions guide how to design the practice. But we also learned that reading about someone else's trauma can have a healing, consolatory effect on persons suffering from similar traumas. In my own literary trauma course, it was about creating ethical awareness among the students about how to read trauma narratives, but also about focusing on my area of expertise, which is meticulous reading and attentiveness to literary language. In the creative writing context, it was about being aware that transforming the trauma into literature changes one's perspective as well as taking the process step by step and avoiding writing about what feels too upsetting and painful.

But I want to conclude by criticizing Carello and Butler's view, with the help of educational theorist Gert J.J. Biesta. Carello and Butler's trauma-informed perspective comes from a concept called trauma-informed care, a framework developed to improve clinical practice and social service delivery,[38] and they believe this is also highly relevant to educational settings. To be *trauma-informed* is, according to Carello and Butler, to understand:

> how violence, victimization, and other traumatic experiences may have figured in the lives of the individuals involved and to apply that understanding to the provision of services [...] so that they accommodate the needs and vulnerabilities of trauma survivors [...]. A central tenet of this view is that individual safety must be ensured through efforts to minimize

the possibilities for inadvertent retraumatization, secondary traumatization, or wholly new traumatizations in the delivery of services.[39]

It may sound obvious, and considerate, to not expose one's students to risk. And I'm not advocating presenting potentially upsetting material to students just to shock them. But the error I think Carello and Butler make is that they too quickly equate the care sector's provision of services with education. In a care setting their safety-first approach is probably of high importance, but education is not a service delivered to "accommodate the needs and vulnerabilities" of the students. Education requires a willingness of the participating student to grow by having their existing world view shattered, and changed, and this can never be a risk-free endeavor. As teachers from most fields know, staying safe is somewhat opposed to learning new skills, engaging in life and growing as a human being. Gert J.J. Biesta explains this well in *The Beautiful Risk of Education* (2013).

Biesta sees education "as an act of creation" – a creation of the student's subjectivity, and in creation, he emphasis, risk always plays a central role. To give risk a central place in education is important because it prevents the subjects involved from turning into machine-like beings. Trying to minimize the risks in educational settings is also to create an atmosphere where there is no tolerance for failure. "The quest for certainty [...] keeps us away from engaging with life itself," which is risky, uncertain, unpredictable and frustrating.[40] Biesta points out that if "the possibility of subjectivity," "the event of subjectivity" – "those situations in which we are called [...] to take responsibility" – is to happen in class, then the important things for educators is: "[D]o not keep our students away from such experiences, do not shield them from any potential intervention of the other." This, of course, comes with a risk, but "it is only when we are willing to take this risk that the event of subjectivity has a chance to occur."[41]

Carello and Butler mention how literary scholar Shoshana Felman (1991) describes her literature students' reactions to viewing interviews with Holocaust survivors as "a shattering experience." The students were overwhelmed and disconnected. And Carello and Butler find it "alarming [...] that some educators appear to interpret these symptoms as evidence of effective teaching and learning rather than as potentially harmful or undesirable."[42]

But, as my own experience as a student in creative writing shows, as well as Biesta and Pennebaker's research and several of the bibliotherapy studies mentioned above, being shaken, having one's worldview shattered, is also an inalienable part of the development toward new knowledge and perspectives, and an important reason why people with various traumas turn to literature and art. As Franz Kafka famously put it:

> I think we ought to read only the kind of books that wound or stab us. If the book we're reading doesn't wake us up with a blow to the head,

what are we reading for? [...] A book must be the axe for the frozen sea within us.[43]

My discussion above can be summarized in the following applications for a broader pedagogical setting:

1) If learning is the primary goal, both teacher and students involved must be willing to take a risk.
2) Every student group is vulnerable in its own unique way; an educator teaching potentially traumatic material must be sensitive and assess what the group in question can handle and how to discuss the material in a way that will make the students grow as human beings.
3) Teaching traumatic material should include a discussion of the ethical challenges the traumatic material poses and how we can be responsible as readers.
4) If the student group is to work with subjects that are traumatic on a personal level for some of them, it is important that the teacher keep the focus on their area of expertise and what the course aims to teach. Students who want to share personal experiences might do so, but no one should be pushed to share painful experiences in order to create a powerful learning situation.

Notes

1 "catharsis," *Merriam-Webster's Encyclopedia of Literature*, Merriam-Webster (1995), 217. Audre Lorde, "The Transformation of Silence into Language and Action," *Sister Outsider: Essays and Speeches* (Trumansburg, NY: Crossing Press, 1984) [1978], 41.
2 *Trauma and Literature*, ed. J. Roger Kurtz (Cambridge: Cambridge University Press, 2018), 1–2.
3 For more on how trauma theory has been reflected in contemporary fiction and culture see, for instance, Anne Whitehead, *Trauma Fiction* (Edinburgh: Edinburgh University Press, 2004), or *The Future of Trauma Theory: Contemporary Literary and Cultural Criticism*, ed. Gert Buelens, Samuel Durrant and Robert Eaglestone (Abingdon: Routledge, 2013).
4 *The Routledge Companion to Literature and Trauma*, ed. Colin Davis and Hanna Meretoja (London: Routledge, 2020). Lucy Bond and Stef Craps, *Trauma* (Routledge, 2020). Other examples of noticed trauma publications are Jeffrey C. Alexander, *Trauma: A Social Theory* (Malden: Polity, 2012) and Roger Luckhurst, *The Trauma Question* (London: Routledge, 2008).
5 Janice Carello and Lisa D. Butler (2014) "Potentially Perilous Pedagogies: Teaching Trauma Is Not the Same as Trauma-Informed Teaching," *Journal of Trauma & Dissociation*, 15:2 (2014), 153–168.
6 In the anthology *Bibliotherapy*, ed. Sarah McNicol and Liz Brewster (London: Facet Publishing, 2018) case studies from Canada, Uruguay, Australia, the UK and Scotland, and the USA are presented. For an overview of bibliotherapy in the Nordic Countries, see Cecilia Pettersson, *Biblioterapi* (Stockholm: Appell förlag, 2020).

7 Forthcoming: Båth, Katarina, "Trauma as Literature – Literature as Therapy. A dialogue between current bibliotherapeutic practices and literary trauma studies," *The Book As Cure: Bibliotherapy and Literary Caregiving from the First World War to the Present*, eds. Siobhan Campbell, Sara Haslam and Edmund King (Palgrave Macmillan, London, forthcoming 2022/2023).
8 Carello and Butler 2014, 162.
9 Liz Brewster, "Bibliotherapy: A Critical History," in *Bibliotherapy*, 5.
10 *Att tiga eller tala. Litteraturterapi – ett sätt att växa*, ed. Juhani Ihanus, swe transl. Ann-Christine Relander (Helsingfors: BTJ Kirjastopalvelu, 2004), 7.
11 Päivi Kosonen,"Towards Therapeutic Reading," *Scriptum* Vol 5, Issue 2, 2018, 2018, 25
12 Juhani Ihanus "Litteratur och terapi," *Att tiga eller tala*, 7, 22–23, 28–30.
13 Kosonen, "Towards Therapeutic Reading," 34.
14 Ibid., 37, with reference to Christopher Bollas, *Being a Character: Psychoanalysis and Self Experience* (London: Routledge, 1993) and Sirkka Knuuttila, *Fictionalising Trauma: The Aesthetics of Marguerite Duras's India Cycle* (Helsinki: University of Helsinki 2009).
15 Arleen McCarty-Hynes and Mary Hynes-Berry, *Biblio/Poetry Therapy: The Interactive Process: A Handbook*. (St. Cloud, MN: North Star Press, 2012) [1986].
16 Pettersson 2020, 66, Brewster 2011, 6.
17 Pettersson, 2020, 63–66 with reference to Laura J. Cohen, *Bibliotherapy. The Experience of Therapeutic Reading from the Perspective of the Adult Reader*, diss. (New York: New York University, School of Education, Health, Nursing and Arts Professions, 1992) and Elizabeth Brewster, *An Investigation of Experiences of Reading for Mental Health and Well-Being and the Relation to Models of Bibliotherapy*, diss. (Sheffield: University of Sheffield, 2011).
18 Pettersson, 2020, 63–66, Brewster 2011, Cohen 1992.
19 Pettersson 2020, 65, Brewster 2011, 216. See also Cecilia Pettersson, "Psychological Well-being, Improved Self-confidence and Social Capacity: Bibliotherapy from a User Perspective," *Journal of Poetry Therapy*, 31, 2018, 124–134.
20 Pettersson 2020, 69–77.
21 For my above-mentioned article about bibliotherapy and trauma theory, I interviewed Pia Bergström and Eva Bergstedt, bibliotherapy practitioners and teachers of the course "The Bibliotherapeutic Work Procedure" at Ersta Sköndal University College, Stockholm, Sweden. I also interviewed a Swedish Shared Reading practitioner, Åsa Sarachu. Shared Reading is a concept developed in the UK, with the aim of bringing "people together in small groups to read aloud a book, short story or poem." Advocates of Shared Reading explicitly avoid calling their practice bibliotherapy, since they want to stress the nonhierarchical form of the reading group, but the concept has some similarities with creative, interactive group bibliotherapy. http://www.thereader.org.uk/about/whatwedo/#whatissr
22 Nicholas Mazza, *Poetry Therapy: Theory and Practice* (New York: Brunner-Routledge, 2003), 4 with reference to Arthur Lerner, "Poetry Therapy Corner," *Journal of Poetry Therapy*, 7, 54–56.
23 Carello and Butler 2014, 155.
24 Emily T. Troscianko, "Literary reading and eating disorders: survey evidence of therapeutic help and harm," *Journal of Eating Disorders* 6, 8 (2018).
25 Bergström, P. & Omsén, E. (red) (2016). *Du jag vi. Om att ha en förälder i fängelse*. Stockholm: Buff Stockholm. I interviewed Bergström about the project in fall 2018.
26 Eva Selin, *Läsklubb pågår! En metodbok om högläsning som biblioterapi* (Lund: BTJ Förlag, 2019).

27 We read central theoretical texts such as Cathy Caruth, Dori Laub and Shoshana Felman, Kali Tal, and newer theoretical texts, among other texts from *Contemporary Approaches in Literary Trauma Theory,* ed. Michelle Balaev (2014) and Laurie Vickroy, *Trauma and Survival in Contemporary Fiction* (2002). The fiction selection consisted of some classics such as Dostoevsky, Perkins Gilman, Toni Morrison and Art Spiegelman, and more recent Scandinavian literature, including Vigdis Hjorth, Johanna Frid and Yahya Hassan. I tried to select disparate works that embodied various forms of trauma in different genres.
28 We read Susan Sontag's "Regarding the Pain of Others" (2004) and I integrated perspectives from Martin Modlinger and Philipp Sonntag, *Other People's Pain: Narratives of Trauma and the Question of Ethics* (2011) in the discussion.
29 Here, the above-mentioned Modlinger and Sontag's anthology, *Other People's Pain: Narratives of Trauma and the Question of Ethics* (2011) is one example; another is Hanna Meretoja and Colin Davis' 2017 initiative "Trauma Narratives and the Ethics of Reading": a symposium arranged by the research circle Narrative and Memory: Ethics, Aesthetics, Politics, dedicated to "the ethical challenge which trauma narratives pose, as they radically bring into question our responsibility as readers, scholars, subjects, and citizens": https://narrativeandmemory.com/call-2/
30 Parul Sehgal, "The Case Against the Trauma Plot," *The New Yorker,* Dec 27, 2021.
31 Herbert Marcuse, *The Aesthetic Dimension: Toward a Critique of Marxist Aesthetics* (Boston: Beacon Press, 1978).
32 Ethel Spector Person, "How to work through erotic transference" *Psychiatric Times,* Vol 20, No 7, 2003.
33 Benjamin, *Like Subjects, Love Objects,* 160–161.
34 The interview was conducted via Zoom in spring 2022. I have called her Amanda here (which is not her real name).
35 Lorde, "Silence into Language and Action," 40.
36 James W. Pennebaker, *Writing to Heal: A Guided Journal for Recovering from Trauma & Emotional Upheaval* (2004), 4–11.
37 Pennebaker 2004, 15.
38 Carello and Butler 2014, 156, with reference to Harris and Fallot, 2001.
39 Carello and Butler 2014, 156.
40 Gert JJ Biesta, *The Beautiful Risk of Education* (Boulder: Paradigm Publishers, 2013), 17.
41 Biesta 2013, 23.
42 Carello and Butler 2014, 159. With reference to Felman (1991) "Education and crisis, or the vicissitudes of teaching," *American Imago,* 48(1).
43 Kafka states this in a letter to his friend Oskar Pollak in 1904. The English translation of the quote can be found on Goodreads page "Quotable quotes": https://www.goodreads.com/quotes/237620-i-think-we-ought-to-read-only-the-kind-of

References

Alexander, Jeffrey C., *Trauma: A Social Theory* (Malden, MA: Polity, 2012).
Balaev, Michelle, ed., *Contemporary Approaches in Literary Trauma Theory* (Basingstoke: Palgrave Macmillan, 2014).
Benjamin, Jessica, *Like Subjects, Love Objects: Essays on Recognition and Sexual Difference* (New Haven, CT: Yale University Press, 1995).
Bergström, P. and E. Omsén (red), *Du jag vi. Om Att Ha En Förälder I Fängelse* (Stockholm: Buff, 2016).
Biesta, Gert J.J., *The Beautiful Risk of Education* (Boulder, CO: Paradigm Publishers, 2013).

Bollas, Christopher, *Being a Character: Psychoanalysis and Self Experience* (London: Routledge, 1993).
Bond, Lucy and Stef Craps, *Trauma* (London: New Critical Idiom, Routledge, 2020).
Brewster, Elizabeth, *An Investigation of Experiences of Reading for Mental Health and Well-Being and the Relation to Models of Bibliotherapy*, diss. (Sheffield: University of Sheffield, 2011).
Buelens, Gert, Samuel Durrant and Robert Eaglestone, eds., *The Future of Trauma Theory: Contemporary Literary and Cultural Criticism* (Abingdon: Routledge, 2013).
Carello, Janice and Lisa D. Butler, "Potentially perilous pedagogies: Teaching trauma is not the same as trauma-informed teaching," *Journal of Trauma and Dissociation*, 15(2), (2014), 153–168.
Caruth, Cathy (ed.) *Trauma: explorations in memory*, (Baltimore: Johns Hopkins, 1995).
Cohen, Laura J., *Bibliotherapy: The Experience of Therapeutic Reading from the Perspective of the Adult Reader*, diss. (New York: New York University, School of Education, Health, Nursing and Arts Professions, 1992).
Davis, Colin and Hanna Meretoja, eds., *The Routledge Companion to Literature and Trauma* (London: Routledge, 2020).
Felman, Shoshana and Dori, Laub *Testimony: crises of witnessing in literature, psychoanalysis and history*. (London: Routledge, 1992).
Ihanus, Juhani, ed. *Att Tiga Eller Tala. Litteraturterapi – Ett Sätt Att Växa*, swe. transl. Ann-Christine Relander (Helsingfors: BTJ Kirjastopalvelu, 2004).
Knuuttila, Sirkka, *Fictionalising Trauma: The Aesthetics of Marguerite Duras's India Cycle* (Helsinki: University of Helsinki, 2009).
Kosonen, Päivi, "Towards therapeutic reading," *Scriptum*, 5(2), (2018), 25.
Kurtz, J. Roger, ed., *Trauma and Literature* (Cambridge: Cambridge University Press, 2018).
Lorde, Audre, "The transformation of silence into language and action," *Sister Outsider: Essays and Speeches* (Trumansburg, NY: Crossing Press, 1984 [1978]).
Luckhurst, Roger, *The Trauma Question* (London: Routledge, 2008)
Marcuse, Herbert, *The Aesthetic Dimension: Toward a Critique of Marxist Aesthetics* (Boston, MA: Beacon, 1978)
Mazza, Nicholas, *Poetry Therapy: Theory and Practice* (New York: Brunner-Routledge, 2003).
McCarty-Hynes, Arleen and Mary Hynes-Berry, *Biblio/Poetry Therapy: The Interactive Process. A Handbook* (St. Cloud, MN: North Star Press, 2012 [1986]).
McNicol, Sarah and Liz Brewster, eds., *Bibliotherapy* (London: Facet Publishing, 2018).
Merriam-Webster's Encyclopedia of Literature (Springfield, MA: Merriam-Webster, 1995).
Modlinger, Martin and Philipp Sonntag, eds., *Other People's Pain: Narratives of Trauma and the Question of Ethics* (Oxford: Peter Lang, 2011).
Pennebaker, James W., *Writing to Heal: A Guided Journal for Recovering from Trauma & Emotional Upheaval*, (2004), 4–11 (Oakland, CA: New Harbinger Publisher).
Pettersson, Cecilia, "Psychological well-being, improved self-confidence and social capacity: Bibliotherapy from a user perspective," *Journal of Poetry Therapy*, 31(2), (2018), 124–134.
Pettersson, Cecilia, *Biblioterapi* (Stockholm: Appell förlag, 2020).
The Reader, "What We do," https://www.thereader.org.uk/what-we-do/#whatissr (retrieved 2022.05.30).

Sehgal, Parul, "The case Agaist the trauma plot," *The New Yorker*, December 27, 2021. https://www.newyorker.com/magazine/2022/01/03/the-case-against-the-trauma-plot (retrieved 2022.05.30).

Selin, Eva, *Läsklubb pågår! En: metodbok om högläsning som biblioterapi* (Lund: BTJ Förlag, 2019).

Sontag, Susan, *Regarding the Pain of Others* (London: Penguin, 2004).

Spector Person, Ethel, "How to work through Erotic Transference," *Psychiatric Times*, 20(7), (2003). https://www.psychiatrictimes.com/view/how-work-through-erotic-transference (retrieved 2022.05.30).

Troscianko, Emily T., "Literary reading and eating disorders: Survey evidence of therapeutic help and harm," *Journal of Eating Disorders*, 6 (2018), 8.

Vickroy, Laurie, *Trauma and Survival in Contemporary Fiction* (Charlottesville, VA: University of Virginia Press, 2002).

Whitehead, Anne, *Trauma Fiction* (Edinburgh: Edinburgh University Press, 2004).

11
TRIGGER WARNINGS WITH CONSCIENCE

Presenting Texts About Sexual Assault With Respect

Rose Gubele

When I was a graduate student, I had a class in which we watched the film *Once Were Warriors*. Released in 1994, the movie tells the story of a Māori woman, her children, and her abusive husband. This experience occurred long before trigger warnings were used in media and on college campuses. However, my professor warned us that the film contained some graphic content, including a rape scene. I knew, though, that upcoming assignments would be linked to the film, so if I didn't see it, that would affect my grade in the course. As a result, I was left feeling like I had no choice. I watched the film with my class. During the movie, I remained stiff, tense. I wanted to look away during the rape scene, which involved a 13-year-old girl, but I couldn't move. It all seemed unreal, even after the movie ended and my class started discussing the film. I felt like I was outside of myself. I went home after class. In the middle of the night, I woke up screaming.

As an educator, I never want to put my students through the experience I had in my graduate class. However, I understand the importance of academic freedom, and so I understand the concerns raised against trigger warnings. However, much of the controversy surrounding trigger warnings is based on misinformation concerning trauma and the meaning of trauma and triggers. Because of my own experiences, I also know that trigger warnings alone are insufficient. They must be done in a way that makes trauma survivors feel safe enough to request alternate assignments. Alternate assignments must be allowed for students who have experienced trauma, because PTSD is a recognized disability, and providing trigger warnings and alternate assignments are both accommodations. Trigger warnings, if done correctly, are not a threat to academic freedom, and they can give survivors agency.

DOI: 10.4324/9781003260776-13

Triggers, Trauma, and Accommodations

The beginning of the use of trigger warnings is difficult to pinpoint, but some see it as starting in feminist blogs where trigger warnings were used to alert sexual assault survivors about content that contained references to sexual violence (McNally, 2014). Trigger warnings began to be used in media after that. Later, students at Columbia University raised concerns about a rape scene in a classical text, the University of California at Santa Barbara students asked the university to require trigger warnings, and Oberlin College created a guide to trigger warning usage (Morris, 2015).

Trigger warnings were originally intended to alert students who had experienced trauma of potentially triggering scenes in texts and videos. However, in popular culture, trigger warnings have taken on the meaning of a statement that alerts viewers or readers to any content that could potentially be upsetting. The debate concerning trigger warnings is divided among professors and students and has focused on wide-ranging concepts, from trauma recovery to academic freedom (Bentley, 2017). Some of the arguments leveled against trigger warnings suggest that students are asking for them because they are "uncomfortable with the points of view expressed in the classroom and by individual faculty members" (Bass & Clark, 2015, par. 2). Students have been accused of "rebelling against certain assignments, topics, or speakers" (Bass and Clark, 2015, par. 5). Some see trigger warnings as against all that academia supports, as voiced by the American Association of University Professors: "The presumption that students need to be protected rather than challenged in a classroom is at once infantilizing and anti-intellectual" (Committee A on Academic Freedom and Tenure, 2014, par. 3).

Arguments like these assume that students are asking for trigger warnings because they are uncomfortable with course material; however, asking for trigger warnings because of past trauma is different:

> There is a difference between discomfort and trauma. The difference between the two terms has often been ignored in the trigger warning debate. Discomfort jolts us out of our prior perspectives—even if only momentarily. Students can learn and continue to learn *through* discomfort. Trauma, on the other hand, does not simply jolt us out of our own perspectives. Trauma completely disrupts our focus and makes learning virtually impossible.
>
> *(Rae, 2016, p. 95, emphasis in original)*

As Angela M. Carter points out, the "'debate' about trauma in the classroom has been for the able-bodyminded among us"; for those of us who have experienced trauma, we have no choice, "our experiences of trauma shape how we move through the world" (2015, par. 1).

Much of the debate concerning trigger warnings reveals a misunderstanding of what the term "trigger" means. To be "triggered" isn't to be offended or upset by content. The word comes from psychology. Used in the *DSM-V*, the word means an external event or sensory experience which causes the sufferer to experience intrusive memories of trauma. The term is often used in discussions of PTSD, where triggers can be anything that reminds the trauma survivor of the initial traumatic experience (American Psychiatric Association, 2013).

The word "trauma" is frequently misused and applied to any unpleasant situation, but trauma is much more than that. In *Unclaimed Experience: Trauma, Narrative, and History*, Cathy Caruth defines trauma as "the response to an unexpected or overwhelming violent event or events that are not fully grasped as they occur" (2016, p. 94). In sum, trauma is an event that is so severe that the trauma survivor's mind can't process what is happening at the time it occurs. Because the survivor does not completely understand the trauma at the time it happens, memories of the event intrude upon their consciousness in the form of "flashbacks, nightmares, and other repetitive phenomena" (Caruth, 2016, p. 94). Flashbacks and nightmares are not bad memories; they force trauma survivors to reexperience the initial traumatic event. These intrusive memories can be triggered by external sensory input. Of course, teachers cannot control all potential triggers. A scent can be a trigger, for example. However, graphic depictions of sexual violence in literature and film could definitely trigger a sexual-assault survivor.

Though the debate about trigger warnings is complex and multilayered, some of the arguments in favor of trigger warnings are focused on protecting students from retraumatizing experiences. Many of the arguments against trigger warnings that suggest students are being overly sensitive are offensive when considering students with PTSD. In short, forcing students with PTSD to be retraumatized can cause them to have long-lasting symptoms which can include insomnia, depression, irritability, difficulty concentrating, and suicidal ideation, symptoms that could impede their ability to complete any classwork at all (American Psychological Association, 2013, pp. 275–276, 278). PTSD is a recognized disability, so trigger warnings are considered by many to be a disability accommodation:

> To be triggered is to mentally and physically re-experience a past trauma in such an embodied manner that one's affective response literally takes over the ability to be present in one's bodymind. When this occurs, the triggered individuals often feel a complete loss of control and disassociation from the bodymind. This is not a state of injury, but rather a state of disability.
>
> *(Carter, 2015, par. 7)*

I believe that students can be both challenged and protected. As an educator, I always strive to do both. I ask my students to grapple with new and controversial ideas as well as address difficult topics. I want them to think critically and raise questions about the messages they receive. However, I also want them to be safe, and I believe that academia doesn't do enough to protect students. I see trigger warnings not as a way out for students who want to avoid difficult topics but as an accommodation for students with PTSD.

Teachers who include material that depicts sexual violence should consider using trigger warnings as an accommodation. Among survivors of sexual trauma, "81% of women and 35% of men report significant short-term or long-term impacts such as Post-Traumatic Stress Disorder (PTSD)" (National Sexual Violence Resource Center, 2015, par. 9). This is an important consideration for teachers because students experience high rates of sexual assault. According to the National Sexual Violence Resource Center, "one in five women and one in sixteen men are sexually assaulted while in college," and over 90 percent of the victims of sexual violence on campus "do not report the assault" (2015, par. 19). These figures suggest that in each of the classes we teach, we are likely to have at least one sexual assault survivor.

Universities also don't do enough to help sexual assault survivors. Although most universities provided the minimum amount of information required by Title IX, universities do not offer sufficient support for survivors:

> Most schools failed to provide information on important topics such as consent, victim blaming, date and acquaintance rape, and physical and psychological effects of sexual assault. As such, information largely focused on policies, victim services, and the immediate aftermath of assault and thus did not take a perpetrator-focused view of rape prevention (e.g., focusing on combating rape myths). Similarly, there was not a common focus on universal victim support (e.g., combating victim blaming and rape myths). Thus, colleges and universities appear to favor a solely procedural and crisis-focused approach to sexual assault, as opposed to a feminist, prevention-focused, or joint approach.
>
> *(Lund & Thomas, 2015, p. 537)*

In addition, the lack of education about sexual assault on campuses can thwart its prevention. A study conducted of over 2,000 undergraduates found that misconceptions about rape, or "rape myths" which were believed by many undergraduates, caused them to not intervene if they saw a rape in process (McMahon, 2010). Sexual assault survivors on college campuses also experience more severe trauma because they are not protected by their universities. In situations where sexual violence occurs in an institution that is trusted to provide safety, survivors experience "betrayal trauma" because the institution failed to protect them (Smith, 2013, p. 120). Survivors on college campuses are left with minimal institutional support and a sense of betrayal, as well as shame and self-blame.

Sexual Assault and Native Americans

If we view trigger warnings as a disability accommodation, we should be required by law to provide them. Given the high rate of sexual assault on college campuses, teachers need to understand that students in each of their classes will be trauma survivors. Presenting literature or films with scenes of sexual violence to students in college is, then, very tricky. Also, in my experience, trigger warnings do not do enough to help trauma survivors. Telling students that trauma is coming doesn't make the trauma less severe, in the same way that telling someone they are going to be hit by a car would lessen the severity of their pain. But those who have concerns about trigger warnings express even greater concerns for alternate assignments, calling this practice censorship and a threat to academic freedom. As a teacher, I don't want to ever cause my students trauma. But I also don't want to censor important content.

I teach a Native American literature course in a small town in rural western Missouri. Missouri has no federally recognized Indian tribes, and my area is populated by non-Indian people here who know very little about Native Americans. Many of the people in Missouri have no exposure to Native Americans except what they see in the media, so they tend to believe all of the most egregious stereotypes. I bear the responsibility of educating this population. To both dispel stereotypes and accurately portray the realities that Native Americans face daily I introduce my students to a variety of texts featuring a range of indigenous experiences. I have long believed that trauma is an important aspect to introduce because it has touched so many Native Americans. It also has touched our students, so this is an important topic for them to make cross-cultural connections.

Rape is one of the many traumas my class covers. I don't approach the subject lightly. I am aware that many of my students are probably sexual assault or childhood sexual abuse survivors. Though the subject is very difficult for both me and my students, it is vitally important for me to cover it so that my students understand colonization more fully. Rape and colonialism are inextricably linked. In "Father God and Rape Culture," Paula Gunn Allen argues that rape and colonialism both come from the same ideology, "the 'civilized' belief that the strong must prevail over the weak, the superior over the inferior, the violent over the peaceful, and the order of patriarchy over all, leads inexorably to rape" (1998, p. 66). As an "exercise in power," rape "is a fundamental result of colonialism" (Brownmiller, 1993, p. 256; Deer, 2015).

In addition, I find that most non-Natives are unaware of the extent to which sexual trauma impacts Native Americans. Native women (and I would argue, men and Two-Spirits as well) have a greater risk of being raped than non-Natives. An Amnesty International report states that "Native women are more than 2.5 times more likely to be raped or sexually assaulted than women in the USA in general" (2006, p. 2). According to the 2010 National Intimate Partner and Sexual Violence Survey, 26.9 percent of American Indian or Alaska Native women have been raped during their lives (Black et al., 2011, p. 3). The survey also stated that 49 percent of American Indian or Alaska Native women have experienced some kind of sexual violence during their lives (Black et al., 2011, p. 20). These numbers, though already extremely high, almost certainly do not portray the extent of the trauma experienced by Native women:

> Amnesty International's interviews with survivors, activists and support workers across the USA suggest that available statistics greatly underestimate the severity of the problem. In the Standing Rock Sioux Reservation, for example, many of the women who agreed to be interviewed could not think of any Native women within their community who had not been subjected to sexual violence.
> *(Amnesty International, 2006, p. 2)*

Skewed perceptions of Native women compounded by an insufficient and racist legal system make prosecution difficult, if not impossible (Deer, 2015, pp. 101–102, 105). This is, in part, because "federal prosecutors decline to prosecute 67 percent of sexual abuse cases" (Erdrich, 2013, par. 5).

One of the reasons for the low prosecution rate is the difficulty with jurisdictional issues that arise when rapes are committed on reservation land, especially if they are committed by non-Native offenders. According to a 1978 Supreme Court ruling, tribes do not have jurisdiction over non-Natives. The Minnesota Indian Women's Resource Center argues that this gap has attracted predators to reservation lands, and reports in Minnesota have noted an increase in the number of rapes on reservations around the time of hunting season (Erdrich, 2013, par. 6). More than 80 percent of men who rape Native women are non-Native (Erdrich, 2013, par. 5). In short, the statistics suggest that white men go hunting for women to rape on reservation lands because they know it is unlikely that they will be prosecuted.

Trigger Warnings in a Native American Literature Class

Trigger warnings are not a threat to academic freedom, but as I say at the beginning of this chapter, alone they are not enough. In my own experience that I recounted earlier, my teacher did warn the class that a traumatic scene was coming. However, at the time, I didn't know that I had PTSD, and I had no idea that it was considered a disability for which I could receive accommodations. All I knew was I wanted to do well in class, and to do that, I believed I had to face a traumatic scene. The aftereffects of that day in class were far-reaching. I plunged into an episode of major depression, and though I did receive treatment and support from my university, I had to cut back on my coursework. It took me much longer to complete my MA because of the experience. An alternate assignment would have been helpful for me. However, alternate assignments aren't always possible.

As someone living daily with PTSD, I know what I am asking of my students when I introduce them to traumatic content. However, as an educator, I also know that in some cases, the traumatic content must be covered. We can't, for example, stop teaching students about important, but traumatic, historical events. We come close to censoring our teaching when we do that. Even if we did provide alternate assignments for all potentially traumatizing material, it would not be possible to completely shield our students. Students with PTSD could be triggered by a scent or the color of a room. However, there are things we can do to make it safer for students who have PTSD. In the following section, I discuss my process as I teach a Native American Literature class. I use the following steps to support students: 1) I provide a trigger warning at the beginning of the course, both in writing and verbally; 2) I provide ways for students with PTSD to opt out of the most explicit traumatic content; 3) whenever possible, I include required texts that don't depict graphic depictions of traumatic events; 4) I establish a safe atmosphere that encourages students to come forward; and 5) I listen and offer access to support services.

Provide a Trigger Warning at the Beginning of the Course, Both in Writing and Verbally

It is important to me that my students know about how sexual violence affects Native Americans, so I created a trigger warning that serves as the beginning of my method for working respectfully with survivors. I place the trigger warning in my syllabus, so the students see it when we go over the document at the beginning of the semester. Simply providing the trigger warning alone is not sufficient. I discuss it with the class on the first day of the semester. Students must know if there is traumatic content coming at the beginning of the course. That will enable them to drop the class without incurring fees if they are not ready to face the issues raised in the class. Below is the note that I include in my syllabus:

> **A Note to Survivors**
>
> Several of the course readings deal with sexual assault or sexual abuse. I have all of these readings labeled with trigger warnings. I know that these readings will be difficult, but I am asking you to read these if you are able. I don't make this request lightly. Most Native Americans know at least one friend who has been violated; many of us have many friends and family members who have experienced it. I am asking the class to read these pieces of literature because of the enormous impact that sexual assault has had on Native American communities. Also, because many Native Americans live on reservation land, questions of jurisdiction make

it difficult to prosecute offenders. To understand Native American culture and Native American literature, this very painful issue has to be addressed.

However, I know that for survivors, these pieces can be very traumatic to read and can trigger nightmares and depression. I want to find a balance—I need you to know the facts concerning sexual assault and American Indians, but I respect your healing process, and I don't wish to cause you further trauma. Please speak to me if you find that you cannot face some of the readings. I ask that you know the details about tribal jurisdiction and other issues concerning sexual assault and Native Americans. But many of the readings on this topic can be avoided. I will only test you on *The Round House*, but not the other readings that have been marked with a trigger warning, so you can avoid them if that is what you need. You may miss class on days we discuss these pieces, but make sure to get notes from a trusted classmate, or ask me, and I will get notes from someone for you.

In this statement to survivors, I show respect and understanding. I don't come out and say that I have PTSD, I say that the material "can trigger nightmares and depression," which suggests that I understand PTSD. I want to be sure that they know that they can trust me, that I am a safe person for them to talk to, if they fear that the material will be too much for them to handle at the present moment. Healing is a process, and I want students to know that I respect their healing process. Healing should not be forced.

Provide Ways for Students With PTSD to Opt-Out of the Most Explicit Traumatic Content

I respect their decisions about what content they can and cannot read. I don't want them to feel ashamed or reluctant to talk to me. The important thing is to let them know that they have a choice. When a person is raped, their control is taken away by the rapist. If I force students to view material that they are not ready to see, I risk traumatizing them not only with the material but with my actions. So, I make sure that my students have the power to say no to content (Rae, 2016).

It's important to note that any discussion of sexual assault will trigger some survivors, even if we don't read material that depicts traumatic scenes of sexual violence. Just talking about the issue can be too much. This is why I include my trigger warning in the syllabus at the beginning of the semester. My course is one of two possible courses that students who are seeking a Bachelor of Science in Education can take at my institution. In other words, they don't have to take my class—they can seek out another course to fulfill their requirements. So, if they are unable to face the material we cover, they can drop without harming their chances of graduating on time.

Include Required Texts That Don't Depict Graphic Scenes of Trauma

I assign *The Round House* by Louise Erdrich. This is a text I require all of my students to read, even survivors. The novel deals with sexual assault, but the actual assault is not shown in the novel. For this reason, it's a good choice for survivors, but it also is helpful to educate those who don't know much about sexual assault. In *The Round House*, Erdrich brings all the complex legal issues surrounding rape on reservation land into play. The novel tells the story of Geraldine Coutts who is brutally raped in the grounds of the Round House, a location that sits at the intersection of "Tribal trust, state, and fee" land (Erdrich, 2012, p. 160). Because each class of land is governed by different authorities (tribal, state, and federal authorities), the prosecution of the crime seems unlikely. Additionally, Geraldine is raped by a non-Indian man, another factor that will hinder the prosecution of the crime.

The assault occurs before the beginning of the novel, and the story is told from the point of view of Geraldine's son, Joe, who is only 13. The novel reads like a mystery novel—rather than focusing on the crime, Erdrich focuses on who did it and how to bring them to justice. The characters, especially Joe, engage in novice investigating, and the reader is drawn into the mystery. Joe becomes an Indian Hardy Boy or Nancy Drew, adopting the amateur sleuth role, a popular formula that the dominant culture knows very well.

In the first part of the novel, Joe and his father find Geraldine bleeding and injured. At first, Joe doesn't know what happened to his mother. He shoves aside the thought of rape when a racist white woman in the hospital waiting room introduces the idea (Erdrich, 2012, p. 9). Readers see Joe struggle with not knowing, not wanting to know and then realizing what he has known all along, and his struggles mirror the reader's reactions. From the beginning, though, Joe is the focus of the novel, not Geraldine. It is only because Joe loves his mother, and wants everything to go back to the way it was, that the reader focuses on Geraldine's trauma.

What Erdrich's audience needs to hear is that rape does not just impact the person who is attacked. As Deborah Miranda argues, "The ripples of a rape spread in every direction. How we respond to rape determines whether those ripples continue to be destructive, or move towards restoration" (2010, p. 105). Rape is a difficult topic to discuss. However, through Joe, the readers see that rape is not an isolated crime—it affects the entire family. The men in the story desperately wish to help Geraldine, but they can't. Joe's father, Bazil, is a tribal judge, and he is powerless to help his wife. Joe tries to help, even though he is only 13. The women in the story are aware that this could happen to them. The whole community is scarred by the trauma (Tharp, 2014). As Julie Tharp points out, "Despite the emotional difficulty," the novel "creates an approach that seems almost calculated to attract and transform readers" (2014, p. 29).

Erdrich teaches readers lessons through Joe. Readers with no experience with sexual trauma learn as he learns; they see what helps and what does not. Joe is old enough to understand initially what happened to his mother, but not old enough to grasp the full complexity of the trauma. He grows up quickly, and readers grow with him. They learn about post-traumatic stress, as they see Joe face his mother's change in behavior. Readers see the complex jurisdictional issues which make prosecuting rape so difficult as they see Joe work with his father and read tribal law books to find some way to prosecute the offender. They see Joe become jaded.

The Round House can be triggering, but it is far easier for survivors than a book with an explicit rape scene. The novel is the reason I put the trigger warning in my syllabus and discuss it with them at the beginning of the semester. Depending on where a survivor is in her healing process, she may not be able to read and discuss a novel like *The Round House* without completely dismantling her life. I give students the opportunity to drop the class if that's what they need.

Establish a Safe Atmosphere That Encourages Students to Come Forward

I work to create a safe environment in my classroom because I know that "For students who have experienced the abusive exercise of power that characterizes sexual assault, heightened anxiety in a context that is already organized around power disparity can be a trigger" (Crumpton, 2017, p. 138). As a teacher, I am the one in a position of power. My goal is to demonstrate my vulnerability so that my students perceive me on more equal terms. In my class, I don't shy away from difficult topics. I talk about PTSD and its symptoms. I tell students that they can come to me if they need alternate assignments and I promise them that I will listen without judgment. In my experience, I found that teachers had one of two reactions to material that depicts sexual trauma. My teachers would either not talk about it at all, or they would push too hard and ask too many questions, which made me feel uncomfortable. When survivors do come to me, I don't press them with questions, but I listen if they trust me enough to tell me what happened to them. I also say things in class to make survivors feel safe. For example, in my trigger warning, I mention some of the symptoms of PTSD. This lets students know that I understand what they are facing and how serious it is.

I never say anything to suggest that we all have to learn to deal with difficult topics (which is something some of my teachers said to my classes when I was in school). Statements like that suggest that everyone is coming from the same set of experiences, and nothing can be farther from the truth. Some students do not know anything about sexual assault. Some believe rape myths they have heard. Some have histories of trauma that make the material too difficult to bear. The challenge is to educate the first two kinds of students without causing further trauma to the third group.

Listen and Offer Access to Support Services

Whenever a survivor comes to talk to me about sexual assault, I provide her with resources, such as the university's counseling center. It's important to understand that many of our students don't realize that they have PTSD. I have talked to many students who came to me simply to explain why they were not doing well in class; they then stated that their difficulties in the class started because they were raped. Often, survivors blame themselves for not being able to concentrate on their work. When students make these kinds of statements, I suggest that they talk to a counselor. I tell them that they could be having symptoms of PTSD or depression and that there are things that can be done to help them. I tell them that what they have experienced (the sexual assault) and what they are experiencing (likely symptoms of PTSD) are not their fault. I have also walked them over to the counseling center.

Trigger Warnings Across Disciplines

Though my class is a literature class, the same approach can easily be used in other subjects, such as history, sociology, women and gender studies, film studies, and communication. My method is not complex, but it is difficult to do because it involves taking personal risks. I don't hide my emotions. I can't remain emotionless when talking about the harm that sexual assault causes, and I don't try. I warn the students ahead of time about the course content, support them, and I don't back down. I have ideas that I want to cover in class, and I make sure that we do. I am empathetic and compassionate to my students, but I don't omit important course content.

It is also difficult because finding materials that address traumatic subjects respectfully is a challenge. I will be using sexual assault and abuse for my examples, but the same can be said of any kind of traumatic content. Textbooks often adopt the same strategy that I have seen teachers adopt when discussing traumatic topics—avoid or overemphasize. Neither method is helpful. Trauma is a part of life—we have to talk about it, and we have to talk about the emotions that come up when it is discussed.

Not addressing trauma in class can have long-term effects that perpetuate the stigma surrounding sexual assault. For example, Carolyn Byerly reviewed several journalism textbooks and she "found that journalism textbooks typically address the problem of whether and when to name rape victims, but otherwise provide no comprehensive discussion of rape or its reporting" (1994, p. 62). This is a crucial issue, since news reporters interview rape victims. The focus of the textbooks fosters programs that emphasize reporting strategies "rather than developing knowledge and understanding of specific kinds of victimization and how to use this knowledge to develop sensitive, effective interviews and stories" (Byerly, 1994, p. 64). This means that new journalists go out into the field where they interview rape survivors with no real training concerning how to talk to victims of trauma. This presents a scenario where survivors could be further traumatized.

Too much emphasis on trauma can be just as harmful. Janice Carello and Lisa Butler examined several classes from a variety of disciplines where instructors required students to write about personal traumas. They found that "Instructors' accounts of their pedagogical practices suggest that their students are experiencing retraumatization and/or secondary traumatization in response to coursework" (2013, p. 158). In these classes, students were often unaware of the content of the course before enrolling and were required to write about traumatic events in explicit detail in order to do well in the classes (Carello & Butler, 2013). This kind of approach can cause serious harm to survivors and can be exploitative.

Omitting discussions of rape in the class is not helpful for survivors because, ultimately, it perpetuates the stigma surrounding sexual assault. However, overemphasizing rape to the point where students are required to write about their traumas, retraumatizing them in the process, is certainly not helpful either. A good model for how to address rape in the classroom comes from Rosalyn Cooperman, Melinda Patterson, and Jess Rigelhaupt who describe a freshman-level political science course entitled "Race and Revolution." The course focuses on women and the Civil Rights Movement. As the authors point out, discussions of the Civil Rights Movement in political science classes often emphasize male Civil Rights leaders. Women, though included, are "often treated as accidental heroes rather than leaders in their own right" (2016, p. 558). Cooperman, Patterson, and Rigelhaupt use Rosa Parks as an example. While Parks has been portrayed as "a tired seamstress whose refusal to give up her seat on the bus laid bare a nation's consciousness about the evils of racial segregation," she was actually an activist long before the incident on the bus (2016, p. 558). Many textbooks present the stereotypical view of Parks, so the authors introduce students to two books: *At the Dark End of the Street: Black Women, Rape, and the Rise of Black Power* by Danielle McGuire and *The Rebellious Life of Mrs. Rosa Parks* by Jeanne Theoharis. The books describe Parks' role as investigator for the NAACP and discusses Parks' investigation into the gang rape of a black woman named Recy Taylor in 1944, a crime that was not prosecuted. The men who raped Taylor were white, a common occurrence at that time in the south (2016, p. 559).

The rape is not the focus of the class, but it is an important part of the story. Parks was motivated by the injustice she saw to bring about change. Rape is not fixated upon in this lessen nor is discussion of it avoided altogether. The class reveals what rape truly is: "It is nothing more or less than a conscious process of intimidation by which all men keep all women in a state of fear" (Brownmiller, 1993, p. 15). Though Brownmiller focuses on gender in the previous quote, rape is also a tool of colonial power and racial dominance, and that is how it is presented here.

Understanding what rape really is helps students to understand power dynamics at play between men and women, between people of color and the dominant society, and in any other situation involving unequal power dynamics. This kind of an approach to discussions of rape educates all students. Students who are not survivors begin to look at rape as something more than sexual. Survivors begin to see how their abusers tried to take their power away. As Mary A. Nyangweso argues, "Sexual violence as a social reality can only be taught effectively if we interrogate the complex social variables that inform it" (2017, p. 180).

Final Comments

When I was in school, I was certain that I was alone. I didn't think my instructors or other students would understand anything that was happening to me. That was, in part, because no one ever talked about PTSD symptoms, depression, or mental health. Sexual assault was not a subject discussed either. It's important for teachers to know that though it can be triggering for survivors to hear classroom discussions about rape, not talking about sexual assault at all can be isolating. I think isolation is worse than being triggered. After I saw the film I describe early in this chapter, I sought out the work of Deborah Miranda, a poet who was raped when she was seven by a family friend (Miranda, 1996). Miranda had just released her first book of poetry, *Indian Cartography*, and the book includes poems about the rape and her healing process. Reading Miranda's work made me feel less alone. Not facing trauma is even more harmful in some ways than facing it. As Miranda writes:

> The loss itself is never denied in a healthy recovery; a person who says, "Oh, I was raped, but it's been twelve months and I'm over that now," is continuing to act as a victim; voiceless, unacknowledged even to herself. Silence may allow a victim to become somewhat functional, but the energy necessary to labor under that kind of unresolved trauma is draining and limits your ability to form relationships, live fully, and be a creative, fulfilled human being.
>
> *(2010, pp. 104–105)*

For me, and for other survivors I know, silence is death. Facing trauma is hard, but a necessary step to healing. Though the experiences I had in that class were extremely difficult, I am not sorry that they happened. The timing was not ideal, but then, there is never a good time to face past trauma. What transpired in that class caused me to pursue my own wellness, which was an important step that helped me live my life.

I am in no way suggesting that teachers act as counselors. Most of us, except for those of us trained in psychology, are not prepared to do that, and could cause more harm than help if we tried. However, what I am suggesting is that if we truly want academic freedom, we have to be willing to talk about trauma ourselves. I have seen many teachers who are eager to present a book or film that features a rape scene because they value academic freedom, and then they refuse to talk about it in class or they talk around it. It is difficult to discuss topics like sexual assault in class, so I understand this, but presenting material and not discussing it is very harmful to survivors. It suggests that they are unspeakable.

Every time I discuss sexual trauma in my own classes it is difficult for me. Seeing students who I recognize as survivors tears at my soul. I don't do it because of academic freedom, though I value academic freedom. I do it because so few people know the extent of the impact sexual trauma has had on Native communities. So few survivors understand the power dynamics involved in sexual violence. My students remember my lessons. Many of my students are future K-12 teachers, and I keep in touch with them and know that they take my lessons to their own students. The work I do is serious, and difficult, but vitally important. I think that's the mindset we need to adopt, to teach information that students must know to make this world a better place, and do it with respect and compassion.

References

Allen, P. G. (1998). Father god and rape culture. In *Off the reservation: Reflections on boundary-busting, border-crossing loose canons* (pp. 63–83). Beacon Press.

American Psychiatric Association. (2013). *Diagnostic and statistical manual of mental disorders, fifth edition*. American Psychiatric Publishing, Inc. https://doi.org/10.1176/appi.books.9780890425596

Amnesty International. (2006). *Maze of injustice: The failure to protect indigenous women from sexual violence in the USA*. https://www.amnestyusa.org/pdfs/mazeofinjustice.pdf

Bass, S. A., & Clark, M. L. (2015, September 28). The gravest threat to colleges comes from within. *The Chronicle of Higher Education*. https://www.chronicle.com/article/the-gravest-threat-to-colleges-comes-from-within/?cid=gen_sign_in

Bentley, M. (2017). Trigger warnings and the student experience. *Politics*, 37(4), 470–485. https://doi-org.cyrano.ucmo.edu/10.1177/0263395716684526

Black, M. C., Basile, K. C., Breiding, M. J., Smith, S. G., Walters, M. L., Merrick, M. T., ... Stevens, M. R. (2011). *The national intimate partner and sexual violence survey: 2010 summary report*. The Centers for Disease Control and Prevention, National Center for Injury Prevention and Control. http://www.cdc.gov/ViolencePrevention/pdf/NISVS_Report2010-a.pdf

Brownmiller, S. (1993). *Against our will: Men, women and rape*. Fawcett Columbine. (Original work published 1975).

Byerly, C. M. (1994). An agenda for teaching news coverage of rape. *The Journalism Educator*, 49(1), 59–69. https://login.cyrano.ucmo.edu/login

Carello, J., & Butler, L. (2013). Potentially perilous pedagogies: Teaching trauma is not the same as trauma-informed teaching. *Journal of Trauma and Dissociation*, 15(2), 153–168. https://doi.org/10.1080/15299732.2014.867571

Carter, A. M. (2015). Teaching with trauma: Trigger warnings, feminism, and disability pedagogy. *Disability Studies Quarterly, 35*(2). https://dsq-sds.org/article/view/4652/3935

Caruth, C. (2016). *Unclaimed experience: Trauma, narrative, and history*. Johns Hopkins University Press. (Original work published 1996).

Committee A on Academic Freedom and Tenure. (2014). *On trigger warnings*. American Association of University Professors. https://www.aaup.org/report/trigger-warnings

Cooperman, R., Patterson, M., & Rigelhaupt, J. (2016). Teaching race and revolution: Doing justice to women's roles in the struggle for civil rights. *PS: Political Science and Politics, 49*(3), 558–561. http://www.jstor.org/stable/24771768

Crumpton, S. M. (2017). Trigger warnings, covenants of presence, and more: Cultivating safe space for theological discussions about sexual trauma. *Teaching Theology and Religion, 20*(2), 137–147. https://doi.org/10.1111/teth.12376

Deer, S. (2015). *The beginning and end of rape: Confronting sexual violence in native America*. University of Minnesota Press.

Erdrich, L. (2013, February 26). Rape on the reservation. *New York Times*. https://www.nytimes.com/2013/02/27/opinion/native-americans-and-the-violence-against-women-act.html

Erdrich, L. (2012). *The round house*. HarperCollins Publishers.

Lund, E. M., & Thomas, K. B. (2015). Necessary but not sufficient: Sexual assault information on college and university websites. *Psychology of Women Quarterly, 39*(4), 530–538. https://doi.org/10.1177/0361684315598286

McMahon, S. (2010). Rape myth beliefs and bystander attitudes among incoming college students. *Journal of American College of Health, 59*(1), 3–11. https://doi.org/10.1080/07448481.2010.483715

McNally, R. J. (2014). Hazards ahead: Five studies you should read before you deploy a trigger warning. *Pacific Standard: The Science of Society, 7*. https://psmag.com/hazards-aheadthe-problem-with-trigger-warnings-according-tothe-research-4f220f7e6c7e#.7jn7u493c

Miranda, D. (2010). "Saying the padre had grabbed her": Rape is the weapon, story is the cure. *Intertexts, 14*(2), 93–112.

Miranda, D. (1996). Silver. In N. Maglin & D. Perry (Eds.), *"Bad girls"/"good girls": Women, sex and power in the nineties* (pp. 125–133). Rutgers University Press.

Morris, L. V. (2015). Editor's page: Trigger warnings. *Innovative Higher Education, 40*(5), 373–374. https://doi.org/10.1007/s10755-015-9342-7

National Sexual Violence Resource Center. (2015). *Info and stats for journalists: Statistics about sexual violence*. https://www.nsvrc.org/sites/default/files/2015-01/publications_nsvrc_factsheet_media-packet_statistics-about-sexual-violence_0.pdf

Nyangweso, M. A. (2017). Intersectionality, education, and advocacy against sexual violence. *Journal of Feminist Studies in Religion, 33*(1), 180–182. https://doi.org/10.2979/jfemistudreli.33.1.24

Rae, L. (2016). Re-focusing the debate on trigger warnings: Privilege, trauma, and disability in the classroom. *First Amendment Studies, 50*(2), 95–102.

Smith, C. P., & Freyd, J. J. (2013). Dangerous safe havens: Institutional betrayal exacerbates sexual trauma. *Journal of Traumatic Stress, 26*(1), 119–124. https://doi.org/10.1002/jts.21778

Tharp, J. (2014). Erdrich's crusade: Sexual violence in the round house. *Studies in American Indian Literatures, 26*(3), 25–40. https://login.cyrano.ucmo.edu/login

12
LGBTQ+ TRAUMA-INFORMED PEDAGOGY IN A TRANSNATIONAL CONTEXT

Jason Lee, Beverley Hancock-Smith, Zara Hooley, and Eleanor McSherry

Introduction

Well-being in universities became even more of a focus due to the global pandemic (2019–2022), but financially many universities were already under-resourced, which had an impact on how they dealt with trauma. Without more investment, we could find students who are unknown to their instructors educated solely via automated processes. The dangers of turning education into a dehumanising process have been illustrated for at least half a century (Illich, 1971). Within such a climate, how then can teachers consider LGBTQ+ trauma-informed pedagogy (TIP)? Unless detailed interviews take place, it is unlikely teachers will know their students' backgrounds, whether they be LGBTQ+ or have experienced some form of trauma, or both. TIP can focus on large traumatic events, such as those involving indigenous populations, or the Holocaust, and specific materials can be used, including those that take a nuanced approach to LGBTQ+ relationships (Lee, 2018). In the context of teaching creative writing, empathy and a heightened sensitivity to those present in the workshop is necessary. There are several books that tackle the psychology of this process (Lee, 2014).

Suggesting a move away from a supplier and consumer relationship in education is not new either (Illich, 1971), but this point still needs making. In creative subjects, such as film and television degrees, even at undergraduate level, some universities do interview students in groups, but can we always expect students to talk personally about themselves in a group format? The two case studies that follow explore this. It can be predicted that those suffering from trauma will be less confident, more anxious, and less likely to enter the classroom in the first place; attain the grades necessary to enter university; or attend interviews.

DOI: 10.4324/9781003260776-14

Worryingly, some research on trauma-informed pedagogy emphasises compliance as being an attribute a teacher wants from their student. Of course, teachers at all levels want their students to engage with the topic, but the use of the term compliance suggests a rigidity that is not benign for creative learning. According to Sharp, to have a truly trauma-informed approach we need to change the foundations of the university. As Sharp states, we live in a rape culture, students need to unlearn experiences, plus an instructor must realise that trauma and triggering do not always happen in the way we expect (Sharp, 2022, pp. 13–39). If we do not know our students, there is always the danger of re-traumatisation, plus we should continue to examine intersectional influences including disability.

Why LGBTQ+ as a Focus?

The extent of the persecution experienced by sexual minorities and gender non-conformists throughout the 20th century (Plummer, 2000; Adam, 2004; Jennings, 2007a; Doan, 2017) gives justification to an approach which foregrounds sexuality and gender identification as a relevant contemporary axis of oppression. The depiction of LGBTQ+ people as dangerous and immoral and in need of containment to the private domain (Adam, 2004) has cast a long shadow into the 21st century. Latterly, the fight to protect authentic self-expression and achieve equality in civil liberties has long occupied activists from the transgender and genderqueer movement (Monro, 2005; Hines, 2007; Coll-Planas and Missé, 2021). Nevertheless, pervasive social scripts around appropriate behaviour and presentation of self still abound, and LBGTQ+ individuals experience daily microaggressions (Nadal et al., 2016). This minority stress (Meyer, 2003), combined with a higher likelihood of having undergone traumatic life experiences (Craig et al., 2020), arguably make the needs of LGBTQ+ students unique.

Labels of any sort can be problematically reductive. As discussed by Weeks et al. (2001, p. vii; see also Hicks, 2011, p. 14), labels can be tied to constructed ideas of respectability and belonging, identity, and differentiation. The naming or labelling of a sexual or gender identity minority is a political act; therefore, this needs to begin with the idea of categories as part of the shifting sands of what it means to belong within society. In terms of transnational differences, labels are culturally contextual and dependent on the unique political history of the locality. As discussed by Coll-Planas and Missé (2021), categorisations around gender identity developed differently in the environment of post-Franco dictatorship of Barcelona. A more fluid definition emerged, compared to the medicalized "transexual" emphasis in other Western countries. Some homogenisation of terms is necessary to achieve a discussion, however, this loss of cultural context should not be ignored.

Where possible, this chapter is built on an LGBTQ+ inclusive perspective and will use that acronym when it accurately reflects the populations in the studies discussed. Originally theorized within the context of racial discrimination, microaggression theory (Sue and Capodilupo, 2008) is a useful lens to understand the experience of minority groups. Microaggression can be defined as behaviours and statements, often unconscious, that transmit aggressive or pejorative communications, particularly to members of an already targeted group (Nadal et al., 2016). Despite the perception that overt displays of prejudice or hostility towards minority groups has become less common, research indicates that people tend to hold implicit and explicit bias which affect the way they interact with minority individuals (Nadal et al., 2016).

Discussion of microaggressions has become particularly pertinent within the liberal setting of UK universities. Microaggressions are subtle and covert (Sue and Capodilupo, 2008) but have a negative effect on self-esteem particularly when occurring in an educational context (Nadal et al., 2014). Nadal, Rivera, and Corpus (2010) discussed eight themes of microaggressions related to LGBTQ+ people, ranging from the use of heterosexist or transphobic terminology to the denial of LGBTQ+ oppression. Theme two speaks most directly to the presentation of authentic self within the classroom. This theme gives an overview of behaviours that endorse gender-conforming and heteronormative cultures in which LGBTQ+ people are expected to hide their sexual orientation or gender identity. This literature indicated that LGBTQ+ individuals, and specifically LGBTQ+ students, experience a range of subtle heterosexist and gender-conforming social norms which materialise through microaggressions in their everyday lives. Meyer (2003) proposes that the constant regulation of self within this environment of stigma and prejudice has a causal relationship to the higher rates of mental illness in LGBTQ+ populations. This negotiation of stigma and prejudice is framed as minority stress theory (Meyer, 2003).

LGBTQ+ Trauma

It has been argued that the extra burden of minority stress explains mental health disparities in LGBTQ+ populations (Meyer, 2003). It is certainly true that young people with a minority sexual orientation (Miranda-Mendizábal et al., 2017) or minority gender identification (Craig et al., 2020) are more likely to attempt suicide than their heterosexual peers. It is also apparent that this trend does not appear to be decreasing with increasing access to basic civil rights over time (Friedman et al., 2011). The relationship between LGBTQ+ specific factors and mental health is discussed by Gnan et al. (2019) within a UK university setting. Gnan et al. demonstrate that LGBTQ+ factors are associated with a higher suicide risk and suggest that specific attention is needed for the most vulnerable LGBTQ+ student groups such as female, bisexual, and transgender individuals.

The ongoing experience of minority stress for students should not be underestimated but there is also evidence to suggest that LGBTQ+ people are also more likely to have experienced early-life trauma (Craig et al., 2020; Wang et al., 2021). Craig et al. (2020) found that exposure to adverse childhood experiences was consistently high for all populations within this community, especially pansexual, transgender and gender diverse youths. No causality is implied in this research; however, a correlation was found between LGBTQ+ identities and high levels of family dysfunction and emotional abuse. Craig et al. suggest that the combination of the higher levels of adverse childhood experiences and identity-based minority stressors merge to put the emotional well-being of this group into a higher risk category. This finding is echoed by Friedman et al. (2011) who found that LGBTQ+ youths were 3.8 times more likely to have suffered sexual abuse than heterosexual peers. An increased risk was also apparent across experiences of parental physical abuse (Friedman et al., 2011).

The drawing together of this body of evidence highlights that LGBTQ+ students are at a higher risk of trauma, both from everyday microaggressions and early-life experiences. LGBTQ+ individuals are at a higher risk of experiencing assault at school, or missing school through fear (Friedman et al., 2011). Starting university marks another beginning. This can be an opportunity to reinvent oneself and find a friendship group drawn from a larger and more diverse population than secondary school. Conversely it also marks a series of "coming out" moments; new people, new educators, and the need to tell our identity stories repeatedly. Coming out can take on a different meaning for different people, but for most it is a transformative process (Guittar, 2013). Guittar (2013) found that for some it is about self-affirmation, but for others it is about sharing their sexuality to enable them to be their full authentic self in moments of social connection.

These "coming out" moments can be highly stressful; indeed, they can trigger "psychological ill-health," including anxiety and depression and PTSD symptoms (Zavala and Waters, 2021, p. 1359). In terms of TIP, teachers need to be aware of this. It can be argued that enduring these high stress "coming out" moments is crucial for building relationship with others, as Degges-White (2012) discusses in her investigation of lesbian support communities. She found that friendship was "contingent on mutual self-disclosure," but for many lesbians, "freedom to engage in this process [...] is not always guaranteed" (Degges-White, 2012, p. 17). The difficulty of building relationships with peers without honest self-disclosure is evident, but it could be argued that non-disclosure of self may also have an adverse effect on relationships with lecturers and other colleagues. Gnan et al. (2019) found that university experiences relating to outness was worthy of specific investigation in their study on mental health and suicide.

As Case Study I makes clear, one issue is the need for students to repeatedly "come out" if they are going to engage in the honest self-disclosure needed for learning in the creative space. Part of that practice must operate at an institutional level. As discussed by Gnan et al. (2019), out LGBTQ+ staff can arguably play a role in mitigating minority stress in a higher-education setting. An environment in which LGBTQ+ staff feel comfortable about presenting their authentic selves is only part of the solution. More supportive environments are associated with less abuse, polices that protect sexual minority youths and programmes that train professionals need implementing, plus empowering youths is important, regardless of sexual orientation, so they can intervene on behalf of sexuality minority youths (Friedman et al., 2011, p. 1492).

Craig et al. (2020) characterised the most effective interventions as "affirmative and trauma-informed" (p. 9), while Gnan et al. (2019) issued their higher-education call to arms. They suggest that this educational setting could be a site of prevention and healing for LGBTQ+ people, but it is currently being underused. The creative writing classroom, distinct in its moments of self-disclosure, is arguably the perfect place to enact some of the practices to enable post-traumatic growth. As discussed by Zavala and Waters (2021), the act of self-disclosure can be a moment of healing and positive transformation, but only if it is supported in a way that manages distress and promotes growth. There is a delicate balance and Case Studies I and II reveal some of the challenges and opportunities.

Part I: Case Studies

Case Study I

To disclose or not to disclose, that is the question. What follows is a reflection on LGBTQ+ visibility and its impact on trauma-informed writing pedagogy.

"Write what you know" is the time-honoured advice given to writers. Whether that writing is wholly autobiographical or entirely fictional work, it is arguably impossible to separate "self" from creative outputs, nor should we seek to. Our context, lived experience, and perceptions of the world and how we move through it run through our creative outputs like words through a stick of rock. Guy de Maupassant and many other writers make this point. But what if those words invoke trauma, fear, threat? We ask students to share their writing, and by proxy, themselves. It is a risk. Writing is risky. We want to empower students to take risks with their work, without putting themselves at risk. To do this, we must create a calm, supportive, empowering environment. But Imad's view of trauma-informed pedagogy goes further, arguing that an educator is required to be more than just a curator and creator of this environment; they must embody this too (Imad in Baker, 2022). As Bev Hancock-Smith explains here, to create a learning and teaching environment in which students feel empowered to bring their whole selves into the classroom, I must do so too.

I am a lecturer. I am playwright. I am a lesbian. Which part of my identity is appropriate to disclose? How does being "out" impact the dynamic of a classroom? How does this intersect with professional boundaries? Does disclosing my sexuality empower others to be their authentic selves? And if so, by omitting this part of my identity am I unwittingly reinforcing a heteronormative, or worse, homophobic learning environment? This reflection considers the visibility of LGBTQ+ identities in the classroom and the impact on TIP in a creative writing context.

Trauma is not only limited to a traumatic event, but how that event is experienced and what effect that experience has on the nervous system (Sar and Ozturk, 2008; Imad in Baker, 2022). In other words, the effect is more important than the event itself. By this definition, trauma is subjective; the same event can be experienced differently by different individuals (Imad in Baker, 2022). During my 13 years teaching in FE, HE, and adult education, I have encountered countless trauma-experienced students: students who have experienced rape, suffered from domestic violence, drug abuse, homelessness; experiences I would not hesitate to label "traumatic." In contrast, a class outing to the theatre to watch a production of the play we were studying, as part of a level three Access to Huminites module, did not to me flag as traumatic. Indeed, quite the opposite. But for one student, the bustling foyer, the noise, the crowds, proved overwhelming. She arrived at the theatre, she spotted me and her classmates huddled in the bar before the performance began, my students delighting in the fact that they were permitted to drink (they were all of legal age, I hasten to add) and me, frantically counting heads, handing out tickets and ensuring everyone had a pen and paper to make notes; and she could not come in. For this student, this event represented trauma. A trauma I had been completely unaware of. Whilst a trauma-informed approach may not have prevented this incident, it would certainly have provided a more supportive space in which the student may have felt empowered to voice her anxieties. I could have met her outside. We could have waited for the crowds to subside before taking our seats. I did not. And both her learning and mental well-being suffered as a result.

If we accept, as I do, an inclusive definition of trauma as one that "encompasses chronic or toxic stress" and that regular exposure to stress, threat, and microaggressions can be experienced as trauma (Tyles, 2021, p. 299), then an LGBTQ+ student operating in a heteronormative educational system is arguably at risk of trauma. Although I have experienced heterosexism on an almost hourly basis in my professional life, I have encountered little overt homophobia, perhaps in part due to the negative correlation between homophobia and increasing levels of academic attainment (Ohlander, Batalova and Treas, 2005). However, I am mindful that my LGBTQ+ students do not necessarily share this privilege, particularly within compulsory education settings.

Cultural and institutional homophobia and heteronormativity in the UK education system has been well documented (Batten et al., 2020; Ripley, 2012). According to Stonewall's School Report (2017), 45 per cent of students identifying as LGBTQ+ experience homophobic bullying within the secondary education system. Not surprisingly, then, rates of school refusal, self-harm, and suicidal thoughts are alarmingly high for this population (Stonewall, 2017). Students also reported poor responses from schools in tackling homophobic bullying and a dearth of LGBTQ+ issues in the curricula: 40 per cent of respondents had never been taught anything around LGBTQ+ issues at school.

The curricula essentially erases LGBTQ+ existence (McCormack, 2012). Viewing these formative educational experiences through a trauma-informed lens, I must be mindful of my students' experiences through the compulsory education system. Some of my students will have been educated under the shadow of Britain's homophobic Section 28. Indeed, some of my students have been educated in one of the 69 countries that still have laws that criminalise homosexuality (Paletta, 2020). Creating a safe, welcoming, inclusive learning environment in which all students, regardless of sexuality, race, ethnicity, age, or gender, can thrive is a necessity for all learning but is especially relevant for the learning which takes place in the creative writing classroom.

Creative writing can be viewed as a process of meaning-making and self-discovery (Moriarty and Adamson, 2019). We ask our students to share their work and, by proxy, themselves on a regular basis. Sharing creative writing, or indeed any writing, can feel akin to standing in front of the class naked. We shed our layers, make ourselves vulnerable, ask others to bear witness. If sharing a polished piece of writing feels like this, then sharing an early draft of work is the equivalent of standing in front of the class naked, only this time pointing out all your flaws; the wobbly bobbly bits that you feel ashamed of and ordinarily try to conceal. Sharing early drafts, we share ourselves, flaws and all. But this should not be confused with therapy, or as Cardell and Douglas (2016, p. 10) describe it: "classroom as clinic." Nor should self-disclosure be conflated with authenticity (MacCurdy, 2000, p. 160).

How, then, can we support our students to strive for authenticity in their work without causing harm to self? In striving to deliver a trauma-informed approach to pedagogy, Imad cites several core principles which align with creative writing pedagogy (Imad in Baker, 2022). As trauma-informed educator, it is my responsibility to create and maintain a safe, inclusive and empowering space. At the start of every creative writing course, I ask the students to collectively write and sign "rules of engagement" or contract in which they agree as a cohort on rules, values and boundaries within the session. This invariably covers areas such as respecting each other, giving time to speak, providing supportive and constructive feedback to help develop our practice.

Another core principle which can be applied directly to creative writing pedagogy is autonomous learning – offering students options and choices (Imad in Baker, 2022). Drawing on self to write must not lead to re-traumatisation (Talyes, 2021) and educators need to be mindful of stimulus material and offer students choice in their curricula (Imad in Baker, 2022). Creative writing allows students to select and explore their own themes and subject matter. Yes, many students do select difficult or painful issues to write about and yes, many do not view or label these experiences as "traumatic." But frequently their experiences fall under the broader definition of trauma previously discussed, reinforcing the need for a TIP approach (Tayles, 2021, p. 299).

TIP also acknowledges that we do not learn in a vacuum. Students do not always arrive at class calm, focussed and ready to learn. Nor do educators. I begin each session with a starter activity designed to help transition to a state of mind that is receptive to learning. I make learning clear and transparent using aims and objectives: What are we doing? Why are we doing this? How does this link with the wider programme? This, in turn, can serve to reduce anxiety about what will be taking place in the session. I utilise inclusive language in these aims – "today we will …" – and often I will carry out the activity with the students too, assuming dual role of educator and learner. In one amusing example, I had asked students to draft a paragraph critiquing a journal article we were studying. I set a timer and asked them to be prepared to share their drafts with a partner at the end of the time. I too used the time to write my paragraph, which I later displayed on the screen. Far from being an exemplar, my paragraph was met with some derision with one bold student stating: "that's rather a long and rambling sentence Bev." "I know I replied. Writing's hard, isn't it?"

The final principle I want to draw on is that of educator as a "buffering role model" who embodies the principles of trauma-informed practice (Tayles, 2021). Mindful of her own self-care and resilience, she describes how her own self-regulation provides capacity to act as a "buffer" for her students. For Tayles (2021) the "buffering role model" also includes honest disclosure, sharing not only her writing process with her students, but also her wider identity as a mother, wife, teacher, and their impact on her resilience. I too take this approach with my students and find my acknowledgement of my eternal imposter syndrome, and the painful process I find writing to be, is often well received by students. By acknowledging my own fears and self-doubts, I seek to normalise these feelings in others and to explore together strategies to overcome this. But how does my disclosure of writing process and self-doubt segue with my identity as gay woman?

In her paper "'Undoing' the self," Allen (2011) presents several motivators for LGBTQ+ educators' disclosure in the classroom: from the politically motivated dismantling of heteronormative narratives to the pedagogically motivated "teachable moment." Batten et al. similarly position being "out" as a "key pedagogical tool towards reducing homophobia among youth" (Batten et al., 2020, p. 201). As a gay lecturer then, does my pedagogy compel me to "come out?" Although I am "out" in all aspects of my personal life, in my capacity as an educator, I "come out" selectivity.

Why do I choose to disclose my sexuality to my creative writing students specifically whilst omitting this information with other groups? Returning to

Allen's motivators to disclose, she cites the necessity to portray "an authentic self" (2011, p. 83). An idea echoed by Wolfe (2009), who states she owes it to herself and all her students to be out for her own self-actualisation and to pave the way for others to do the same. This resonates with creative writing pedagogy which necessitates authenticity and veracity. How can we ask our students to bring their whole selves to the classroom, if we do not do the same in return?

Which leads to Allen's final motivating factor: "the imperative for providing role models ... (re)affirming the students' sense of self" (Allen, 2011, p. 84). Here the necessity to act as a buffering role model is part a TIP approach; the need to be open, honest and make myself vulnerable from creative writing pedagogical stance; and the moral, personal and political imperative of challenging the heteronormality of the classroom unite. A triad of evidence compels me to be out, to be proud, to enable students whatever their identity to be able to do the same too. I must bring my whole self to the classroom. Will you bring yours too?

Case Study II

This next case study examines scriptwriting classes in the Republic of Ireland with regard to the issues of authenticity and trauma, especially with students who are declared or not as members of the LGBTQ+ community. We examine how the pedagogy used creates a space in line with not only trauma-informed teaching principles, but also how it benefits all student learning. Context: class sizes – 10–40 students; course length – 6–12 weeks; students: diverse, undergraduates and lifelong learners; contexts: Republic of Ireland in universities, technical colleges, educational training boards, and community-based programmes; class/workshop length – two hours. Whilst this course was not designed as a therapeutic class, it does contain elements (strategies and practices) that encourage openness in discussion and can contribute to the alleviation of traumatic stress for the students, especially for those from the LGBTQ+ community.

These classes are underpinned by trauma-informed principles, which are creating a space that is physically, emotionally, socially and academically safe, that is, trustworthy and transparent, that allows for support and an opportunity to connect, where collaboration is fostered and mutual, where students are made to feel empowered, have a voice and, importantly, have choice. Students are encouraged to understand their rights in the classroom, are provided the space to grow and change as writers, all the while developing their craft (Zingarelli-Sweet, 2022; University of Denver, 2022). This incorporates the principles of Universal Design for Learning (engagement, representation, action and expression), multiple means of engagement and its guidelines providing options for recruiting interest, sustaining effort and persistence and self-regulation (McCarthy and Butler, 2015), all underpinning this trauma-informed pedagogical approach.

While these principles did not form a part of the conscious design of the course, they are very much a part of the ethos of the facilitator, a person who has their own personal trauma stories and has worked with people who have experienced different types of trauma (mental health, disability, war, etc.). To facilitate creativity, learning and authentic storytelling, this case study will discuss the main elements that have been developed over many years of practice in class: lecturer (facilitator) introductions, a student contract, facilitated discussion as interaction and the creation of a community of writers; these are adapted to suit each different group of students. The first lectures are structured to focus on forming a good foundation for communication in class and to create a bond between teacher and students, also between the students. This contains an ice-breaker activity which begins with the lecturer introducing themselves, telling the students a bit about their background. Each student is then asked the same questions. This allows for the facilitator to give bespoke relatable examples in following classes. In relation to course material, it encourages an exchange of knowledge and experiences between participants, and it supports student interaction. This type of approach is like Angelo and Cross's "Background Knowledge Probe" (1993, pp. 121–125) but adapted.

Very few students make declarations, in the first class, of trauma, but it can be obvious in their ideas and writing exercises as the course progresses. It is imperative for students to be able to be their authentic selves as writers, so they need to feel that the group will be receptive to any story. To create a safe space for discussions, the course/module begins with a student/lecturer contract, which clearly states the rules of the class, class etiquette, the expectations of the lecturer and what the student receives in return. This forms a solid foundation for openness, transparency and student safety. This contract has worked so well it is now a formative part of all my courses. All this information in the first class allows for the students to see the expectations of the lecturer. The ice-breaker exercise and the student contract are just two important examples of simple pedagogical elements that can be used to create a trauma safe space, but they are only part of it.

The following classes are typically broken into two parts: one-hour academic lecture (PowerPoint, screenings and film-script case studies), and the second-half group discussion on their weekly writing assignments. After creating the foundation for the safe space, with the earlier pedagogical elements as outlined, the discussion section, the second hour of the class, creates not only a temporary writer's community, which is invaluable in the academic experience, especially for students who struggle with their writing, but also incorporates the guiding principles of trauma care: safety, choice, collaboration, trustworthiness and empowerment (Institute on Trauma and

Trauma-Informed Care, 2015). This is where the students are told they now exist in a "circle of trust" on this course; the idea came from the film, *Meet the Fockers* (Roach, 2010).

The main exercise of this new community is to every week send each other their written assignment two days before class, then in class present and discuss their work with the group. The discussion group opens an opportunity for each student to be comfortable in sharing their work, experiences, and discussing their opinions with their contemporaries. While this can be a very hard experience and exposing, it can also be very freeing. The activity of deconstruction, dissemination, questioning and making connections with their classmates fosters critical skills where the student develops their ideas into, in some cases, better, more authentic stories. It should be noted that a student does not have to participate in the exercise, but this has never happened. This exercise creates the opportunity, anecdotally, to explore personal stories about trauma; some students have shared and have found a very supportive reception.

Students also learn how to accept constructive criticism, to see this feedback as necessary and, more importantly, they learn when and how to stick up for their story, which they need to do as writers. This peer-led, tutor-facilitated and reflective constructive exercise, as a part of a community of writers, is also a way for the students to not only demonstrate knowledge but to be active learners. In this space, students are encouraged to share their life experiences where they compare their perspectives and views; this is also an opportunity to plan and set personal learning goals with their peers and as individuals. The facilitator makes sure every student has a voice and gets heard (McCarthy and Butler, 2015, pp. 7–8); every student has their time to speak. This approach is heavily influenced by Shulman's discussion on how a teacher creates an innovative and nurturing learning space (Shulman, 2018). These discussions are a form of "active learning" as stated by Perrone and McCarthy in McCarthy and Butler (2015, p. 5), who concluded that when students are comfortable with the class format and know the lecturer, interaction is made easier. This section of the class is also underpinned by the trauma-informed principles that were stated at the beginning of this case study; students feel safe, connected, empowered, collaboration is fostered and mutual; most importantly, they also have a choice not to participate.

This case study illustrates how simple elements and multiple ways of interacting are an integral part of the scriptwriting class structure and that student voice and participation are not only a vital part of the teaching process but also an integral part of authentic story creation, whether the student declares or not. The elements discussed here cultivate the development of the relationships between teacher and students which allow for the students to feel comfortable in expressing their authentic selves in class, and even afterwards, as many students have formed writing groups. The structure has evolved over many years and through feedback from each cohort, but it is also underpinned by good teaching and learning practice and TIP principles. There is no doubt it will still go on changing as the groups of students change.

Part II: Voices, Trauma, Childhood

We have seen how authenticity is central to LGBTQ+ TIP, especially in terms of creative writing and screenwriting in the UK and the Republic of Ireland. That creativity is seen as a threat is partly down to fear; creativity begins by stepping into the unknown. Heteronormative ideology claims spaces to assert the status quo. Authenticity in terms of LGBTQ+ queering of these spaces can subvert the status quo. Similarly, acknowledging the power of the imaginary self means we can begin to subvert it (Boulter, 2007, p. 62). In writing practice this can include partly relinquishing the search for our own voice through working with and for the reader. There are different pedagogical approaches that can inform LGBTQ+ TIP. So, welcoming the competing voices of characters, "to find our voice we must lose it … in the voices of others" (Boulter, 2007, p. 62). Paradoxically, to do this involves knowing yourself and having a core authenticity, a form of "coming out" to yourself. This is where TIP helps, as explained above.

To find yourself you must lose yourself; "to find their voice the writer must know, at whatever level of conscious or unconscious imagining, their own intentions as an artist" (Boulter, 2007, p. 68). Following Freud, to the writer, words are deeds. Boulter is writing about fiction when she comments that every word is caught between the conventions of the literary, the languages of the world, and our own "voice." This is relevant for other forms, such as screenwriting, where the reader in this instance is the co-conspirator. In terms of LGBTQ+ experience and TIP in a North American context, this view is partly antithetical to the Amherst Artists & Writers (AAW) Group manifesto that begins with – "1. The teacher believes that the student possesses at least one unique, powerful voice that is appropriate for expressing his or her own lived experience, memory, and imagination" (Schneider, 2003, p. 320).

The AAW manifesto goes on to command the tutor to tease out the primary voice of the student, through teaching craft, convincing the student of the "value, beauty, and power" of their own voice (Schneider, 2003, p. 321). We might question the over-identification of voice, authenticity and identity, in the sense that writing concerns the imagination, which is arguably beyond identity. These are AAW guidelines, but the style they are written in suggests a form of pedagogic dogmatism, implying if the teacher does not do so they are failing the student. What if the student fails to find their voice, or does not feel safe to express their voice? It is important to question whether the complexities of the voice concerning the context, story, character or social structures should be as important as the "real," "primary," "authentic" voice that is coaxed from the writer.

Winnicott (1971) and Russ (2003) relate children's pretend play with creative writing and primary processes (Kaufman and Kaufman, 2015). Importantly, "aesthetic cognition may involve representational manipulation of emotional experiences," and what distinguishes humans from other primates is this feature (Kaufman and Kaufman, 2015, p. 254). Children who use play well can maintain more emotional memories and have better access to these memories than those who cannot use play to deal with emotions. Research in this context found that expressing negative affect was important (Kaufman and Kaufman, 2015, p. 256). This is significant within a LGBTQ+ TIP creative writing context. We need to take what students write seriously but should not automatically assume that if the student is writing from the first person about suicide, for example, that they are suicidal.

To advance a positive psychology for the group we can set exercises, such as: write about your safest, most beautiful, place in the world. This often leads to an excellent setting for a screenplay via caressing the divine details in a Nabakovian sense, moving from surface level prose. Taking this childhood paradigm into adulthood, a creative writer has a greater ability to play and to access these memories in play, ritualistically and artistically, translating them to the wider community. As Ingmar Bergman put it with regard to his screenplays, he had maintained an open channel with his childhood. At night, between sleeping and waking, he entered the door of his childhood where everything was as it had been (Kaufman and Kaufman, 2015, p. 257). This is the root of transrational well-being which leads to creativity, rather than anxiety; awareness of this is useful for TIP, especially in a creative writing context.

How do we resurrect the past, or tap into the eternal which includes the past, present and future? Through a focus on the transrational, these false time boundaries become immaterial. We observed that those who identify as LGBTQ+ are more likely to have had childhood trauma, although there is no causal effect. How creativity deals with early childhood trauma is an interesting area full of many voices, the theory being that those constricted by unresolved mourning use this unresolved grief and identity issues in their transformative creative work (Kaufman and Kaufman, 2015, p. 257). Teachers need to be educated about and aware of this. In the classroom, teachers need to be conscious of homophobia and transphobia and bias, challenging this behaviour. As Case Studies I and II show, a TIP approach is sensitive and aware of the needs of the class, and benign pedagogy concerns establishing and building positive boundaries for relationships rather than merely imparting information. This is relevant for teachers in different disciplines, including the sciences, especially when we acknowledge how mental health is central to students – especially, as has been explained, LGBTQ+ students – flourishing in all contexts. Often, students will take subjects outside their major subjects. Teachers need to share between themselves what they know about students, so LGBTQ+ TIP flourishes across institutions

Conclusions

We have seen how levels of the authentic self inform writing, plus how the curriculum erases LGBTQ+ experience. This reflects in laypersons' terms on the New Critical mantra that there is nothing outside the text, but in New Criticism the structure and unity of a text contains "subterranean connections with its author," such as a verbal icon that corresponds to an author's intuition (Selden et al., 2013, p. 157). The importance of a sensitive approach to childhood and memory needs to be maintained. We outlined practical ways of TIP in an LGBTQ+ context, including creating a contract, buffering, self-regulating, the importance of choice, and co-creation. It should be emphasised no pedagogic context is a therapeutic situation. Overall, what is needed is a revolution addressing both the methods of teaching and the goals of learning (Illich, 1971, p. 84). Authenticity on the part of the student and of the lecturer was addressed in Case Study 1. It is crucial to have contact with our own inner nature and this is part of the concept of originality (Taylor, 1992, p. 29), essential for TIP and learning. Case Studies I and II offered ways for the teacher to create an environment that is beneficial for TIP in an LGBTQ+ context. This is shown to be active rather than passive.

In Virginia Woolf's essay *On Being Ill* (1926) and her novel *Mrs. Dalloway* (1925), her defence of "madness" is a defence of interiority, constituted as an interiorised space of psychic freedom, resisting the interpretive authority of heteronormative patriarchal experts. With identity normally carved through external measures set by heteronormative standards, reflecting Freud's performance principle, especially in a selfie-obsessed culture, an alternative internality such as that proposed by Woolf is needed to redress the balance. This is where TIP in an LGBTQ+ context is crucial, and experiencing the transrational is vital, because it requires engaging with the complex world of interior life and emotions which many try to avoid (Lee, 2010). This has an even more powerful meaning in an LGBTQ+ context, and in a pedagogic context this is complex; students need the freedom to explore, with the group leader being more of a facilitator. Imagination and intellect are at play in creative writing workshops, and this can confirm our humanity; and if we are encountering beauty, the subject discovers, "harmonious relations," "in the manifestation of the unrestricted play of its own faculties" (Lee, 2017, p. 10).

We observed that the effect of trauma is sometimes more significant than the event that caused the trauma. There is also what is termed vicarious trauma, which film scholars claim comes from watching visual material, including documentaries, termed "post-traumatic cinema" (Joy, 2020, p. 21). Teachers need to be conscious of this when using cinema, whether realist film or not, in screenwriting workshops for example. In an international context there will be variations. Each government influences, or even dictates, education. How radical we might want to be is framed by certain realities; concurrently, sexual identities and subcultures have become fragmented (Mottier, 2008, p. 121) and this could be part of a subversion.

Case Study I explained certain adaptations that bring about TIP and how openness works in this LGBTQ+ context, while Case Study II analysed how this may not be so overt or conscious but will still have impact. Part II revealed how there are different transnational approaches to creative writing pedagogy, and we can see how this relates to literary theory and philosophy and to concepts of authenticity via writing. Outside the creative writing and screenwriting classroom, in other disciplines, self-disclosure might not be so appropriate, and we saw in Case Study II that this should be an individual choice. There is a danger with prioritising authenticity, in that a person expressing their authentic self may contravene someone else's emotional boundaries. Optimistically, we might be in a radical position to frame pedagogy beyond traditional structures (Illich, 1971, p. 84). This is, using a term borrowed from sexualities studies, more fluid – to be less dictated to by existing paradigms, including standard pedagogic terminology. In this fashion, LGBTQ+ experience informs TIP to enhance the experience of all.

References

Adam, B. D. (2004) 'Care, intimacy and same-sex partnership in the 21st century'. *Current Sociology*, 52(March), pp. 265–279.

Allen, L. (2011) '"Undoing" the self: Should heterosexual teachers "come out" in the university classroom?' *Pedagogy, Culture and Society*, 19(1), pp. 79–95.

Angelo, T. A. and Cross, P. K. (1993) *Classroom Assessment Techniques: A Handbook for College Teachers*. San Francisco, CA: Jossey-Bass.

Baker, K. (2022) 'Mays Imad on trauma-informed pedagogy'. *The National Teaching and Learning Forum*, 31(2), pp. 5–6.

Batten, J., Ripley, M., Anderson, E., Batey, J. and White, A. (2020) 'Still an occupational hazard? The relationship between homophobia, heteronormativity, student learning and performance, and an openly gay university lecturer'. *Teaching in Higher Education*, 25(2), pp. 189–204.

Boulter, A. (2007) *Writing Fiction: Creative and Critical Approaches*. London: Palgrave.

Cardell, K. and Douglas, K. (2018) 'Why literature students should practise life writing'. *Arts and Humanities in Higher Education*, 17(2), pp. 204–221.

Coll-Planas, G. and Missé, M. (2021) 'The (trans)formation of identity: The evolution of categories related to gender diversity in the case of trans-activism in Barcelona (1978–2010)'. *International Journal of Iberian Studies*, 34(1), pp. 23–45.

Craig, S. L., et al. (2020) 'Frequencies and patterns of adverse childhood events in LGBTQ+ youth'. *Child Abuse and Neglect*, 107(April), p. 10462.

Degges-White, S. (2012) 'Lesbian friendships: An exploration of lesbian social support networks'. *Adultspan Journal*, 11(1), pp. 16–26.

Doan, L. (2017) 'Queer history/queer memory: The case of Alan Turing'. *GLQ*, 23(1), p. 113.

Friedman, M. S., et al. (2011) 'A meta-analysis of disparities in childhood sexual abuse, parental physical abuse, and peer victimization among sexual minority and sexual nonminority individuals'. *American Journal of Public Health*, 101(8), pp. 1481–1494.

Gnan, G. H., et al. (2019) 'General and LGBTQ-specific factors associated with mental health and suicide risk among LGBTQ students'. *Journal of Youth Studies*, 22(10), pp. 1393–1408.

Guittar, N. A. (2013) 'The meaning of coming out: From self-affirmation to full disclosure'. *QSR*, 9(3), pp. 169–187.

Hicks, S. (2011) *Lesbian, Gay and Queer Parenting*. Basingstoke: Palgrave Macmillan.

Hines, S. (2007) *TransForming Gender: Transgender Practices of Identity, Intimacy and Care*. Bristol: Policy Press.

Illich, I. (1971). *Deschooling Society*. London: Calder & Boyars.

Jennings, R. (2007a) *A Lesbian History of Britain: Love and Sex between Women Since 1500*. Westport, Connecticut: Greenwood World Publishing.

Joy, S. (2020) *The Traumatic Screen – The Films of Christopher Nolan*. Bristol: Intellect.

Kaufman, A. and Kaufman, J., eds. (2015) *Animal Creativity and Innovation*. New York: Academic Press.

Lee, J., ed (2010) *Cultures of Addiction*. New York: Cambria.

Lee, J. (2014) *The Psychology of Screenwriting*. New York: Bloomsbury.

Lee, J. (2017) *Sex Robots – The Future of Desire*. London: Palgrave.

Lee, J. (2018) 'Are you kidding? Re-assessing morality, sexuality, and desire in *Kids*'. *Film International*, 16(3), pp. 27–40

McCarthy, M. and Butler, B. (2015) 'How can Teaching for Understanding act as a vehicle for the principles and guidelines of Universal Design for Learning?', presented at Conference on UDL: License to Learn, Dublin Castle, March.

McCarthy, M. and Anderson, C. (2000) *Writing and Healing: Toward an Informed Practice*. Misssouri: NCTE.

McCormack, M. (2012) 'The positive experiences of openly gay, lesbian, bisexual and transgendered students in a Christian sixth form college'. *Sociological Research Online*, 17(3), pp. 229–238.

Meyer, I. H. (2003) 'Prejudice, social stress, and mental health in lesbian, gay, and bisexual populations: Conceptual issues and research evidence'. *Psychological Bulletin*, 129(5), pp. 674–697.

Miranda-Mendizábal, A., et al. (2017) 'Sexual orientation and suicidal behaviour in adolescents and young adults: Systematic review and meta-analysis'. *British Journal of Psychiatry*, 211(2), pp. 77–87.

Mizzi, R. C. and Star, J. (2019) 'Queer eye on inclusion: Understanding Lesbian and Gay student and instructor experiences of continuing education'. *The Journal of Continuing Higher Education*, 67(2–3), pp. 72–82.

Monro, S. (2005) *Gender Politics*. London: Pluto Press.

Moriarty, J. and Adamson, R. (2019) '"Storying the self": Autobiography as pedagogy in undergraduate creative writing teaching'. *Journal of Writing in Creative Practice*, 12(1–2), pp. 91–107.

Mottier, V. (2008) *Sexuality*. Oxford: Oxford University Press.

Nadal, K. L.,Rivera, D. P., and Corpus, M. J., (2010) 'Sexual orientation and transgender microaggressions in everyday life: Experiences of lesbians, gays, bisexuals, and transgender individuals'. In D. W. Sue (Ed.), *Microaggressions and Marginality: Manifestation, Dynamics, and Impact* (pp. 217–240). New Jersey: Wiley.

Nadal, K. L., Whitman, C. N., Davis, L. S., Erazo, T. and Davidoff, K. C. (2016) 'Microaggressions toward lesbian, gay, bisexual, transgender, queer, and gender queer people: A review of the literature'. *Journal of Sex Research*, 53(4–5), pp. 488–508.

Nadal, K. L., Wong, Y., Griffin, K. E., Davidoff, K. and Sriken, J. (2014) 'The adverse impact of racial microaggressions on college students' self-esteem'. *Journal of College Student Development*, 55(5), pp. 461–474.

Ohlander, J., Batalova, J. and Treas, J. (2005) 'Explaining educational influences on attitudes toward homosexual relations'. *Social Science Research*, 34(4), pp. 781–799.

Paletta, D. (2020) 'ILGA world updates state-sponsored homophobia report: "There's progress in times of uncertainty"'. The International Lesbian, Gay, Bisexual, Trans and Intersex Association. [Online] Available at: https://ilga.org/ (Accessed August 2022).

Plummer, K. (2000) 'Mapping the sociological gay: Past, presents and futures of a sociology of same sex relations'. In Sandford, T., Schuyf, J., and Duyvendak, J. W. (Eds.), *Lesbian and Gay Studies: An Introductory, Interdisciplinary Approach*. London: SAGE Publications.

Ripley, M., Anderson, E., McCormack, M. and Rockett, B. (2012) 'Heteronormativity in the university classroom: Novelty attachment and content substitution among gay-friendly students'. *Sociology of Education*, 85(2), pp. 121–130.

Roach, J. (2010) *Meet the Fockers*. United States: Universal Pictures.

Russ, S. (2003) 'Play and creativity: Developmnetal issue's'. *Scandanavian Journal of Educational Research*, 47(3), pp. 291–303.

Sue, D. W. and Capodilupo, C. M. (2008) 'Racial, gender, and sexual orientation microaggressions: Implications for counseling'. In Sue, D. W. (Ed.), *Counseling the Culturally Diverse: Theory and Practice* (5th ed., pp. 105–130). Hoboken, New Jersey: Wiley.

Selden, R., Widdowson, P. and Brooker, P. (2013) *A Reader's Guide to Contemporary Literary Theory*. Harlow: Pearson Longman.

Schneider, P. (2003) *Writing Alone and With Others*. Oxford: Oxford University Press.

Sharp, K. J. (2022) 'Teaching trauma: Sexual violence and the Kairoti space of the first-year writing classroom'. In Marshall, J. E. and Skibba, C. (Eds.), *Trauma-Informed Pedagogy* (pp. 13–29). Bingley: Emerald.

Stonewall. (2017) 'School report'. June 2017. [Online] Available at: https://www.stonewall.org.uk/school-report-2017 (Accessed 9 August 2022).

Tayles, M. (2021) 'Trauma-informed writing pedagogy: Ways to support student writers affected by trauma and traumatic stress'. *Teaching English in the Two-Year College*, 48(3), pp. 295–313.

Taylor, C. (1992) *The Ethics of Authenticity*. Cambridge, MA: Harvard University Press.

University of Denver Office of Teaching and Learning. (2022). *Trauma-Informed Pedagogy*. Available at: https://inclusive-teaching.du.edu/content/trauma-informed-pedagogy#tip (Accessed 23 July 2022).

Wang, Y. et al. (2021) 'Methods of attempted suicide and risk factors in LGBTQ+ youth'. *Child Abuse and Neglect*, 122(April), p. 105352.

Weeks, J., Heaphy, B. and Donovan, C. (2001) 'Same sex intimacies: Families of choice and other life experiments'. *Contemporary Sociology*, (31), p. 410.

White, A. J., Magrath, R. and Thomas, B. (2018) 'The experiences of lesbian, gay and bisexual students and staff at a further education college in Southeast England'. *British Educational Research Journal*, 44(3), pp. 480–495.

Winnicott, D.W. (1971) *Playing and Reality*. London: Penguin Books.

Wolfe, S. J. (2009) 'I. Using the L-word: Coming out in the classroom'. *Feminism and Psychology*, 19(2), pp. 181–185.

Woolf, V. (1926) *On Being Ill*. London: Hogarth Press.

Woolf, V. (1925) *Mrs Dalloway*. London: Hogarth Press.
Zavala, C. and Waters, L. (2021) 'Coming out as LGBTQ +: The role strength-based parenting on posttraumatic stress and posttraumatic growth'. *Journal of Happiness*, May, pp. 1359–1383
Zingarelli-Sweet, D. (2022) 'Keeping up with…trauma-informed pedagogy'. Association of College and Research Libraries (ACRL). Available at: https://www.ala.org/acrl/publications/keeping_up_with/trauma-informed-pedagogy (Accessed 23 July 2022).

LIST OF CONTRIBUTORS

Whitney J. Archer (they/she) is the Director of the Hattie Redmond Women & Gender Center at Oregon State University where they are also a doctoral student in women, gender, and sexuality studies. Whitney's work focuses on anti-racist feminist praxis in higher education.

Katarina Båth is a Senior Lecturer in comparative literature at Umeå University, Sweden. She specializes in romanticism, psychoanalytic literary criticism, literary trauma studies, and creative writing. Båth earned her PhD from Uppsala University, Sweden, in 2017.

Brynn Fitzsimmons (they/them) is a PhD candidate at the University of Kansas, USA, in English – Rhetoric and Composition. Their research interests include disability studies, health and body rhetorics, activist and abolitionist rhetoric, and community writing (particularly citizen journalism).

Rose Gubele is currently an Associate Professor of English at the University of Central Missouri, USA, where she teaches courses in writing, rhetoric, and American Indian literature. She received her PhD in Rhetoric and Composition at Washington State University. Her research focuses on race and mental disabilities.

Cassandra L. Hall is a care worker and teacher whose interests include disability justice, Jewish and feminist rhetorics, reproductive justice, and feminized genres and cultural productions, including romance and memoir. Cassandra completed their doctoral and MA degrees in women, gender, and sexuality studies (queer studies minor) at Oregon State University, USA.

List of Contributors

Beverley Hancock-Smith is a playwright and Lecturer. Previous plays include *Adrift* for Action Transport Theatre and *Into the Blue* for the Arcola Theatre. She works as a Senior Lecturer in the Centre for Learning and Study Support at De Montfort University, UK, where she is also an LGBTQ+ role model.

Zara Hooley has taught in higher education for 12 years and is a Senior Lecturer in Academic Writing at De Montfort University, UK. Her PhD is on investigating the friendship-making processes of same-sex couples during transition to parenthood. She is an active member of the Centre for Reproduction Research and is published in the areas of pedagogy, sexuality, and adoption.

Dennis Kombe is an Associate Professor of Mathematics Education at California State University Monterey Bay. His work focuses on making rigorous mathematics accessible to a wide range of learners. His scholarly interests explore ideas on teacher preparation and beliefs on mathematics and science teaching and learning. He has diverse collegiate and secondary teaching experiences, having worked with high school and college students drawn from rural and urban school settings in Kenya and Botswana, as well as South Carolina and California.

Emma L. Larkins (she/her) is a PhD candidate in the women, gender, and sexuality studies program at Oregon State University, USA. She holds MA degrees in college student administration and women, gender, and sexuality studies. Her research draws upon histories of student-led activism, using principles of feminist accountability to reduce sexual violence in higher education.

Sarah Le Pichon received her PhD in French Studies from UT Austin, USA. She is a middle- and high-school teacher in the Humanities Department at Fusion Academy in Austin, which offers an alternative, student-centered approach to education.

Jason Lee (CJP Lee) is a Professor of Film, Media, and Culture at De Montfort University, UK, and is currently a British Academy Innovation Fellow. Lee is the author/editor of 20 books, including *Nazism and Neo-Nazism in Film and Media*.

Vanessa Lopez-Littleton is an Associate Professor of Public Administration and Nonprofit Management and Chair of the Department of Health, Human Services, and Public Policy at California State University, Monterey Bay, USA. She is a racial equity scholar whose work focuses on advancing critical consciousness and erasing anti-Black racism in public organizations.

Steve Lundy is a project manager and online course developer at the University of Texas, USA, in Liberal Arts Instructional Technology Services (LAITS). He is also an occasional Lecturer for the Department of Classics, from which he received his PhD in 2013.

Eleanor McSherry is a program coordinator/designer and Lecturer for Hibernia College Dublin and University College Cork, and a PhD student with Maynooth University, all in Ireland. She lectures on autism and disability studies and film: film script, policy, practice, law, advocacy, and representation.

Angela (AK) Moore currently works as the Program Development Specialist for Diversity & Inclusion at the University of Nevada, USA. Her background is in modern rhetoric, composition pedagogies, and LGBTQIA2+ program development.

Kriti Prasad is a MD Candidate at the University of Minnesota Medical School, USA. Her scholarship and advocacy focus on clinician stress and burn-out, antiracism in medical education, and organizational initiatives in trauma-informed care. Kriti will be applying to Internal Medicine/Primary Care residency programs in the 2022–2023 cycle.

Pritha Prasad is an Assistant Professor of English at the University of Kansas (KU), USA. As a scholar and teacher of critical race and ethnic studies, feminist studies, and queer studies, her research focuses on how cultural, political, and educational institutions negotiate the politics of race and racism in the wake of racial unrest. At KU, Pritha teaches undergraduate and graduate courses in cultural studies and rhetorics, rhetoric and composition studies, and critical university studies.

Ernest Stromberg is Professor of Rhetoric and Communication at California State University, Monterey Bay, USA. He teaches courses in dialogue and deliberation, written communication, American Indian Studies, and literature. He is the editor and co-author of *American Indian Rhetorics of Survivance* and many articles on culture and literature in a variety of journals and book collections.

Carina M. Buzo Tipton (she/her) is a Queer Chicana PhD candidate in women, gender, and sexuality studies at Oregon State University, USA. Her scholarship focuses on feminist institutional change. Carina is also a DEI consultant and trauma-informed birth doula. To learn more about her work visit www.cmbt.space.

Christine Valdez is a licensed clinical psychologist with expertise in trauma. She is an Associate Professor of Clinical Psychology at California State University, Monterey Bay, USA, where she teaches undergraduate courses on the application, research, and theory of psychology. Her research program examines outcomes of trauma and factors implicated in recovery and growth.

INDEX

A
AAW *see* Amherst Artists & Writers
ableism 66, 79
ACE *see* adverse childhood experiences
ACE and adverse meditation effects 94
Active Minds 19, 25
adverse childhood experiences (ACE) 94
advice: horizonal 102–103; vertical 102–103
American Psychiatric Association 3–5, 14–15, 45, 150
American Psychiatric Association (APA) 14
American Psychological Association 45, 89, 150
Amherst Artists & Writers (AAW) 174
Amnesty International 152–153
anti-Black murders 70
anti-black racism: action plan 50; and bold leadership 47
anxious attachment 96
APA *see* American Psychiatric Association
authority: figure(s) 8, 100, 101, 103, 108; in higher education 100; -related traumas 8, 100; scale 104
autonomy: in relationship 125

B
behavioral manifestations of PTSD symptoms: attachment **17**; behavioral control **17**; dissociation 15, **17**, 44; increased arousal **17**; self-concept **17**; cognition **17**
bibliotherapeutic: practice 132; process 134, 135
bibliotherapy 8, 133–136, 141–142; and trauma recovery 136; applied field of 132; creative 8; definition of 132
BIPOC *see* Black Indigenous and people of color
Black liberation 49
black teachers/faculty: as role models 48
Black Indigenous and people of color (BIPOC) 70, 75–76
breath as trigger and re-stimulator 96
burnout: COVID-related 69; prevention of 108; reduction of 109; teacher 44

C
care:-oriented relationships 7, 70–71; transformative 58
catharsis 131, 134, 136
China virus *see* COVID-19
chronic anxiety 89
cis-heteropatriarchal foundations 60
Civil Rights Movement 159
clinical depression 2
collaborative: activities and group projects 125; learning activities 116–118
collective psyche 2
collectivist cultures 49

Index

colonialism: 66, 152; British 77; European 76; histories of 85; legacy of 66; rape and 152
complex trauma: and chronic problems 15
contact tracing 57–58
counseling assistance 2
COVID: grammar 56–57, 59; vocabularies 65
COVID-19, 74–76
COVID-19 pandemic 1, 33, 56, 65, 69, 84, 119, 127; and digital learning 36; impact of 9
creative writing: and psychological wellbeing 140; classroom 167, 169; risks of in trauma class 141–142
creative writing: and pedagogical implications of 143; course 139; pedagogy core pricinples 169
critical: consciousness 46, 48–51; instructional pedagogy 36
critical race theory (CRT) 44–46
CRT *see* critical race theory
culture of care 49

D
Dalloway (Woolf) 176
decolonization of higher education 46, 48
depressive symptoms 96
Diagnostic and Statistical Manual of Mental Disorders (DSM) 14
Diagnostic and Statistical Manual of Mental Disorders (3rd Edition) 3–4
Diagnostic and Statistical Manual of Mental Disorders (5th Edition) 4, 5, 9, 14, 45, 150
dismantling anti-black racism: checklist for 51; strategies for 48–49; teachers' checklist for 52
domestic violence 14, 168
drug abuse 135, 168

E
emotional disorders 3
epigenetic inheritance 45
Eurocentric values 44, 46
exposure therapy 139

F
first-year seminar (on trauma): and awareness raising 24; and course assignments 23; and creation of safe environment 22; and peer-support programs 25; and positive change 24; and social connectedness 23; and student traumatic stress 21; content of 22
Floyd, George 70, 73

G
gender non-conformists 164
global climate crisis 9, 75

H
healing-centered: future 68; institutional practices 55; practices 56
heteronormative ideology 174
homophobia 7, 168, 170, 175

I
Indian Cartography (Miranda) 160
institutional betrayal 18, 62
institutional teaching-learning spaces 67
institutionality 60, 66, 78
intersubjective love 138
intrapsychic love 138
intrusive memories 14, 150

K
Kung flu *see* COVID-19

L
LGBTQ+ 164, 166–167, 170; community 171; depiction of 164; identities 166, 168; student groups 165; students 164–166, 168, 175; visibility 167
LGBTQ+ TIP 174–175
literary trauma studies 131–132, 136–137; and escapism 135
literary trauma theory 8, 132

M
mandates: as opportunity 62; in higher education 61; limitation of 61
MasculinUT 38
MBSR *see* mindfulness-based stress reduction
meditation: adverse effects of 93; as trauma recovery technique 97; benefits of 93
Meet the Fockers (film) 173
mental health: benefits 90, 92; challenges 21, 89, 97; disorders 2, 89, 90
Mental Health First Aid 25

microaggression(s): theory 165; against LGBTQ+ 164, 165; as trauma 168
mindfulness: interventions 95; meditation 90–95, 97; meditation practices 96; practices 121; practicing 23, 90; training 23, 96
mindfulness program outcomes 23
mindfulness-based cognitive therapy (MBCT) 90
mindfulness-based: meditation practice 98; stress reduction 3, 90, 92
mindfulness-based stress reduction (MBSR) 3, 7, 90, 95
mindfulness-based stress reduction program 95
Minnesota Indian Women's Resource Center 153

N

NAMI *see* National Alliance on Mental Illness
National Alliance on Mental Illness (NAMI) 24
National Center for Trauma-informed Care (NCTIC) 13
National Sexual Violence Resource Center 151
Native Americans and sexual trauma 152
NCTIC *see* National Center for Trauma-informed Care

O

On Being Ill (Woolf) 176
online existence 1

P

pedagogical partnership program 19
peer-review: in trauma-informed syllabus 123; questions 124
piety meaning 101
positive regard 106–107
post traumatic slave syndrome 5
posttraumatic stress disorder (PTSD) 3, 16, 45, 90, 95, 131, 150, 153–154, 158,
posttraumatic stress disorder symptoms 14
problem-posing education (Freire's idea) 122
psychoanalytic: process 134; theory texts 138
psychological: distress 2; support 2
PTSD *see* posttraumatic stress disorder

PTSD: and academic performance 21; and adverse meditation effects 94; and sense of belonging 18; in college students 16; symptoms 16, 20, 35, 160, 166; symptoms of 5, 16, 95, 157, 158

R

racial: discrimination 165; hierarchy 44; ideology 44; prejudice 44; trauma symptoms of 45; violence 46
racialized: complexities 47; oppression 48
racism: anti-Black 6–7, 43–44, 46–47, 49, 50–53; history of 7; structural 43–44, 47, 51
rape 156–157; as tool of colonial power 159; discussions of 159–160; victims 158
rape prevention 151
retraumatization: 25, 35, 95, 108–110, 116, 141; reduction of 31; risk of 35, 132
rhetorics: Asian 85; cultural 77; curative 65; institutional 70, 84
Round House (Erdrich) 156–157

S

SAMHSA *see* Substance Abuse and Mental Health Services Association
schizophrenia 89
secondary trauma(tization) 4, 6, 35, 40, 108, 110, 116, 141, 159; definition of 109
sexual abuse 15, 136, 152, 153, 154, 166
sexual assault 151–152, 154; psychological effects of 151; stigma of 158
sexual violence: 151, 160; and trauma 149; depictions as trauma trigger 150
Standing Rock Sioux Reservation 153
state-sanctioned: violence 76
student (emotional) wellness 3, 5–6, 89, 97
Substance Abuse and Mental Health Services Association (SAMHSA) 43, 118, 127,
suicidal tendencies 2

T

teaching trauma risks 137
therapeutic transference 139
third spaces 39
Third World feminists 72, 85
TIP *see* trauma-informed pedagogy

TIP community 34, 39\40; network 39; planning 40
tips to support PTSD students 154–157
transference definition 139
transphobia 175
trauma: age of 2; and academic freedom 161; and academic success 23; and authority 108; and collaborative activities 125; and collaborative learning 115, 116, 117; and cultural violence 5; and disability 116; and feelings of safety 18; and interpersonal violence 16; and its manifestations 43, 44; and marginalized students 20; and peer support 19; and positive regard 102; and traumatic stress 116; and triggers 148; and violence 15; and wellbeing 14; and writing 127; and writing feedback 124; as cultural experience 4; authority-related 8, 100, 101, 105, 106; awareness 22; awareness of 13, 131; betrayal 151; chronic stress and 123; combat 135; commodification of 137; complex 15, 16; compounding stressors of 16; conceptual evolution of 38; cultural 5; definition of 5, 9, 14, 30, 45, 71, 168, 170; definition of (Caruth) 150; embodied experiences of 65, 67; external reminders of 14; -focused: professional development training 33; historic 5; historical 7, 20, 22, 57; institutional 35, 62, 65; institutional responses to 62; intergenerational 5, 7, 57; internal reminders of 14; manifestations of 150; media representations of 4; medicalization of 29; narratives 136, 137, 141; negative effects of 45; negative emotions of 15; peak age of 15; postcolonial 7; psychiatric disorders related to 15; psychoanalytic study of 137; psychological 6, 14, 15, 17, 21, 45, 95; psychological re-experiencing of 14; racial 44, 45, 46, 48, 49, 50, 77; recovery 21, 149; recovery and healing from i 5, 6; responses 14, 24; risk factor for 15; sexual 151, 152, 157, 161; societal awareness of 13; studies 3, 4, 35; survivors 4, 21, 24, 96, 126, 141, 148, 150, 152; symptoms of 5, 13; systemically inflicted i 6; theory 133; through creative writing 140;

understanding of 3, 5, 13, 38, 60, 117; vicarious 176
trauma exposure: 15–16, 21, 23, 33, 132; and socioeconomic status 16; problem of 33; rates of 21, 23; risk for 16
trauma recovery: and productive relationships 97; and reflective writing 121
Trauma Recovery Centers 25
trauma-inflicting oppression 131
trauma-informed: advocacy 34; approaches to meditation 92; best practices in higher education 29; care 13, 29, 56, 59, 62, 141; care 62; care practices 58; classroom 33, 50; coalition on campus 32; cornerstones 105–109; education practices 109; educators 37; frameworks 63, 75; institutional care 67; institutional practices 62; instruction 37; integration of meditation 95; interaction 117; intervention 31; interventions 36, 126; measures 33; networks 35, 39, 40; pedagogies 50, 57; positive education 18, 20; practice 116; practices 6, 21, 30, 31, 33, 39, 40, 56, 57, 58, 63, 64, 84; practitioners 37; practitioners 66; praxis 7, 61; principles 8, 22, 25, 32, 171, 173–174; programming 31; research 108, 110, 111; responses 66; scholars 66; scholarship 8; school 32; schools 32; support 40; syllabus 119; syllabus and small group discussion 120; sylabus and creating safety 125; syllabus prompts 119, 120; teacher-learners 66; teaching i 33, 34, 35, 59, 81, 118, 132, 171; training and student posttraumatic stress 32; work 67; work requirements 56; writing pedagogy 167
trauma-informed pedagogies: 9; and authority 100; approaches to 9
trauma-informed pedagogy: 34, 40, 72, 117–118, 166, 168, 170; and bibliotherapy 131; for higher education 4; insights 136; LGBTQ+, 163; policies 29, 33; project of 1; research on 164; workshops 38
trauma-informed pedagogy (TIP) 6, 163
trauma-informed pedagogy pillars: safety 17–18; trustworthiness and transparency 18–19; peer support and

mutual self-help 19; collaboration and mutuality 19–20; empowerment, voice, and change 20; cultural, historical, and gender issues 20
trauma-sensitive approaches 97
Trauma-Sensitive Mindfulness (Treleaven) 95
traumatic experiences 141; as vehicle for healing 3; complex 14; effects of 6, 97; restimulation of 94; treatment of 36; types of 14
traumatic stress: clinical manifestations of 6; symptoms 20
traumatizing: conditions reproduction 39; effects 43
trigger warnings 39, 148, 150, 152; across disciplines 158; and academic freedom 148; asking for 149; use of 149
triggering effects 43

U
unresolved traumatic stress 6

V
Voices Against Violence 34, 36, 38

W
whisper networks 62, 64
White Lion (slave ship) 44
white supremacist: capitalist patriarchy 60; cis-heteropatriarchy 62, 63
white supremacy: culture of 43, 44, 56
wholeness: advantages of 64; meaning of 63; medicine of 63
World Health Organization 1
wound culture 136
Wright, Daunte 73
writing: as healing 8; therapeutic benefits of 3
Wuhan virus *see* COVID-19

Z
zeitgeist 137

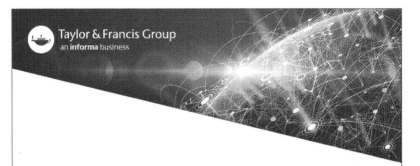

Printed in the United States
by Baker & Taylor Publisher Services